Exploring Data

An Introduction to Data Analysis for Social Scientists

Second Edition

Catherine Marsh and Jane Elliott

polity

First published in 2008 by Polity Press

Polity Press
65 Bridge Street
Cambridge CB2 1UR, UK

Polity Press
350 Main Street
Malden, MA 02148, USA

ISBN-13: 978-0-7456-2282-8
ISBN-13: 978-0-7456-2283-5(pb)

A catalogue record for this book is available from the British Library.

Typeset in 10 on 12 pt Sabon
by Servis Filmsetting Ltd, Stockport, Cheshire
Printed and bound in Great Britain by MPG Books Ltd, Bodmin, Cornwall

The publisher has used its best endeavours to ensure that the URLs for external websites referred to in this book are correct and active at the time of going to press. However, the publisher has no responsibility for the websites and can make no guarantee that a site will remain live or that the content is or will remain appropriate.

For further information on Polity, visit our website: www.polity.co.uk

This edition is accompanied by a website at www.polity.co.uk/exploringdata

This book is dedicated to Jamie and Geoffrey, Cathie's sons, who were born during the writing of the original edition of the book. It is also dedicated to Joe, who I hope will find this book useful.

Contents

Detailed contents   ix
List of figures   xiii
Acknowledgements   xxi

Introduction   1

Part I Single Variables

1   Distributions and Variables   7
2   Numerical Summaries of Level and Spread   35
3   Scaling and Standardizing   57
4   Inequality   76
5   Smoothing Time Series   93

Part II Relationships between Two Variables

6   Percentage Tables   117
7   Analysing Contingency Tables   141
8   Handling Several Batches   161
9   Scatterplots and Resistant Lines   191
10 Transformations   212

Part III Introducing a Third Variable

11 Causal Explanations   235
12 Three-Variable Contingency Tables and Beyond   254
13 Longitudinal Data   277

References   293
Index   299

Detailed contents

List of figures   xiii
Acknowledgements   xxi

Introduction   1

Part I   Single Variables

1   Distributions and Variables   7
   1.1   Preliminaries   7
   1.2   Variables on a household survey   8
   1.3   Reducing the number of digits   12
   1.4   Bar charts and pie charts   13
   1.5   Histograms   13
   1.6   From interval level to ordinal level variables – recoding   18
   1.7   Household level data   19
   1.8   Using SPSS to produce bar charts, pie charts and histograms   24
   1.9   Conclusion   32
   Exercises   32

2   Numerical Summaries of Level and Spread   35
   2.1   Working hours of couples in Britain   35
   2.2   Summaries of level   37
   2.3   Summaries of spread   40
   2.4   Other locational statistics   43
   2.5   Choosing between measures   45
   2.6   Obtaining summaries of level and spread using SPSS and Excel   47
   2.7   Individual and aggregate level data   52
   2.8   Hours worked by age   53
   2.9   Comparing working hours across Europe: the Working Time
          Directive   54
   2.10 Conclusion   55
   Exercises   55

3	**Scaling and Standardizing**	57
	3.1 Data are produced not given	57
	3.2 Adding or subtracting a constant	58
	3.3 Multiplying or dividing by a constant	58
	3.4 Standardized variables	61
	3.5 The Gaussian distribution	66
	3.6 Standardizing with respect to an appropriate base	71
	3.7 Has the Equal Pay Act worked?	72
	3.8 Conclusion	73
	Exercises	74
4	**Inequality**	76
	4.1 Prosperity and inequality	76
	4.2 Income and wealth	77
	4.3 Measuring inequality: quantiles and quantile shares	81
	4.4 Cumulative income shares and Lorenz curves	83
	4.5 Desirable properties in a summary measure of inequality	85
	4.6 The Gini coefficient	86
	4.7 Alternative measures of inequality	88
	4.8 Conclusion	90
	Exercises	90
5	**Smoothing Time Series**	93
	5.1 Time series	93
	5.2 Smoothing	94
	5.3 The aim of smoothing	94
	5.4 Tough on crime, tough on the causes of crime?	96
	5.5 Opinion polls	99
	5.6 Techniques	101
	5.7 Residuals	107
	5.8 Refinements	109
	5.9 Conclusion	110
	Exercises	110

Part II Relationships between Two Variables

6	**Percentage Tables**	117
	6.1 Introduction	117
	6.2 Higher education: a question of access?	117
	6.3 Proportions, percentages and probabilities	119
	6.4 NS-SEC: a new measure of social class?	120
	6.5 Contingency tables	121
	6.6 Percentage tables	124
	6.7 Good table manners	126
	6.8 Producing contingency tables using SPSS	129
	6.9 Simplifying tables by recoding variables and collapsing categories	130
	6.10 Conclusion	138
	Exercises	138

7	**Analysing Contingency Tables**	141
	7.1 Which way should proportions run?	141
	7.2 The base for comparison	142
	7.3 Summarizing effects by subtracting proportions	144
	7.4 Properties of *d* as a measure of effect	146
	7.5 How large a difference in proportions is a 'significant' difference?	147
	7.6 Calculating the chi-square statistic – innocent until proven guilty?	148
	7.7 Calculating chi-square using SPSS	156
	7.8 Conclusion	157
	Exercises	158
8	**Handling Several Batches**	161
	8.1 Unemployment – an issue of concern	161
	8.2 Counting the unemployed	162
	8.3 Regional variation in unemployment rates	163
	8.4 Boxplots	167
	8.5 Outliers	168
	8.6 Multiple boxplots	171
	8.7 Decomposing the variation in unemployment rates	172
	8.8 Moving to the individual as a unit of analysis and using a statistical test	174
	8.9 The T-test	176
	8.10 Obtaining multiple boxplots using SPSS	182
	8.11 One-way analysis of variance	183
	8.12 Using SPSS to carry out a one-way analysis of variance	186
	8.13 Conclusion	188
	Exercises	189
9	**Scatterplots and Resistant Lines**	191
	9.1 Introduction: lone parents and deprivation	191
	9.2 Scatterplots	192
	9.3 Lone parents	193
	9.4 Linear relationships	194
	9.5 Where to draw the line?	195
	9.6 Fitting a resistant line	196
	9.7 Using SPSS to fit a resistant line	199
	9.8 Inspection of residuals	204
	9.9 Further examples	206
	9.10 Conclusion	209
	Exercises	210
10	**Transformations**	212
	10.1 The Millennium Development Goals	212
	10.2 The distribution of GNI per capita	215
	10.3 The log transformation	217
	10.4 The ladder of powers	219

10.5 The goals of transformation   222
10.6 Promoting equality of spread   223
10.7 Alternatives to GNI as a measure of welfare   224
10.8 Unbending curvy lines   225
10.9 Determining the best power for transformation   227
10.10 Conclusion   228
      Exercises   229

Part III   Introducing a Third Variable

11 Causal Explanations   235
11.1 Why did the chicken cross the road?   236
11.2 Direct and indirect effects   238
11.3 Controlling the world to learn about causes   239
11.4 Do opinion polls influence people?   241
11.5 Assumptions required to infer causes   242
11.6 Controlling for prior variables   244
11.7 Controlling for intervening variables   248
11.8 Positive and negative relationships   250
11.9 Conclusion   251
      Exercises   252

12 Three-Variable Contingency Tables and Beyond   254
12.1 Trust and reciprocity   254
12.2 Controlling for a prior variable   255
12.3 Causal path models for three variables   258
12.4 More complex models: going beyond three variables   262
12.5 Logistic regression models   262
12.6 Estimating a more complex model   266
12.7 Interpreting the coefficients in a logistic regression model   268
12.8 Estimating a more complex model – interactions   269
12.9 Age and cohort effects   273
12.10 Conclusion   273
      Exercises   274

13 Longitudinal Data   277
13.1 Introduction   277
13.2 Collecting longitudinal data   278
13.3 Examining change over time   282
13.4 Transition tables   284
13.5 Poverty dynamics   286
13.6 Approaches to the analysis of longitudinal data   287
13.7 Event history modelling   288
13.8 Causality in cross-sectional and longitudinal research   290
13.9 Conclusion   290
      Exercises   291

References   293
Index   299

Figures

1.1   Specimen data from the 2005 GHS (individual file)   10
1.2   Bar chart showing drinking behaviour from GHS specimen data
       (20 cases)   14
1.3   Pie chart showing drinking behaviour from GHS specimen data
       (20 cases)   14
1.4   Histogram of age from the General Household Survey 2005   15
1.5   Histogram of estimated individual alcohol consumption per week   16
1.6A   Histogram of men's estimated individual alcohol consumption
       per week   17
1.6B   Histogram of women's estimated individual alcohol consumption
       per week   17
1.7A   Bar chart of men's estimated individual alcohol consumption
       per week   18
1.7B   Bar chart of women's estimated individual alcohol consumption
       per week   19
1.8   Specimen data from the 2005 GHS (household file)   20
1.9   Bar chart of number of households in each Government Office
       Region in the GHS 2005   21
1.10   Histogram of weekly household income from the GHS 2005   22
1.11   Pie chart of number of cars or vans per household from the
       GHS 2005   23
1.12   Bar chart of number of people in each household in the GHS 2005 24
1.13   Using menus to open a dataset in the SPSS Data Editor   25
1.14   Accessing the SPSS tutorials   26
1.15   Using menus to produce a pie chart   27
1.16   A first dialogue box for pie charts   28
1.17   A second dialogue box for pie charts   28
1.18   The second dialogue box for pie charts with variable 'drinkamt'
       selected   28
1.19   A pie chart of the variable 'drinkamt' shown in an SPSS Output
       Viewer window   29
1.20   Opening the SPSS dialogue box to show the missing values   30

1.21	Creating a bar chart in SPSS	30
1.22	Selecting the 'Simple' bar chart option	30
1.23	Specifying a variable for the bar chart	31
1.24	The bar chart displayed in the SPSS Output window	31
1.25	Histogram of estimated weekly units of alcohol drunk by those defining themselves as 'drink a moderate amount'	33
2.1	Weekly hours worked by men in the 2005 GHS	36
2.2	Weekly hours worked by women in the 2005 GHS	36
2.3A	Men's working hours ranked to show the median	38
2.3B	Women's working hours ranked to show the median	39
2.3C	Men's working hours ranked and showing the upper and lower quartiles	41
2.4	Worksheet for standard deviation of men's weekly working hours	42
2.5	Numerical summaries of hours worked per week	44
2.6	Alternative numerical summaries of hours worked per week	45
2.7	Selecting 'Analyse' and 'Frequencies' in SPSS to obtain descriptive statistics	47
2.8	The Frequencies dialogue box in SPSS	47
2.9	Selecting the descriptive statistics to calculate in SPSS	48
2.10	Running a syntax file in SPSS	48
2.11	Summary statistics for hours worked per week for men and women combined	49
2.12	Using the menus to select a subset of cases	50
2.13	Specifying a condition for selected cases to satisfy	51
2.14	Limiting the analysis to men only	51
2.15	Selecting 'All cases' for analysis	52
2.16	Distribution of total working hours for men and women working full-time in the UK in 2004	53
2.17	Hours of work by age for men in the UK (2004)	53
2.18	Average actual working hours for men and women working full-time (2005, Q1)	55
3.1A	Histogram of weekly alcohol consumption of men who describe themselves as drinking 'quite a lot' or 'heavy drinkers'	59
3.1B	Histogram of daily alcohol consumption of men who describe themselves as drinking 'quite a lot' or 'heavy drinkers'	59
3.2	Extract of data from the General Household Survey showing *weekly* alcohol consumption (drating) and *daily* alcohol consumption (drday)	60
3.3	Volume of household expenditure over time (UK)	61
3.4	Descriptive statistics for reading comprehension and mathematics test scores from NCDS age 16	62
3.5	Scores of reading and mathematics tests at age 16	63
3.6	Creating standardized variables using SPSS	65
3.7	Selecting variables to standardize	65
3.8	The Gaussian distribution	67
3.9	Fixed proportions under the Gaussian curve with mean 0 and standard deviation 1	67

3.10	Histogram of boys' heights at age 16, with superimposed 'normal' curve	68
3.11	Extract from data on boys' heights from the National Child Development Study	69
3.12	Frequency table of boys' heights recoded for comparison with the Gaussian distribution	70
3.13	Male and female earnings 1990–2000: gross earnings in pounds per week for full-time workers on adult rates whose pay was not affected by absence	71
3.14	Male and female earnings relative to medians for each sex	72
3.15	Female earnings relative to male earnings at the same quantile	73
3.16	Scores obtained by nine respondents on three different tests	74
4.1	Lower boundaries of each gross income decile group	81
4.2	Percentage shares of household income, 2003–4	82
4.3	Cumulative income shares: 2003–4	84
4.4	Lorenz curves of income: 2003–4	84
4.5	Trends in income inequality using the Gini coefficient: 1981–2003–4	88
4.6	Trends in income inequality using P90/P10: 1981–2003–4	89
4.7	Two income inequality indicators for OECD countries for 2000 (or 1995 for Belgium and Spain)	91
5.1	Total numbers of recorded crimes: 1965–94	94
5.2	Total number of recorded crimes: unsmoothed	95
5.3	Total recorded crimes 1965–94: smoothed	95
5.4A	Total quarterly recorded crimes 1990–2004: unsmoothed	97
5.4B	Total quarterly recorded crimes 1990–2004: smoothed	98
5.5	Voting intention in Britain: recent trends	101
5.6	Percentage stating they will vote Labour: unsmoothed	102
5.7	Smoothing numbers by replacing the value of the middle month by the median of all three months	103
5.8	Worksheet: running medians and means of three	103
5.9	Percentage intending to vote Labour: comparison of median and mean smoothing	104
5.10	Worksheet for repeated median smoothing and hanning (3RH)	106
5.11	Voting intentions for the three major parties: median smoothed and hanned	107
5.12	Residuals from the 3RH smooth	108
5.13	Creating a value for t_0	109
5.14	Quarterly crime statistics: violent crime 1990–2006	111
5.15	Heights of recruits to the Marine Society	112
6.1	Social class (NS-SEC) background of individuals aged 19 in 2005	119
6.2	Social class background and main activity of those aged 19 in 2005	121
6.3	Three-dimensional bar chart: main activity by class background, young people aged 19 in 2005	122
6.4	Anatomy of a contingency table	123
6.5	Main activity by class background (frequencies)	123
6.6	Main activity at age 19 by class background	124

6.7	Using SPSS to produce contingency tables	129
6.8	Using the 'Cells' button to specify row, column or total percentages	130
6.9	Selecting just row percentages	130
6.10	SPSS output of contingency table family ns-sec by individual's main activity at age 19	131
6.11	Screenshot demonstrating how to recode a variable into a different variable	132
6.12	Specifying a name for the new variable in the process of recoding an existing variable	133
6.13	Screenshot showing the specification of new groups when recoding a variable	133
6.14	Adding variable label and labels for each value	134
6.15	Adding value labels	135
6.16	Reducing the numbers of values	135
6.17	Specifying a third 'layer' variable	136
6.18	Separate tables for young men and women	137
6.19	SPSS output showing contingency table of mother's social position by father's social position	139
6.20	Household size by numbers in poverty	140
7.1	Levels of worry about walking alone after dark 2004–5	142
7.2	Causal path model of age group and fear of walking alone after dark	144
7.3	Quantifying model in figure 7.2	145
7.4	Feeling safe walking alone after dark by gender	148
7.5	Feeling safe walking alone after dark by gender (hypothetical survey of 200 individuals)	149
7.6	Feeling safe walking alone after dark by gender (hypothetical survey of 200 individuals	149
7.7	Feeling safe walking alone after dark by gender – **expected** values if men and women in the population are equally likely to feel unsafe	149
7.8	Feeling safe walking alone after dark by gender – **observed** values following the survey	150
7.9	Computation of chi-square from figures 7.7 and 7.8	151
7.10	Feeling safe walking alone after dark by gender (sample restricted to those of Black Caribbean ethnic origin)	152
7.11	Chi-square for figure 7.10 calculated using SPSS	153
7.12	Feeling safe walking alone after dark by gender (sample restricted to those aged 16–39 of Black Caribbean ethnic origin)	154
7.13	Chi-square associated with figure 7.12, calculated using the SPSS package	154
7.14	Obtaining a value for chi-square using the 'Statistics . . .' button	157
7.15	Specifying the type of statistics required in SPSS	157
7.16	Women's levels of worry about violent crime by age 2005–6	158
7.17	SPSS output of the association between age group and fear of crime focusing just on the men in the British Crime Survey	159
8.1	Unemployment rates across Europe (October 2006)	163

8.2	Sample of unemployment rates by local area in 2005	164
8.3	Local area unemployment in 2005 across all regions in Great Britain: histogram and descriptive statistics	165
8.4	Unemployment rates in the East Midlands in 2005: percentages, histogram and descriptive statistics	166
8.5	Anatomy of a boxplot	168
8.6	Unemployment in the East Midlands in 2005: boxplot	169
8.7	Local unemployment within regions in 2005: multiple boxplots	170
8.8	Worksheet for fitting conditional regional medians	173
8.9	Displaying residuals from conditional regional fit: histogram and descriptive statistics	174
8.10	Boxplots comparing girls' and boys' mathematics scores at age 11	175
8.11	Extract from SPSS output showing T-test results	176
8.12	Screenshot demonstrating T-test in SPSS	178
8.13	Screenshot demonstrating T-test in SPSS: selecting the test variable(s) and grouping variable	178
8.14	Screenshot T-test in SPSS: define groups	179
8.15	T-test output from SPSS comparing boys' and girls' mathematics scores at age 16	180
8.16	Mathematics test scores at age 11 by mother's interest in education: multiple boxplots	181
8.17	Screenshot from SPSS showing the boxplot command	182
8.18	Screenshot from SPSS showing boxplot options	182
8.19	Screenshot from SPSS showing how to define a simple boxplot	183
8.20	Extract from SPSS output showing mathematics scores by mother's reported interest in child's education	184
8.21	Extract from SPSS output showing one-way Anova results	184
8.22	Comparisons between the five groups (defined by mother's interest in education)	185
8.23	Screenshot demonstrating one-way Anova in SPSS	186
8.24	Screenshot demonstrating specification of one-way Anova in SPSS	187
8.25	Screenshot demonstrating specification of post-hoc comparisons for one-way Anova in SPSS	188
8.26	Screenshot demonstrating specification of display options for one-way Anova in SPSS	188
8.27	Boxplots for economic inactivity rates in London and the South East	190
8.28	Results from a one-way analysis of variance examining the impact of father's interest in education on child's mathematics test score at age 11	190
9.1	A scatterplot showing a moderately strong relationship	192
9.2	Lone parent households and households with no car or van, % by region	193
9.3	Lone parent households by households with no car or van: scatterplot	194
9.4	Anatomy of a straight line	195
9.5	Worksheet for calculating a resistant line	197

9.6	Using SPSS to create a scatterplot	200
9.7	Choosing the type of scatterplot in SPSS	200
9.8	Selecting the variables to plot	200
9.9	Percentage of lone parents and car ownership	201
9.10	Using SPSS to add a fit line	201
9.11	Percentage of lone parents and car ownership including a resistant line	202
9.12	Using regression analysis in SPSS to provide an equation for a straight line	202
9.13	Specifying the dependent and independent variables in SPSS	203
9.14	A model summary produced by SPSS	203
9.15A	Using SPSS to save predicted values and residuals as part of the regression analysis	204
9.15B	Using SPSS to save predicted values and residuals as part of the regression analysis	204
9.16	The SPSS output identifying unusually large residuals	205
9.17	Residuals from regression of nocar on lonepar	206
9.18	Unemployment rate and proportion of households that are owner occupied	207
9.19	Scatterplot of mathematics score at age 16 by general ability test score at age 11	208
9.20	Residuals from regression of mathematics score at age 16 on general ability at age 11	209
9.21	Rating of personal happiness by real GNP per head	210
10.1	GNI per capita in 2000 in 20 sampled countries	215
10.2	The distribution of GNI per capita in 2000: boxplot	216
10.3	Distribution of GNI per capita in 2000 within country groups	216
10.4	Logging the numbers in 10.1	217
10.5	Logging GNI per capita in 2000 in 20 selected countries	218
10.6	Life expectancy in the world in 2000: histogram of raw data	219
10.7	Life expectancy in the world in 2000: boxplots of raw and transformed data	220
10.8	The ladder of powers	221
10.9	Logged GNP per capita in 2000 by country group	223
10.10	Life expectancy by GNI per capita in 2000	225
10.11	Cubed life expectancy by logged GNP per capita in 2000	226
10.12	Guide to linearizing transformations for curves	228
10.13	Boxplot of CO_2 emissions per capita	230
10.14	Scatterplot of GNI per capita by CO_2 emissions per capita	231
11.1	Causes of absenteeism	239
11.2	Different causal relationships between variables	243
11.3	The effect of job status on absenteeism: controlling a prior variable	246
11.4	Outcome I from figure 11.3	246
11.5	Outcome II from figure 11.3	246
11.6	Outcome III from figure 11.3	247
11.7	Outcome IV from figure 11.3	247

11.8	Success of application to graduate school by gender and department: an example of Simpson's paradox	248
11.9	The effect of job status on absenteeism: controlling an intervening variable	249
11.10	Other outcomes for figure 11.3	250
12.1	Membership of voluntary organization by social trust	256
12.2	Causal path diagram based on contingency table in figure 12.1	256
12.3	Highest level of qualifications by membership of a voluntary association	257
12.4	Highest levels of qualifications by social trust	257
12.5	Social trust by membership of voluntary association and level of qualifications: causal path diagram	258
12.6	Screenshot of the Crosstabs dialogue box – creating a three-way contingency table	259
12.7	Extract from SPSS output showing a three-way contingency table	260
12.8	Social trust by highest level of qualifications and membership of a voluntary association	261
12.9	Assigning coefficients to figure 12.5	262
12.10	Screenshot of SPSS demonstrating Binary Logistic regression command	263
12.11	Screenshot of SPSS demonstrating Logistic Regressio dialogue box	263
12.12	SPSS screenshot demonstrating the specification of categorical covariates in the model	265
12.13	Parameter estimates	265
12.14	Parameter estimates with two explanatory variables	266
12.15	Parameter estimates for the model with five explanatory variables predicting 'trust'	267
12.16	Model coefficients to predict 'trust' using the original age variable	268
12.17	Bivariate relationship between party identification and views on welfare	270
12.18	Proportion agreeing with higher spending on welfare by party identification by age	270
12.19	The impact of party identification and age on attitudes to welfare spending [model 1]	271
12.20	Screenshot demonstrating a logistic regression including an interaction term	272
12.21	The impact of party identification and age on attitudes to welfare spending [model 2 including interaction terms]	273
12.22	People's inclination to break the law by household income	274
12.23	Destination of school-leavers April 1979	275
12.24	Logistic regression model SPSS output (dependent variable is agreement or disagreement with the statement 'Income differences in Great Britain are too large')	275
13.1	Examples of longitudinal studies	280
13.2	British General Election results 1992 and 1997	283

13.3 British Household Panel Study self-reported voting 1992 and 1997 (Great Britain only) 283

13.4 Transition table cross-tabulating individuals' votes in 1992 by individuals' votes in 1997 (row percentages) 285

13.5 Transition table cross-tabulating individuals' votes in 1992 by individuals' votes in 1997 (column percentages) 285

13.6 Low income dynamics 1991 and 1992, data from the BHPS 287

13.7 Transition table cross-tabulating individuals' votes in 1992 by individuals' votes in 1997 (row percentages) disaggregated by age group 291

Acknowledgements

This second edition of *Exploring Data* builds very directly on the sound foundations provided by the original book, and thanks should therefore be repeated to all those named in Cathie's original acknowledgements, which are reproduced below.

Acknowledgements from first edition

This book has had a long gestation period, and I have accumulated debts to many people *en route*. It was John Bibby who originally suggested collecting material for a data analysis course with a strong exploratory flavour for British students. He and I, together with Tony Weekes from York University and Allan Seheult from Durham University, and with the generous assistance of the Nuffield Foundation, met over a two-year period to exchange views on how data analysis should be taught, to swop ideas for examples and to argue about methods of presentation. This book is a product of those interactions, and my debt to the other three is great. At one point we planned to write the book together; Allan drafted the first version of a chapter on smoothing and Tony produced materials on price indices and SMRs. But four-way collaboration on something as detailed as a textbook proved impossible, and we agreed that I should smooth the materials for publication. Allan, John and Tony now stand in the enviable position of being able to take credit for any of the ways in which this book succeeds, and to blame me for its shortcomings.

There are many others who have helped enormously. Eddie Shoesmith, Diego Gambetta and Archie Levey helped me teach a course based on these materials in earlier years, and provided very stimulating feedback. Tony Wojciechowski, David Calderbank and Christopher Castleton provided essential research assistance, particularly in preparing small datasets. Don Manning and Geoff Mason helped with reproduction of materials.

Many people helped me by answering my queries, or by providing detail for individual chapters: Pat Altham, Sara Arber, R. J. Bennett, Martin Bulmer, Brendan Burchell, Roy Carr-Hill, Jennifer Church, Frank Cowell, Nick Cox,

Angela Dale, Chris Denham, Dave Drew, Roderick Floud, Don Forster, John Fox, Peter Goldblatt, Brian Gooddale, Anne E. Green, Mary Gregory, Ted Harding, Martin Hargreaves, Geoffrey Hawthorn, Sophie Houston, Mark Kleinman, Ian Knight, Peter Laslett, Alistair McCauley, Alison Macfarlane, Ian Miles, Panos Pashardes, David Raffe, Irene Rauta, Bob Redpath, David Rhind, Jan Siltanen, Peter Shepherd, Nigel Walker, Norman Webb, Julie Wells and Jane White.

Others took the task of colleagueship one stage further and read either parts of or all of the manuscript and gave me a multitude of useful comments: John Bibby, Bob Blackburn, Angela Dale, Jim Davis, Tony Giddens, Nigel Gilbert, and the man himself, John Tukey.

I owe three special debts of gratitude. The first is to Dave Marsh, with whom I have argued extensively over the years about most things, the philosophy and practice of data analysis not least among them, and upon whose judgement I have come to depend. The second is to Claire Young, who, as well as providing detailed assistance in many different ways, coordinated the final production of the text, ensuring that the chapters on the disk, the datasets on the computer and the hard copy all corresponded: an amazing achievement. Finally, I want to thank the students studying Social and Political Sciences at the University of Cambridge. They proved pretty scathing critics, but in the most charming and constructive of manners; they helped make the whole enterprise enjoyable.

Acknowledgements from second edition

As one of the students studying Social and Political Sciences at the University of Cambridge (from 1985–7) I remember Cathie Marsh providing us with copies of her draft chapters for the original book and encouraging us to provide her with feedback. *Exploring Data* was then published in 1988, the year after I graduated, and the battered, dog-eared nature of my own copy of the book is evidence of how much I used it when teaching students the basics of how to do quantitative analysis and also as a handy reference in my early research career. As an undergraduate listening to Cathie's excellent lectures on data analysis I never imagined that one day I would be preparing the second edition of the book. It has been a privilege to have the opportunity to work with Cathie's original text and to update the empirical material in the book to produce a second edition. Several people have helped me with material for specific chapters. In particular Alison Walker at the Home Office provided very helpful comments on chapter 7, Francis Jones from ONS offered helpful advice on calculating the Lorenz curves in chapter 4, and Jo Wathan, Ludi Simpson and Mark Brown, at the Cathie Marsh Centre for Census and Survey Research at the University of Manchester, have always provided very prompt and helpful responses to my various queries.

There are a few individuals whom I would particularly like to thank. Brendan Burchell, who taught alongside Cathie in Cambridge, was one of the key people who fostered my initial interest in data analysis and has been very supportive throughout the production of this second edition. Chris Baker has played a vital role in checking over my text and ensuring that tables and figures are correctly labelled and numbered. Emma Longstaff and Jonathan Skerrett at Polity have been extremely patient and encouraging throughout the project. Special thanks are also due to Jon Lawrence whose support has been essential and who made sure that the West Midlands didn't get forgotten in chapter 8!

Formal acknowledgement also needs to be made for all the data used in this book that have been made available via the UK Data Archive at the University of Essex. In relation to the British Crime Survey in chapter 7, material from Crown copyright records made available through the Home Office and the UK Data Archive has been used by permission of the Controller of Her Majesty's Stationery Office and the Queen's Printer for Scotland.

Introduction

No one wants to be just another statistic. Perhaps this is because of the way that statistical descriptions of society often seem to obscure the individual lives that they represent, or perhaps it is because many of the statistics that we hear reported enumerate events that we would like to avoid such as divorce, violent crime and mortality. However, statistics play an important role in the social world. They provide information which bodies such as local authorities or national governments can potentially use to make policy decisions, or which can be used to evaluate the effectiveness of existing policies. Increasingly data and statistics about institutions such as schools, hospitals and police forces have been made available to the general public. This type of data is often published on the basis that it allows individuals to make informed decisions – for example about which secondary school might be best for their child, or which hospital to go to for a hip operation. However, there is also an argument that these types of statistics fulfil a political purpose in reducing the power of professionals by making their performance more visible and allowing for comparisons to be made. This proliferation of statistics has also led to increasing debate about how these figures are constructed. There is a growing recognition that, although numbers are often thought of as 'hard facts' when compared with more subjective case studies or individual narratives, in reality every published statistic is the result of a number of different decisions about how something should be categorized and counted, or not counted. As statistics become ever more ubiquitous, aided by the power and immediacy of the world wide web, so it becomes even more essential that as citizens we possess the statistical literacy to make informed judgements about how to interpret them and how to decode their political purpose.

To understand how to calculate percentages, how to decipher a table and how to interpret a graph requires a feel for numbers. Many people lack confidence in their numerical abilities and many students studying for degrees in the social sciences have been overheard saying 'I'm no good with numbers.' However, the vast majority of people already have a very sound understanding of number. There is no question that people would rather have a 10 per cent pay rise than a 2.5 per cent pay rise. People would rather win a £10 bet placed on the 100 to one outsider than the two to one favourite in a horse race.

This book is not about sophisticated mathematical techniques or complicated formulae. It is about building on the basic understandings we all have about numbers and introducing some straightforward techniques for using numbers to describe the social world. In addition to providing a wide range of examples of how statistics are used in society, the book also aims to describe the nature of some of the main government social surveys in Britain. This book is therefore more about politics than it is about algebra or sums.

The word 'statistics' comes from German and originally referred to pieces of information about the *state*, particularly its military strength. With the birth of industrialism came an interest in social data. For the early Victorians, 'statisticians' were those who collected social information about the inhabitants of emerging capitalist societies. The first volumes of the *Journal of the Royal Statistical Society* were full of articles describing the social conditions of the time. Gradually the word 'statistics' was restricted to quantitative information of that kind, and came to be synonymous with what we would now call 'data', spreading its meaning beyond social data to biological and other types of data. Finally, as theoretical advances were made, particularly in the theory of sampling and of the regularities which random subsets of data display, statistics swapped disciplinary camps and came under the provenance of mathematics.

Mathematical statisticians have solved some very important problems in the area of sampling theory. They can tell us, with some precision, how likely it is that a property of a small sample drawn at random from a larger population holds true for that larger population. In general, they have elaborated the process of *inference*, i.e. generalizing from small samples. Because people who teach mathematical statistics are justly proud of these achievements, inferential statistics tends to occupy a large place in their courses and many books on quantitative data analysis focus almost exclusively on these topics.

However, this book does not set out to be a course in statistical theory. It seeks to restore the emphasis to data analysis and to the detective work involved in sifting through and piecing together numerical evidence about the social world. The techniques which are presented here are designed to help the researcher look at batches of numbers and make sense of them. Some of the best of these techniques were put forward by John Tukey, whose hero is Sherlock Holmes, and whose maxim is 'Seeing is believing.' In fact, Tukey probably did little more than to formalize the kind of logic in use by practising statisticians the world over. The main original sourcebooks are Tukey's *Exploratory Data Analysis* (1977) and Mosteller and Tukey's *Data Analysis and Regression* (1977). A more recent edition including many of the original techniques is Hoaglin, Mosteller and Tukey (2006). The group of techniques that have come to be known as Exploratory Data Analysis (EDA) provide the data analyst with a set of techniques with which to explore numerical data and to gain an understanding of its most salient features through emphasizing graphical display.

Anyone who is eventually going to make a career analysing data must be able to answer the question 'Is your sample size big enough for you to be fairly sure of that?' This is, however, a second-order question in comparison with 'What do these data say?' or 'Might that result be spurious?' This book therefore aims to keep a balance between introducing the main techniques needed for understanding the patterns or stories within the data and discussing how to check whether the patterns that appear are also likely to be found within the wider population of interest. This second edition of *Exploring Data* therefore retains the original book's emphasis on exploring and understanding the patterns to be found within sets of data but also includes an introduction to inferential statistics.

How to use this book

The book is divided into three parts. The first part covers various techniques for examining variables one at a time. The second part covers relationships between two variables. And – you've guessed it – the third covers situations in which a third variable is brought into the picture. Here three stands in for many; once you understand how to manipulate three variables together, you are ready to understand in principle how to extend the techniques to many variables. In many cases the later chapters in the book build on material introduced earlier; however, some chapters are relatively free standing. While some readers may want to work through the book chapter by chapter others may prefer to tackle topics in a different order. We have therefore suggested at or near the beginning of each chapter which others are required reading.

Data analysis is not a spectator sport. No amount of reading about it substitutes for doing it. The exercises at the end of each chapter are therefore an integral part of the book, and should not be skipped. Sometimes they allow illustration of a point which the example used in the chapter did not show. Read the suggested answers that are provided on the accompanying website www.polity.co.uk/exploringdata, but don't be put off if you did something different, or came to rather different conclusions. One of the most important rules of data analysis is that there is no one model that best or uniquely fits a set of data.

Most of the chapters also have an associated appendix that introduces a major data source. They have been put on the accompanying website so that they can be referred to quickly and easily and can be updated as the major government surveys and sources of data are themselves revised and changed.

While the book starts by suggesting some simple pencil and paper techniques for understanding data, the computer has now become an important part of the data analyst's armoury. At the time of writing, a statistical computer package called SPSS (the Statistical Package for the Social Sciences) is widely used by social scientists in the UK and provides a fast, efficient and well-documented interactive package for data analysis (Norusis, 2005). The book therefore includes basic instructions as to how the various techniques described can be accomplished with SPSS (version 13). However, the book is not primarily intended as an instruction manual for the SPSS package and the sections on SPSS can therefore be ignored if you do not have access to it. There are a series of datasets which are used for the computer exercises and which can be used for further exploratory work of your own devising. They are listed and documented on the accompanying website. The datasets have all been deposited at the ESRC Data Archive at the University of Essex, and it is straightforward to download them via the internet.

Key terms are in bold type in the text when they first appear or where they are given a clear definition. The index entry will have a bold page number to direct the reader to such definitions. In this way the index can also be used as a glossary of terms.

Part I

Single Variables

In this first part, methods are introduced to display the essential features of one variable at a time; we defer until the next part the consideration of relationships between variables. This first part is therefore concerned primarily with the accurate and elegant *description* of features of the social world, rather than with their *explanation*.

Description, classification and summary are the cornerstones of the scientific method. The importance of providing a good description should not be underestimated. If the world, natural or social, revealed its key features easily, then people would not have had to struggle over the centuries to develop better methods to describe it; indeed, some of the techniques which we shall present in the forthcoming chapters have only been in use for the past three decades or so.

The part contains five chapters. In the first, we learn how to look at the whole of a distribution, while in the second we concentrate on summarizing key features. Sometimes we need to rework the original numbers to make them more straightforward to summarize, to combine information into complex measures or to purify them of contaminating influences; this is discussed in chapter 3. The special techniques which have been developed for looking at inequality in the distribution of income are treated in chapter 4. Finally in chapter 5 we focus on a technique for examining changes over time in measures such as crime rates and opinion polls. This final chapter of part 1 strictly speaking introduces a second variable – namely time. However, a full discussion of how to analyse the relationship between two variables is delayed until part 2 of the book.

1

Distributions and Variables

How much alcohol do men and women drink each week? How many households have no access to a car? What is a typical household income in Britain? Which country in Europe has the longest working hours? To answer these kinds of questions we need to collect information from a large number of people, and we need to ensure that the people questioned are broadly representative of the population we are interested in. Conducting large-scale surveys is a time-consuming and costly business. However, increasingly information or data from survey research in the social sciences are available free of charge to researchers and students. The development of the world wide web and the ubiquity and power of computers makes accessing these types of data quick and easy. As will be explained in the appendix to this chapter, which can be found on the accompanying website, literally hundreds of pieces of information about thousands of people can now be downloaded directly from data archives such as the UK Data Archive at the University of Essex. The aim of this chapter is to get you started with exploring data. At the end of the chapter are detailed instructions explaining how you can use the 'Statistical Package for the Social Sciences' (SPSS) package to start analysing data and answering the questions posed above. However, before embarking on using software, it is helpful to start by providing a conceptual introduction to the basics of data analysis.

1.1 Preliminaries

Some stylization of the social world is necessary if we are to describe it systematically and provide explanations for why it is as it is. Two organizing concepts have become the basis of the language of data analysis: *cases* and *variables*.

The **cases** are the basic **units of analysis**, the things about which information is collected. There can be a wide variety of such things. Researchers interested in the consequences of long-term unemployment may treat unemployed individuals as their units of analysis, and collect information directly from them. Those who wish to demonstrate the consensus that exists in industrial societies about the relative prestige of various occupations may take the occupation as their unit of analysis, and then show that the average amount of pay or status associated with each is similar in all industrial societies. Historians may collect information on a series of years, and look for similar patterns in such things as the unemployment rate and the incidence of suicide or depression; here years are the units of analysis.

Sometimes it is possible to do research on all the cases one is interested in. For example, the Census of Population aims to cover all people resident in the country on a particular night. In fact it still misses some people, but in principle everyone is covered. However, most research is done on subsets of the total population of interest, and some selection of cases has to be made.

The problem of **sampling** is the problem of ensuring that the cases selected look like the population from which they were drawn in as many respects as possible. One of the greatest intellectual discoveries of the last hundred years has been that **randomly selected** samples differ from the parent population on average in a predictable way. This will be discussed in more detail in chapter 7, but for now it is enough to recognize that sample data are only worthy of attention if there is reason to believe that they resemble the population from which they were drawn in important respects. The smaller a sample is, the less likely it is to resemble its parent population.

Researchers usually proceed by collecting information on certain features of all of the cases in their sample; these features are the variables. In a survey of individuals, their income, sex, age and satisfaction with life are some of the variables that might be recorded. The word **variable** expresses the fact that this feature varies across the different cases. We mean that the individual cases do not all have the same income, and are not all the same sex. We do not mean that income or sex are things that vary for any one person: at any point in time, when the survey is conducted for example, they are fixed.

In this chapter, we will look at some useful techniques for displaying information about the values of single variables, and will also introduce the differences between interval level and ordinal level variables.

1.2 Variables on a household survey

Household surveys have a long tradition in Britain. Almost as soon as capitalism spawned the first industrial slums, pioneers were out with their notepads and pencils, investigating what they called Britain's 'black continents', observing details of lifestyle from the type of dress to the existence of religious pictures on the walls. These early Victorian statisticians were more interested in people's morals than in their means of existence. Later in the nineteenth century, income information began to be sought. These details were usually collected from employers, rather than from the 'untrustworthy' testimony of the poor themselves. Charles Booth's study of *The Life and Labour of the People of London* in the lean years of the 1890s, for example, documented the widespread nature of poverty, not only among the feckless poor, but even among families Booth considered to be 'deserving' (Booth, 1892). However, Booth relied mainly on the testimony of School Board visitors to reach his conclusions.

Nowadays the state has taken over many of the functions of data collection that were previously performed by volunteer, charitable organizations in the nineteenth century. Much of the data collection is required for the administration of an increasingly complex society. Some of the information is required for purposes of social control. But some modern data collection exercises are still motivated by a similar kind of benevolent paternalism, stressing the need for information to gauge whether society is doing a good job in meeting the needs of its citizens.

One official survey which is a modern inheritor of the nineteenth-century survey tradition is the General Household Survey (GHS). It is a multipurpose survey carried out by the social survey division of the Office for National Statistics (ONS). The main aim of the survey is to collect data on a range of core topics, covering household, family and individual information. Government departments and other organizations use this information for planning, policy and monitoring purposes, and to present a picture of households, family and people in Great Britain. The GHS has been conducted continuously in Britain since 1971, except for breaks between 1997 and 1998 (when the survey was reviewed) and again between 1999 and 2000 when the survey was re-developed. It is a large survey, with a sample size of approximately 8,600 households containing over 20,000 individuals, and is a major source for social scientists. You can read more information about the GHS in the appendix to this chapter on the accompanying website. The sample is designed so that all households in the country have an equal probability of being selected. Problems of bias in sample coverage and non-response are dealt with in the appendix.

Interviews are sought with all adults (aged over 16) in the household and basic information is also collected about any children in the household. The data therefore lend themselves immediately to treating either the individual or the household as the unit of analysis. A third unit can also be constructed – the family unit. Researchers interested in poverty and the distribution of income and wealth have viewed the family as the important social group. For simplicity's sake in this chapter we will only focus on the individual and the household levels of analysis. The two datasets we will use in this chapter provide information from the GHS: first about a sample of individuals and second, about a sample of households. As will be shown below, some information makes most sense when it is collected at the level of the individual. For example, we may be interested in how much alcohol individuals drink each week. However, other variables make more sense if we collect the information at the level of the household because each member of the household shares the same facilities. For example, in a survey such as the GHS it is possible just to ask one member of each household how many cars the household has access to and whether the house is rented or owner occupied. These variables can then be understood to apply to the whole household and not just to some individuals within the household.

Figure 1.1 shows a specimen case by variable **data matrix**. It contains the first few cases in a subset of the 2005 GHS. Information about the first individual is contained in the first row, and so on. The age in years of each individual is shown in column 2 and the sex of each individual is in column 3. In Britain the convention is to use the value '1' to indicate a man and '2' to indicate a woman. The first row of data in figure 1.1 is therefore about a 27-year-old man. We can also see that the fourth person in the data matrix is a 6-year-old boy.

Figure 1.1   Specimen data from the 2005 GHS (individual file).

Person-id	Age	Sex	Units of alcohol per week	Drinking classification	NS-SEC5
1	27	1	24	4	5
2	27	2	8	3	1
3	27	2	27	3	4
4	6	1	.	.	−6
5	5	1	.	.	−6
6	77	1	8	2	1
7	65	2	14	3	2
8	51	2	3	2	2
9	33	1	9	3	5
10	25	1	9	2	5
11	49	1	352	5	3
12	16	1	2	1	97
13	66	1	0	1	4
14	65	2	0	1	5
15	47	2	0	−9	2
16	42	1	6	1	2
17	15	1	.	.	−6
18	13	2	.	.	−6
19	47	2	0	1	1
20	44	1	5	1	1

Source: 2005 GHS individual file.

Column 5 contains a variable that indicates individuals' classification of themselves in terms of the amount of alcohol they usually drink. It has five ranked categories:

1. hardly drink at all
2. drink a little
3. drink a moderate amount
4. drink quite a lot
5. drink heavily

The estimated amount that each person drinks per week is given in column 4. This has been calculated based on people's answers to several detailed questions in the GHS about the quantities of different types of alcohol drunk. This variable is measured in 'units of alcohol' where one unit of alcohol is obtained from half a pint of normal strength beer, lager or cider, a single measure of spirits, one glass of wine or one small glass of port, sherry or other fortified wine. We can see that the second and third individuals in the data matrix shown in figure 1.1 both classify themselves as 'drink a moderate amount' even though there is a substantial difference in the number of units of alcohol they have been estimated to consume over the last week. Information about drinking behaviour is not collected for those under 15. A dot '.' in columns 4 and 5 indicate this lack of data for person 4 and person 5 in the data matrix. It is also interesting to note that in this small sample of twenty people from the GHS there is one person who appears to drink 352 units of alcohol per week. Even though this 49-year-old man classifies himself as a heavy drinker it seems unlikely that he drinks quite this much. Large datasets should always be scrutinized for data values that are almost certainly mistakes, before further analysis is carried out.

It should also be remembered that it is difficult to obtain reliable information about drinking behaviour, partly because people tend to underestimate the amount of alcohol they consume. In particular, drinking at home is likely to be underestimated because quantities are not measured in the way they would be in licensed premises such as pubs. Social surveys such as the GHS are known to record lower levels of alcohol consumption than would be expected given data on the amount of alcohol that is sold.

The social class of each individual is shown in column 6. Most British schemes for placing people in social classes have relied on grouping them on the basis of occupation. The National Statistics Socio-Economic Classification (NS-SEC) is shown here. It has been used for all official statistics and surveys since 2001 and has replaced Social Class based on Occupation (SC), which was formerly the Registrar General's Social Class classification, and Socio-economic Groups. The NS-SEC is based on detailed occupational coding and information about employment status (whether an individual is an employer, self-employed or employee). The NS-SEC is an important variable for social scientists and will be discussed in more detail in chapter 6. For most analyses a version of NS-SEC is used that has eight classes or categories.

However, in the example in figure 1.1 the simpler five-category version is used, which has the following classes.

1. Managerial and professional occupations
2. Intermediate occupations
3. Small employers and own account workers
4. Lower supervisory and technical occupations
5. Semi-routine occupations

In any survey there will be instances of **missing values** for particular variables; it is quite common, for example, to find 10 per cent of respondents failing to provide income information. Some arbitrary numbers are usually chosen to mean 'missing'; any case for which a valid code has not been obtained is then given this value. The numbers −1 and −9 are frequently used to represent a missing value. There are often a number of different reasons why a case may have missing data on a particular variable. For example, an individual may refuse to answer certain questions in a survey or some questions may not be applicable to particular groups of individuals. In large-scale surveys such as the GHS different numbers are routinely used to indicate different types of missing data. In the example above we saw that a dot '.' was used to indicate that data had not been collected on a variable for an individual because that individual was a child. In addition it can be seen that person number 12 has a '97' recorded for the variable NS-SEC5 this indicates that the information provided about his current occupation was insufficient for an accurate classification to be given. It is important to check whether there are any such arbitrary numbers in any dataset before you analyse it, particularly when the information is held on a machine-readable file rather than on paper. Computers, which know no better, will treat all the numbers the same unless they are explicitly told to do otherwise.

The numbers in the different columns of figure 1.1 do not all have the same properties; some of them merely differentiate categories (as in sex or drinking behaviour) whereas some of them actually refer to a precise amount of something (like years of age, or units of alcohol drunk each week). They represent different **levels of measurement**. When numbers are used to represent categories that have no inherent order, this is called a **nominal scale**. When numbers are used to convey full arithmetic properties, this is called an **interval scale**. The techniques of analysis appropriate for the former differ from those appropriate for the latter. Important mathematical operations can be performed on variables measured on interval scales – we can say that one person drinks twice as much as another – but they cannot be performed on nominal scale variables.

There is a difficult grey area between the two, represented by variables such as social class. The numbers contain information about the supposed rank order of the classes, but we cannot say that those in intermediate occupations (code 2) have half of anything that those in lower supervisory and technical occupations (code 4) have. Measures such as these are known as **ordinal scales**. Many of the variables used by social scientists are measured on **nominal scales** or **ordinal scales** (also referred to as **categorical variables**), rather than **interval scales** (also referred to as **continuous variables**). Many of the techniques described in this book will therefore focus on how to analyse these types of categorical data.

1.3 Reducing the number of digits

One final point should be made before we start considering techniques for actually getting our eyes and hands on these variables. The human brain is easily confused by an excess of detail. Numbers with many digits are hard to read, and important features, such as their order of magnitude, may be obscured. Some of the digits in a dataset vary, while others do not. In the following case:

134
121
167

there are two **varying digits** (the first is always 1). In the following, there are also two varying digits:

0.034
0.045
0.062

whereas in the following case:

0.67
1.31
0.92

there are three varying digits. Two varying digits are almost always all that is necessary to get across the important features of a variable. If, however, we wish to perform calculations on the numbers, it is usually best to keep three varying digits until the end, and then display only two. This rule of thumb produces generally sensible results but there can be exceptions. If, for instance, the values were in the range 199.0 to 200.0, it would probably be necessary to work to four and display three varying digits. Of course, if a computer is doing the calculation, there is no point in reducing the precision at all until the display stage.

There are two techniques for reducing the number of digits. The first is known as **rounding**. Values from zero to four are rounded down, and six to ten are rounded up. The digit five causes a problem; it can be arbitrarily rounded up or down according to a fixed rule, or it could be rounded up after an odd digit and down after an even digit. The trouble with such fussy rules is that people tend to make mistakes, and often they are not trivial. It is an easy mistake to round 899.6 to 890. A second method of losing digits is simply **cutting** off or 'truncating' the ones that we do not want. Thus, when cutting, all the numbers from 899.0 to 899.9 become 899. This procedure is much quicker and does not run the extra risk of large mistakes.

1.4 Bar charts and pie charts

Blocks or lines of data are very hard to make sense of. Prolonged gazing at them is more likely to lead to watery eyes than profound insight. We need an easier way of visualizing how any variable is **distributed** across our cases. How can nominal or ordinal scale variables, such as drinking classification in figure 1.1, be represented pictorially? One simple device is the **bar chart,** a visual display in which bars are drawn to represent each category of a variable such that the length of the bar is proportional to the number of cases in the category. For instance, a bar chart of the drinking classification variable in figure 1.1 is shown in figure 1.2.

A pie chart can also be used to display the same information. It is largely a matter of taste whether data from a categorical variable are displayed in a bar chart or a pie chart. In general, pie charts are to be preferred when there are only a few categories and when the sizes of the categories are very different. Figure 1.3 displays the same data as figure 1.2 but in the form of a pie chart rather than a bar chart.

Bar charts and pie charts can be an effective medium of communication if they are well drawn. For example, since there is not always an inherent ordering in the categories, thought has to be given to the order in which to display them.

1.5 Histograms

Charts that are somewhat similar to bar charts can be used to display interval level variables grouped into categories and these are called **histograms**. They are constructed in exactly the same way as bar charts except, of course, that the ordering of the categories is fixed, and care has to be taken to show exactly how the data were grouped.

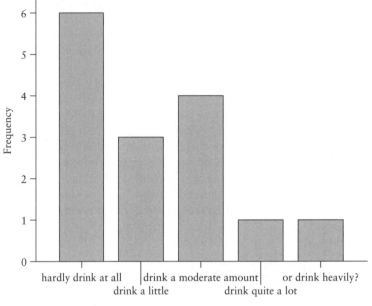

Amount of alcohol respondent drinks

Source: Column 5 of figure 1.1.

Figure 1.2 Bar chart showing drinking behaviour from GHS (2005) specimen data (20 cases).

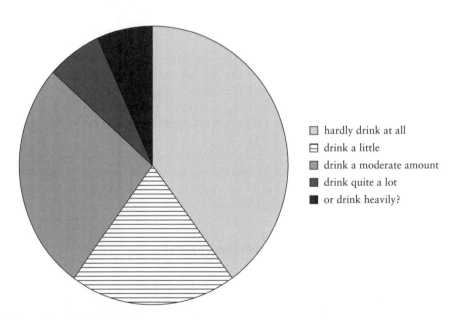

Source: Column 5 of figure 1.1.

Figure 1.3 Pie chart showing drinking behaviour from GHS specimen data (20 cases).

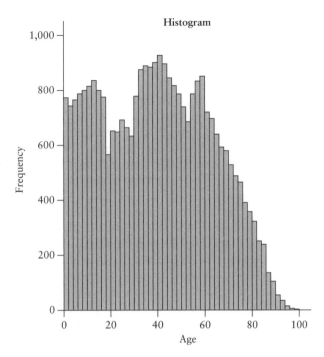

Source: Data from the GHS 2005.

Figure 1.4 Histogram of age from the General Household Survey 2005.

Features visible in histograms

Histograms allow inspection of four important aspects of any distribution:

level   What are typical values in the distribution?

spread   How widely dispersed are the values? Do they differ very much from
           one another?

shape   Is the distribution flat or peaked? Symmetrical or skewed?

outliers   Are there any particularly unusual values?

We will discuss each of these attributes and define each of these important
terms formally in subsequent chapters. In this chapter, they will be used fairly
loosely.

If we look at figure 1.4 we might consider an age of 40, a value near the middle
of the distribution, typical of the values represented here. Careful inspection of the
histogram shows that there are over 800 individuals in the GHS sample who are
40 or 41 years old. (We might, however, want to argue that there was another
typical value at around 12 or 13 years old.)

The distribution has four separate humps or peaks, two more major and two
more minor. This is why it was hard to find an obvious typical value. Distributions
with one peak are called **unimodal**, and those with two peaks are called **bimodal**.
Bimodal distributions should always make us wonder if there are not two rather
different groups being depicted in combination, which would be better analysed

separately. In this case there are four peaks which reflect the current age structure of the British population. These peaks are largely due to fluctuations in the birth rate over the years but this will also be moderated somewhat by immigration and by differential response rates to the survey among groups of people of different ages.

There are other things to notice about the shape of the display. The lower **tail** (end) of the age distribution ends abruptly – no one can be less than 0 years old! But the upper tail **straggles** up slightly from age 80 to age 100. This is what we would expect from a common-sense understanding of life-expectancy in Britain. This slightly bunched up lower tail and straggling upper tail is evidence that the distribution is slightly **skewed**. A more extreme example of a skewed distribution can be seen if we look at the histogram in figure 1.5.

Alcohol consumption is an extremely skewed variable. There is a 'floor effect' in that nobody can drink less than nothing, and the histogram shows that the majority of people in the sample drink fewer than 20 units of alcohol per week. However, we can also see that a small number of individuals drink over 80 units of alcohol per week. This is equivalent to more than five and a half pints of beer per day or nearly two bottles of wine per day. In this example, given that we know that women tend to drink substantially less than men on average, and given that the recommended maximum weekly intake of alcohol is much lower for women than it is for men, it makes sense to display the data separately for men and women in two different histograms.

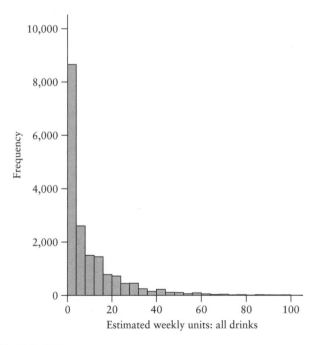

Source: GHS 2005 individual data.

Figure 1.5   Histogram of estimated individual alcohol consumption per week.

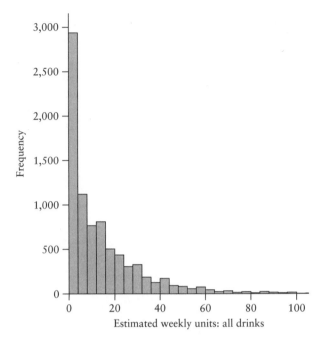

Source: GHS 2005 individual data.

Figure 1.6A   Histogram of men's estimated individual alcohol consumption per week.

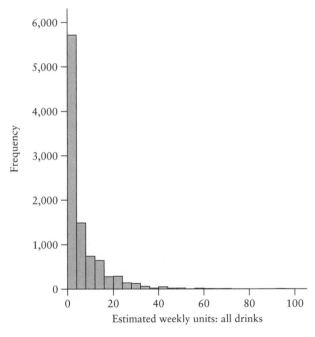

Source: GHS 2005 individual data.

Figure 1.6B   Histogram of women's estimated individual alcohol consumption per week.

1.6 From interval level to ordinal level variables – recoding

In some instances, although a variable has been recorded in a survey at interval level, it can be instructive to group the values of that variable to form a smaller number of categories. For example, given that the maximum recommended weekly intake of alcohol is 21 units for men and 14 units for women it is helpful to recode the interval variable measuring estimated weekly consumption into an ordinal variable with three categories:

- no alcohol drunk (none)
- 1–21 units drunk (moderate drinking)
- over 21 units drunk (heavy drinking)

for **men,** and

- no alcohol drunk (none)
- 1–14 units drunk (moderate drinking)
- over 14 units drunk (heavy drinking)

for **women.** The frequency of individuals in each category can then be displayed using a bar chart or a pie chart.

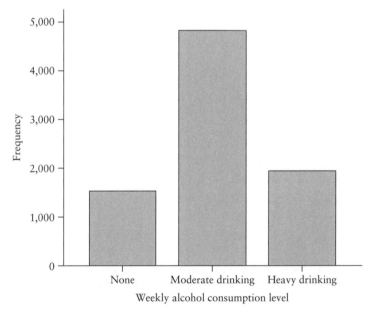

Source: GHS 2005 data.

Figure 1.7A   Bar chart of men's estimated individual alcohol consumption per week.

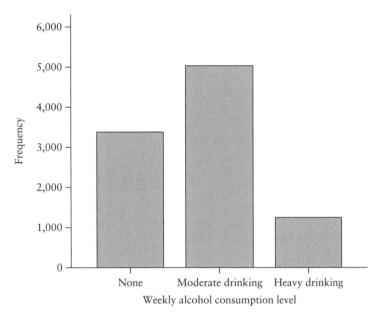

Source: GHS 2005 data.

Figure 1.7B Bar chart of women's estimated individual alcohol consumption per week.

The bar charts show that the distribution of this categorical variable is fairly similar for men and women, with the largest group being the moderate drinkers. However, whereas for men the heavy drinkers outnumber the non-drinkers, for women the non-drinkers outnumber the heavy drinkers.

In a similar way, the variable age could be recoded into a number of categories, and its distribution would then be displayed in a bar chart rather than a histogram. Recoding variables in this way can be particularly useful if the aim is to present results from surveys in simple tables. For example, in table 9.3 of the report on the General Household Survey 2002–3 (published as 'Living in Britain') the maximum daily amount of alcohol drunk last week is shown by sex and for four different age groups, 16–24; 25–44; 45 to 64, and 65 and over. Using tables to examine the relationships between two or more variables will be discussed in more detail in chapters 6 and 7.

1.7 Household level data

The variables discussed so far have been measured at the level of the individual. However, as was outlined above, the General Household Survey also collects data at the level of the household. Figure 1.8 displays some sample data from the GHS 2005 household file.

As is described more fully in the appendix to this chapter, the General Household Survey is based on a clustered sample of households. Some of the

Figure 1.8   Specimen data from the 2005 GHS (household file)

Household id	Region	Weekly household income (pence)	Cars	Persons in household
1	1	22200	1	1
2	1	33205.77	2	3
3	2	21580.77	2	2
4	2	21378.21	2	2
5	4	4250	1	1
6	4	50000	2	1
7	5	384.62	2	1
8	7	162564.1	3	2
9	7	152717.9	4	3
10	8	-8	4	3
11	8	12657.54	1	1
12	8	36769.23	2	2
13	8	31773.08	2	4
14	9	10784.62	1	1
15	9	23730.77	2	2
16	9	57692.31	2	2
17	10	8648.23	2	1
18	10	16528.85	2	3
19	11	55384.62	2	2
20	12	155166.7	3	3

Source: 2005 GHS household file.

information collected is more effectively conceptualized at the level of the household rather than the individual. Figure 1.8 displays a small sample of data from the GHS household file. Only five variables are shown, whereas there are a total of 203 variables in the whole 2005 GHS household dataset. Column 2 of figure 1.8 shows the region in which each household is based; each code refers to a region as follows:

1. North East
2. North West
4. Yorks and Humber
5. East Midlands
6. West Midlands
7. East of England
8. London
9. South East
10. South West
11. Wales
12. Scotland

Region is a nominal level variable. Although the number 1 has been assigned to the North East and the number 2 has been assigned to the North West this is purely arbitrary (and note that due to changes over time in the boundaries and naming

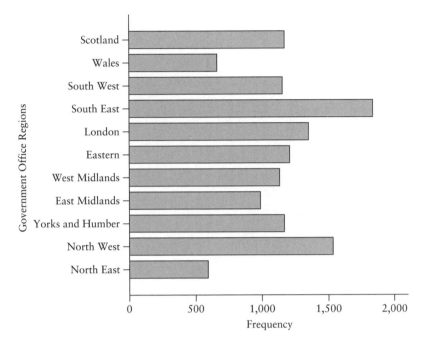

Source: GHS 2005 household data.

Figure 1.9   Bar chart of number of households in each Government Office Region in the GHS 2005.

of regions there is no longer a region number 3). As was discussed above, nominal level variables are best displayed using pie charts or bar charts. Figure 1.9 shows the number of households in each region for the GHS 2005 survey. We can see that there are at least 500 households included in the sample from each region but also that there are approximately three times as many households in the sample from the South East than from the North East. This reflects the total population size of each region.

The weekly income (in pence) for each household is shown in column 3 of figure 1.8. This is an interval level variable and, as discussed above, is therefore best displayed using a histogram. Whereas the original data on weekly household income (shown in figure 1.8) were recorded in pence, in the histogram the variable has been divided by 100 to transform the pence into pounds. This makes the units displayed on the histogram more intuitively interpretable as it is more usual to talk about income in terms of pounds per week. This also underlines the fact that when we are using interval-level variables the numbers are meaningful so that mathematical operations (e.g. addition, subtraction, multiplication, division) can be performed on variables measured on interval scales.

Inspection of the histogram in figure 1.10 reveals that the bulk of households have an income below £1,000 per week and we might consider an income of £500 per week to be a value near the middle of the distribution that is typical of the values represented here. We can also see that there is an upper-income tail that **straggles** up a long way, while the lower end of the income distribution ends

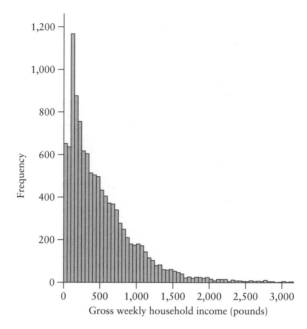

Source: GHS 2005 household data.

Figure 1.10   Histogram of weekly household income from the GHS 2005.

abruptly. This is evidence that the distribution of weekly household income is positively skewed. This is common for most income distributions. It can also be seen
that there are a very few households with incomes above £2,500 per week. These
are a substantial distance from the body of the data and perhaps deserve to be
called 'outliers'.

Column 4 of figure 1.8 shows the number of cars or vans that each household
has access to. This variable is coded as follows:

1. no car or van
2. one car or van
3. two cars or vans
4. three or more cars or vans

Although this variable could almost be treated as an interval-level variable (if
0 indicated no cars, 1 indicated 1 car or van etc.), it takes so few possible values
that it is best thought of as an ordinal variable and displayed as a pie chart or bar
chart.

It can be seen that just over three-quarters of the sample of households in the
GHS 2005 has access to at least one car or van and that of these the majority
have just one car or van. As was highlighted at the beginning of the chapter,
the GHS has been conducted on an annual basis almost continuously in
Britain since the beginning of the 1970s. This makes it an excellent source of
information on social change. For example, in contrast to the figures shown

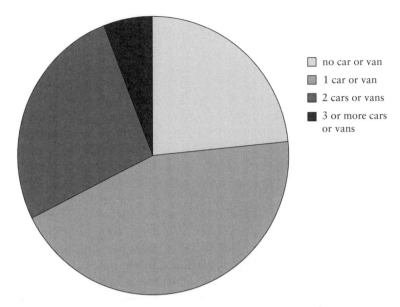

Source: GHS 2005 household data.

Figure 1.11 Pie chart of number of cars or vans per household from the GHS 2005.

above, in 1972 only just over a half of households had access to at least one car or van.

Figure 1.12 displays the number of people in each household in the GHS 2005 (small samples of these data are in column 5 of figure 1.8). We can see that very few households have more than six people living within them and that perhaps the most typical household has two persons living in it. Once again this variable has been included in each year's General Household Survey and this makes it possible to look at change over time. Whereas in 1971 approximately 17 per cent of households were single-person households, this had risen to 22 per cent by 1981, 26 per cent by 1991 and 31 per cent by 2001. The figure given for single-person households in 2002 in the report of the GHS Living in Britain 2002 is 31 per cent. This is slightly different from the figure displayed in figure 1.12 because the data displayed in this chapter are based on unweighted data whereas from 1998 the GHS sample has been weighted to account for non-response (see Appendix D of Living in Britain 2002 for further details).

One of the challenges for those planning and conducting large-scale social surveys such as the GHS is how to keep questions consistent over time in order to be able to measure effectively how behaviour is changing year by year while simultaneously ensuring that questions do not become dated but reflect major societal changes. For example, for the first time in 1979 the GHS introduced questions relating to pre-marital cohabitation for women aged 18 to 49. These questions were then extended to both men and women aged 16 to 59 and to every marriage past and present in 1986. In 1998 a further question was added to find out the number of past cohabitations not ending in marriage. In other words as

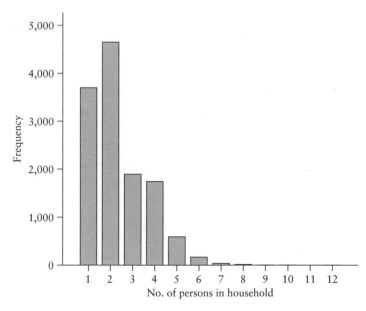

Source: GHS 2005 household data.

Figure 1.12 Bar chart of number of people in each household in the GHS 2005.

cohabitation has become more socially acceptable and more common in Britain the questions in the General Household Survey have changed to reflect this. Large-scale structured interview surveys such as the GHS do not simply measure the characteristics of individuals in a society; they are also a product of that society.

1.8 Using SPSS to produce bar charts, pie charts and histograms

The graphical displays of data in this chapter have all been produced using SPSS (the Statistical Package for the Social Sciences). This software is relatively easy to learn and is widely available to students and researchers through their universities. It is also frequently used by researchers in market research companies, local author-ities, health authorities and government departments. The following section pro-vides a brief introduction to the SPSS package and describes how to use it to produce bar charts, pie charts and histograms. The package itself has tutorials that will guide you through its main features. A useful and comprehensive introductory book on how to use SPSS is the *SPSS 15 Guide to Data Analysis* by Marija Norusis.

Getting started with SPSS

SPSS is a very useful computer package which includes hundreds of different pro-cedures for displaying and analysing data. If you follow the SPSS instructions in

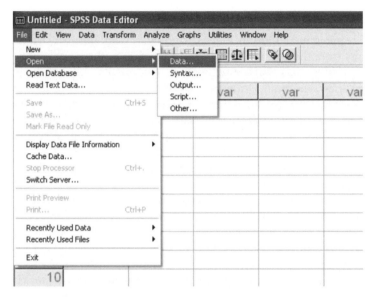

Figure 1.13   Using menus to open a dataset in the SPSS Data Editor.

this book you will be introduced to just a few of the most basic, useful and commonly used procedures. When you first start using the program, don't be overwhelmed by the number of different menus and options that are available. Rather than trying to discover and understand all the facilities that SPSS provides, it is better to start by focusing on mastering just a few procedures.

SPSS has three main windows:

- The Data Editor window
- The Output window
- The Syntax window

When you first open SPSS, the **Data Editor window** will be displayed. This will be empty until you either open an existing data file or type in your own data – in the same way that you would enter data into a spreadsheet like Excel. The emphasis in this book is on using existing data files based on large-scale datasets.

You can open an existing data file using the File menu and then selecting 'Open' and 'Data'. You are then able to browse the directories on your computer until you find the data file that you need.

The data in the SPSS Data Editor are displayed in rows and columns. Each row provides the information about a single case in the dataset. As we have seen in this chapter this could be an individual person or a household. Each column contains the information about a specific variable, and the name of the variable appears at the top of each column. The menus across the top of the Data Editor allow you to access a range of procedures so that you can analyse your data, modify your data and produce tables, pie charts, histograms and other graphical displays.

When you use SPSS to produce a graph, a table or some statistical analysis, your results will appear in an **Output Viewer window**. It is straightforward to copy and paste results from the Output Viewer into a word processing package so that you can integrate tables and charts into a report. You can also save all the contents of the Output Viewer into an Output file so that you can come back to them later. The menus across the top of the Output Viewer are almost identical to those across the top of the Data Editor. There are just a couple of extra menus that allow you to edit your output, but you can ignore these for now! The main two menus that you will be using are the 'File' menu, to enable you to open an SPSS Data file and the 'Analyze' menu, to enable you to create the histograms, bar charts and pie charts discussed in this chapter.

There are two ways of getting SPSS to perform procedures for you. One is to use the menus and then the Dialog boxes that SPSS provides to choose exactly the variables that you want to work with. The second is to type instructions into the **SPSS Syntax window**. SPSS syntax consists of keywords and commands that need to be entered very precisely and in the correct order. The most common reasons for using command syntax are firstly to repeat analyses quickly and secondly to keep a record of what you have done. This is particularly important if you are manipulating or recoding data (for example in section 1.6 above, we discussed grouping the variable describing alcohol consumption from an interval level variable to an ordinal variable). Also, if you are working as part of a research team, using syntax is very valuable for sharing with others exactly what commands you have performed in order to produce your outputs. We will leave further discussion of syntax until chapter 2 and through the rest of the book will highlight both how to use the menus and how to use syntax to get the most out of SPSS.

SPSS Tutorials

The SPSS package itself provides a good introduction to all the main aspects of the program via the Tutorials. In order to view a tutorial, choose 'Tutorial' from the Help menu (see below).

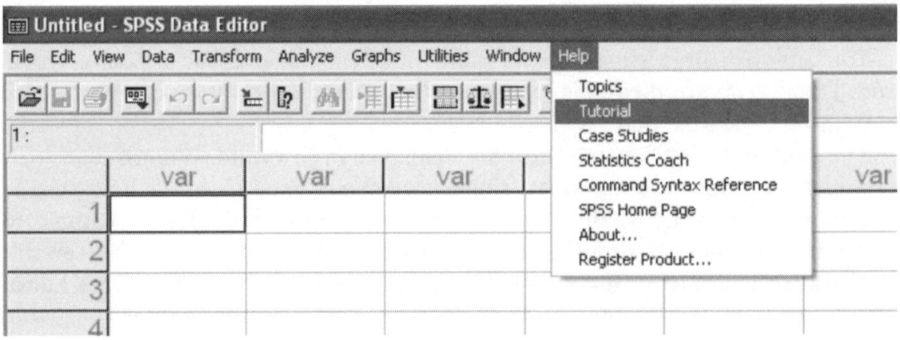

Figure 1.14   Accessing the SPSS tutorials.

A Table of Contents appears and you can select one of the book icons and click it to display more books and topics. As a starting point the tutorial entitled 'Examining Summary Statistics for Individual Variables' is most relevant for consolidating much of the material in this chapter and the next.

Doing your first analysis

Before you can get SPSS to do any analysis, you first need to open a dataset. The following examples use the GHS05_ind_teach.sav file, which is a teaching dataset available from the UK Data Archive. For details of how to download these data see the accompanying website. Once you have the dataset available on your computer, start SPSS and then click on 'File' and 'Open Data' as shown in figure 1.13.

In order to produce a pie chart of drinking behaviour, similar to that shown in figure 1.3, from the menus along the top, choose 'Graphs' and then 'Pie'.

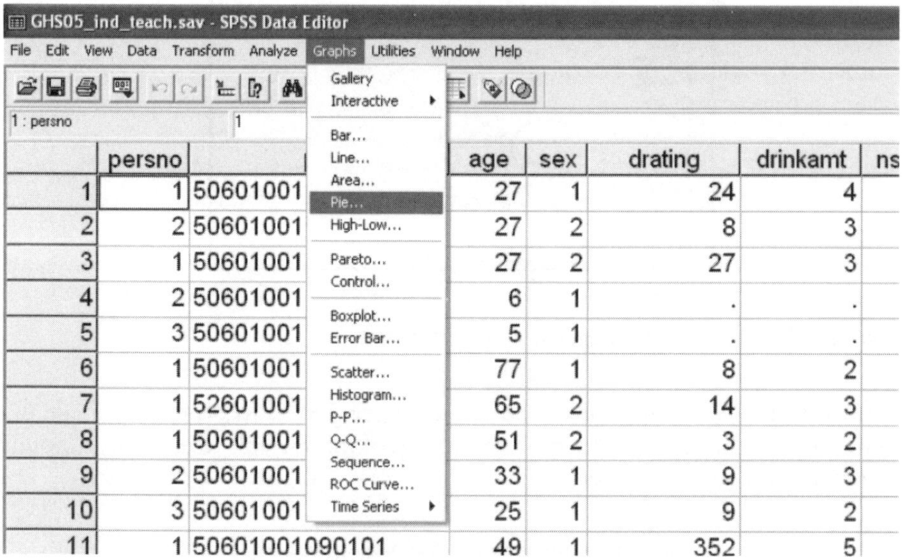

Figure 1.15 Using menus to produce a pie chart.

An SPSS 'dialogue box' will now appear (see figure 1.16). By default this specifies that the data in the chart represent summaries for groups of cases and this is what you want. Next click on the 'Define' button.

A second dialogue box will appear (see figure 1.17). This has a similar structure to many of the dialogue boxes that you will encounter in SPSS. Notice that on the left hand side there is a list of variable names. These are all the variables within the dataset you are using. Use the left mouse button to click on the variable 'drinkamt'. Next click on the little button with an arrow next to the empty box labelled 'Define Slices by:'(circled in figure 1.17). This will move the variable name

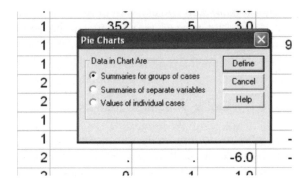

Figure 1.16   A first dialogue box for pie charts.

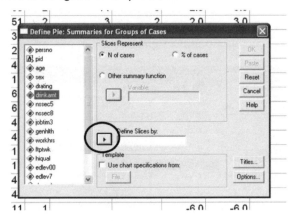

Figure 1.17   A second dialogue box for pie charts.

'drinkamt' into the empty box. You are instructing SPSS to produce a single pie chart where each slice is defined by a category of the variable 'drinkamt; Amount of alcohol respondent drinks'.

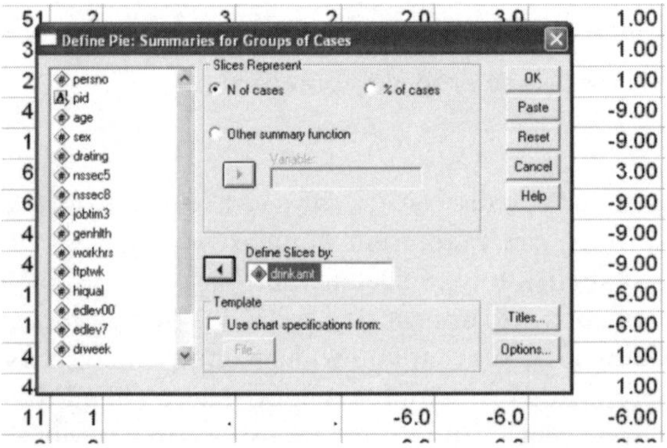

Figure 1.18   The second dialogue box for pie charts with variable 'drinkamt' selected.

Finally, if you click on the button in the top right corner labelled 'OK', SPSS will automatically open an Output Viewer window for you, which will display your first pie chart. You should see something like the pie chart displayed in figure 1.19. This is similar to the pie chart displayed in figure 1.3. However, whereas figure 1.3 is based on only a small subsample of 20 cases from the data file, the pie chart you have just produced summarizes data from the whole GHS sample of 30,069 individuals. The pie chart shows that almost equal numbers of individuals define themselves as 'hardly drink at all', 'drink a little' and 'drink a moderate amount' and only a tiny fraction of the sample define themselves as heavy drinkers. The pie chart shown in figure 1.19 is just a very simple picture with no fancy title, 3D effects, or labels telling you how many individuals are in each slice of the Pie. To take a further step, and to learn how to modify and improve your pie chart, select the Tutorial entitled 'Creating and editing charts'.

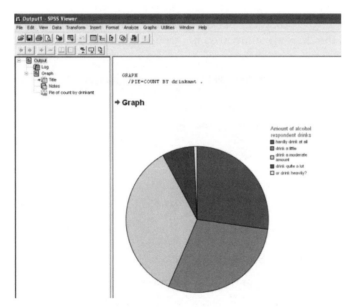

Figure 1.19   A pie chart of the variable 'drinkamt' shown in an SPSS Output Viewer window.

Defining missing values

In the example shown in figure 1.19, the 'missing values' for the variable drinkamt had already been specified for you (remember that missing values occur when there are no data on a particular variable for a case – this was discussed in section 1.2). However, before producing graphical displays of single variables in SPSS you will normally have to tell the computer which values of the variable correspond to 'missing values'. To do this, in the variable view of the data editor in SPSS click on the appropriate row '**genhlth**' of the column headed '**Missing**' and use the dialogue box that appears to specify the three missing values, -9, -8 and -6 and then click the OK button.

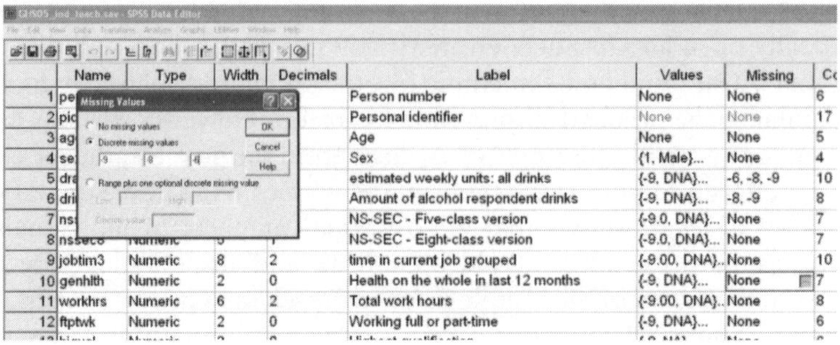

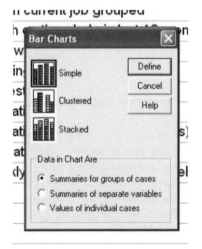

Figure 1.20   Opening the SPSS dialogue box to show the missing values.

Next, from the menus along the top, choose 'Graphs' and then 'Bar'
From the dialogue box that appears, choose the first option 'Simple' and specify that data in the chart are summaries for groups of cases. Next click on the 'Define' button.

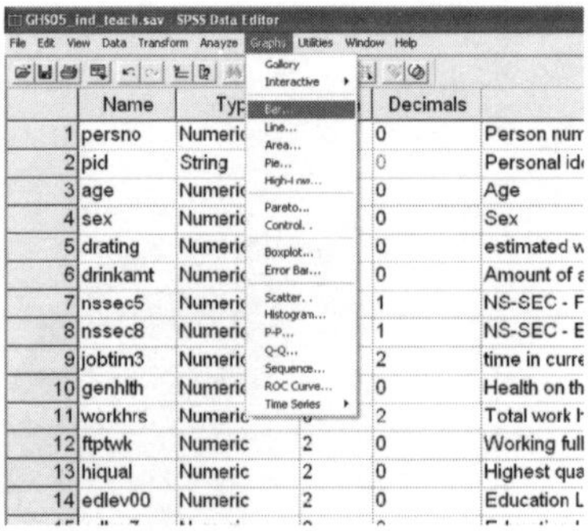

Figure 1.21   Creating a bar chart in SPSS.

Figure 1.22   Selecting the 'Simple' bar chart option.

In the next dialogue box you can specify for which variable you want a bar chart displayed and also choose whether the bars represent the number of cases (N of cases) or the percentage of cases (% of cases) in each category of the variable. Select the variable **genhlth** from the variable list and move it to the 'Category Axis' window by clicking on the arrow button. Finally click on the OK button and the bar chart for the variable **genhlth** will appear in the SPSS output window.

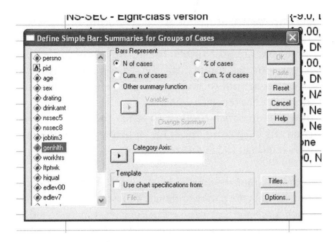

Figure 1.23 Specifying a variable for the bar chart.

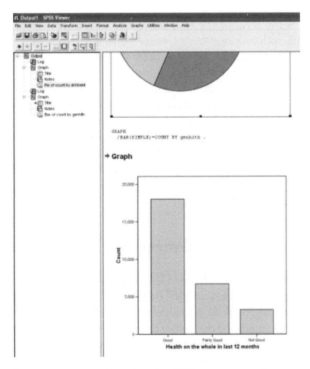

Figure 1.24 The bar chart displayed in the SPSS output window.

1.9 Conclusion

The technical emphasis so far has been on pictorial displays of numerical data. Bar charts and pie charts were introduced as techniques for displaying nominal or ordinal scale variables, and histograms were introduced as an effective way of displaying interval scale variables. The latter allow inspection of the full distribution of values for a sample of cases.

In general, there are four features of any distribution that are worth systematic attention: level, spread, shape and any unusual data values (outliers). At the moment these concepts are still rather fuzzy. We use statements like 'a typical household weekly income is around £500'. After looking at these four features in a histogram, it is often helpful to find numbers to summarize them. That will be the subject of the next chapter.

We should, however, not rush too fast to reach succinct numerical summaries, especially if this means by-passing the stage of display. Brevity may be the soul of wit, but as Aldous Huxley (1958: vii) reminds us:

> The soul of wit may become the very body of untruth. However elegant and memorable, brevity can never, in the nature of things, do justice to all the facts of a complex situation. On such a scheme, one can be brief only by omission and simplification. Omission and simplification help us to understand – but help us, in many cases, to understand the wrong thing.

This chapter has also highlighted the fact that information can be collected and analysed both at the level of the individual and at the level of the household. In the chapters that follow a number of other household surveys will also be introduced. Depending on the type of information that is being examined, it sometimes makes sense to use the household as the unit of analysis while at other times it is more sensible to focus on the individual.

As was also discussed in section 1.7, large-scale government surveys such as the GHS provide extremely valuable information about the way that society is changing. The fact that a number of questions are asked in an identical format year by year means that it is possible to look at trends over time, for example, in terms of the size of households or average alcohol consumption. In addition, the questions included in a large-scale survey such as the GHS will also reflect changing social values and changing policy concerns.

Exercises

1.1 Look at the histogram in figure 1.25. This shows the estimated weekly units of alcohol drunk by those in the GHS who placed themselves in the category of 'moderate drinkers'. What value near the middle of the distribution might be considered typical of the values displayed here? Does this provide a useful summary of the level of the distribution? How would you describe the shape of the distribution (is it unimodal or bimodal, and is it symmetrical or skewed)?

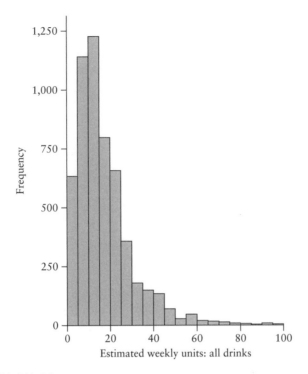

Source: GHS 2005 individual data.

Figure 1.25 Histogram of estimated weekly units of alcohol drunk by those defining themselves as 'drink a moderate amount'.

1.2 Collect a dataset for yourself. You might like to ask some of your friends and acquaintances how many cars there are within their households. Construct a pie chart or a bar chart to display a summary of their answers.

1.3 The following pieces of information are all collected as part of the General Household Survey. In each case decide whether the information is best conceptualized as an interval level (continuous) variable, an ordinal level variable or a nominal level variable.
(a) Sex
(b) Hours worked per week
(c) Marital status
(d) Number of dependent children in the household
(e) Ethnic group

1.4 Using the teaching data set GHS05_ind_teach.sav, use SPSS to produce a bar chart to show the distribution of the variable **genhlth** 'Health on the whole in the last 12 months'. Why would it not be appropriate to try and produce a histogram to display this variable?

1.5 Experiment with producing bar charts, histograms and pie charts for a number of different variables in the teaching dataset GHS05_ind_teach.sav.

Think carefully about which type of graphical display is most appropriate for each variable. Remember that:
(a) Continuous variables can be displayed as histograms.
(b) Categorical (ordinal and nominal) variables can be displayed as either bar charts or pie charts.

2

Numerical Summaries of Level and Spread

It has become something of a cliché that no one on their deathbed ever wished that they had 'spent more time at the office'. There is considerable discussion in the media of 'the long hours culture' and 'work–life balance'. In modern society there is considerable interest in the length of time people spend at work. The measurement of hours that people work is important when analysing a variety of economic and social phenomena. The number of hours worked is a measure of labour input that can be used to derive key measures of productivity and labour costs. The patterns of hours worked and comparisons of the hours worked by different groups within society give important evidence for studying and understanding lifestyles, the labour market and social changes.

In this chapter we will focus on the topic of working hours to demonstrate how simple descriptive statistics can be used to provide numerical summaries of **level** and **spread**. The chapter will begin by examining data on working hours in Britain taken from the General Household Survey discussed in the previous chapter. These data are used to illustrate **measures of level** such as the mean and the median and measures of spread or variability such as the standard deviation and the midspread. In the second part of the chapter, data from the Annual Survey of Hours and Earnings and data from Eurostat on working hours across Europe will be discussed together with the European Working Time Directive.

This chapter leads on very directly from the previous one, and presents summary measures which will be used repeatedly throughout the book.

2.1 Working hours of couples in Britain

The histograms of the working hours distributions of men and women in the 2005 General Household Survey are shown in figures 2.1 and 2.2.

We can compare these two distributions in terms of the four features introduced in the previous chapter, namely level, spread, shape and outliers. We can then see that:

- The male batch is at a higher level than the female batch
- The two distributions are somewhat similarly spread out

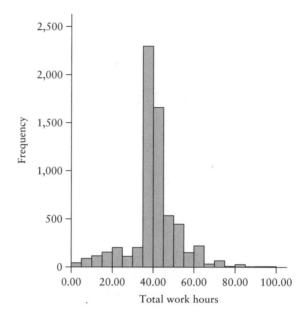

Source: Analysis of data from GHS05_ind_teach.sav.

Figure 2.1   Weekly hours worked by men in the 2005 GHS.

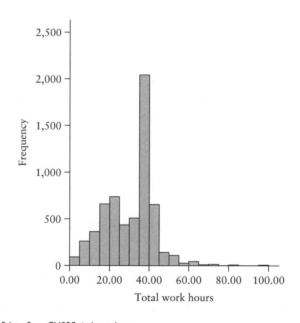

Source: Analysis of data from GHS05_ind_teach.sav.

Figure 2.2   Weekly hours worked by women in the 2005 GHS.

- The female batch is bimodal suggesting there are two rather different underlying populations
- The male batch is uni-modal

Although there are no extremely high values, those working for over 90 hours per week stand out as being rather different from the bulk of the population.

These verbal descriptions of the differences between the male and female working hours' distributions are rather vague. Perhaps the features could be summarized numerically, so that we could give a typical numerical value for male hours and female hours, a single number summary for how spread out the two distributions were, a cut-off point to allow us to count unusual values, or (perhaps more ambitiously) a numerical description of the shape of the distribution.

A summary always involves some loss of information. As the quote from Huxley at the end of the previous chapter reminded us, summaries cannot be expected to contain the richness of information that existed in the original picture. However, they do have important advantages. They focus the attention of the data analyst on one thing at a time, and prevent the eye from wandering aimlessly over a display of the data. They also help focus the process of comparison from one dataset to another, and make it more rigorous.

In this chapter, we will look at different ways of finding a number to summarize the level and spread of a distribution. It is not so easy to suggest numerical summaries for shape, but the problem will be discussed at the end of the next chapter. A more rigorous definition of what are considered to be unusual data points will be given in chapter 8.

2.2 Summaries of level

The **level** expresses where on the scale of numbers found in the dataset the distribution is concentrated. In the previous example, it expresses where on a scale running from 1 hour per week to 100 hours per week is the distribution's centre point. To summarize these values, one number must be found to express the typical hours worked by men, for example. The problem is: how do we define 'typical'?

There are many possible answers. The value half-way between the extremes might be chosen, or the single most common number of hours worked, or a summary of the middle portion of the distribution. With a little imagination we could produce many candidates. Therefore it is important to agree on what basis the choice should be made.

Residuals

Before introducing some possible alternative summaries of level, it is helpful to introduce the idea of a 'residual'. A residual can be defined as the difference between a data point and the observed typical, or average, value. For example if we had chosen 40 hours a week as the typical level of men's working hours, using data from the General Household Survey in 2005, then a man who was recorded in the survey as working 45 hours a week would have a residual of 5 hours. Another way of expressing this is to say that the residual is the *observed data value minus the predicted value* and in this case $45 - 40 = 5$. In this example the process of calculating residuals is a way of recasting the hours worked by each man in terms of distances from typical male working hours in the sample. Any data value such as a measurement of hours worked or income earned can be thought of as being composed of two components: a fitted part and a residual part. This can be expressed as an equation:

$$\text{Data} = \text{Fit} + \text{Residual}$$

As we shall see shortly, if the numerical summaries are fitted to some data and residuals are calculated, one way of evaluating different summaries is by looking for certain desirable properties in the residual distribution.

The median

The value of the case at the middle of an ordered distribution would seem to have an intuitive claim to typicality. Finding such a number is easy when there are very few cases. In the example of hours worked by a small random sample of 15 men (figure 2.3A), the value of 48 hours per week fits the bill. There are six men who work fewer hours and seven men who work more hours while two men work exactly 48 hours per week. Similarly, in the female data, the value of the middle case is 37 hours. The data value that meets this criterion is called the **median**: the value of the case that has equal numbers of data points above and below it. The

Figure 2.3A   Men's working hours ranked to show the median.

Men's working hours (ranked)
30
37
39
40
45
47
48
Median value 48
50
54
55
55
67
70
80

Source: Small random sample of men's working hours from GHS 2005 data.

Figure 2.3B　Women's working hours ranked to show the median.

Women's working hours (ranked)
5
21
22.5
30
32
37
37
Median value　37
38
40
45
48
50
60
80

Source: Small random sample of women's working hours from GHS 2005 data.

median hours worked by women in this very small sample is 11 hours less than the median for men. This numeric summary of the **level** of the data therefore confirms our first impressions from simply looking at the histograms in figures 2.1 and 2.2 that women generally work shorter hours than men.

The median is easy to find when, as here, there are an odd number of data points. When the number of data points is even, it is an interval, not one case, which splits the distribution into two. The value of the median is conventionally taken to be half-way between the two middle cases. Thus the median in a dataset with fifty data points would be half-way between the values of the 25th and 26th data points.

Put formally, with N data points, the median M is the value at depth $(N + 1)/2$. It is not the value at depth $N/2$. With twenty data points, for example, the tenth case has nine points which lie below it and ten above.

Why choose the median as the typical value? It is a point at which the sum of absolute residuals from that point is at a minimum. (An **absolute value** denotes the magnitude of a number, regardless of its sign.) In other words, if we fit the median, calculate the residuals for every data point and then add them up ignoring the sign, the answer we get will be the same or smaller than it would have been if we had picked the value of any other point. This is illustrated in Exercise 2.1 at the end of this chapter.

In short, the median defines 'typical' in a particular way: making the size of the residuals as small as possible. It's not the only definition, but it yields one fixed answer, and it has intuitive appeal. Galton (1907) called it the 'democratic value': any higher or lower, and there would be a majority against. It is determined by information from the whole of the dataset (albeit only the rank order information in most of the dataset).

The arithmetic mean

Another commonly used measure of the centre of a distribution is the **arithmetic mean**. Indeed, it is so commonly used that it has even become known as *the* average. It is conventionally written as $\bar{Y}$ (pronounced 'Y bar'). To calculate it, first all of the values are summed, and then the total is divided by the number of data points. In more mathematical terms:

$$\frac{\sum Y_i}{N}$$

We have come across N before. The symbol Y is conventionally used to refer to an actual variable. The subscript i is an index to tell us which case is being referred to. So, in this case, Y_i refers to all the values of the hours variable. The Greek letter Σ, pronounced 'sigma', is the mathematician's way of saying 'the sum of'.

When we defined 'typical' to mean a point at which half the cases were higher and half lower, thus minimizing the size of deviations from that point, the median fitted the bill. What definition of 'typical' leads us to the mean? It turns out to be the number which makes the sum of the *squared* distances from that point as small as they can be. This is not the most obvious definition of 'typical'. But as we will discuss later, it has important mathematical properties. In any dataset, the absolute magnitudes of deviations are smallest from the median, the squared deviations are smallest from the mean.

So what? Well, one important consequence is that the mean is more affected by unusual data values than the median. The mean of the male working hours in the above dataset is 51 hours, not very different from the median in this case. The mean and the median will tend to be the same in symmetrical datasets. However, if one man who worked very few hours had been included in the sample, the mean would have been seriously affected, but the median would only be slightly altered, if at all. Whether this is a good or a bad thing is discussed below.

2.3 Summaries of spread

The second feature of a distribution visible in a histogram is the degree of variation or spread in the variable. The two histograms of male and female working hours shown in figures 2.1 and 2.2 allow visual inspection of the extent to which the data values are *relatively* spread out or clustered together. The word 'relatively' is important: a single distribution can look very tightly clustered simply because the scale has not been carefully chosen. In figures 2.1 and 2.2 the scale along the horizontal axis ranges from 0 to 100 in both cases, which makes it possible directly to compare the two distributions.

Once again, there are many candidates we could think of to summarize the spread. One might be the distance between the two extreme values (the **range**). Or we might work out what was the most likely difference between any two cases drawn at random from the dataset. There are also two very commonly used measures which follow on from the logic of using the median or mean as the summary of the level.

The midspread

The range of the middle 50 per cent of the distribution is a commonly used measure of spread because it concentrates on the middle cases. It is quite stable from sample to sample. The points which divide the distribution into quarters are called the **quartiles** (or sometimes 'hinges' or 'fourths'). The lower quartile is usually denoted Q_L and the upper quartile Q_U. (The middle quartile is of course the median.) The distance between Q_L and Q_U is called the **midspread** (sometimes the 'interquartile range'), or the **dQ** for short.

Just as the median cut the whole distribution in two, the upper and lower quartiles cut each half of the distribution in two. So, to find the depth at which they fall, we take the depth of the median (cutting the fractional half off if there is one), add one and divide by two. There are 15 cases in the small datasets of men's working hours and women's working hours in figure 2.3A and . The median is at depth 8, so the quartiles are at depth 4.5. Counting in from either end of the male distribution, we see that for men Q_L is 42.5 hours and Q_U is 55 hours. The distance between them, the dQ, is therefore 12.5 hours.

Figure 2.3C   Men's working hours ranked and showing the upper and lower quartiles.

Men's working hours (ranked)	
30	
37	
39	
40	
	$Q_L = 42.5$
45	
47	
48	
48	
50	
54	
55	
	$Q_U = 55$
55	
67	
70	
80	

Source: Small random sample of men's working hours from GHS 2005 data.

The midspread is a rather inexact measure. In datasets with 15 and 16 cases, for example, the quartile is defined as the value of the 4.5th data point in both cases. A fussier rule could be given which would be more precise, and could be implemented on a computer, but it would in practice run more risk of calculating error if done by hand. This formula is easily remembered and applied.

The standard deviation

The arithmetic mean, you will recall, minimizes squared residuals. There is a measure of spread which can be calculated from these squared distances from the mean. The **standard deviation** essentially calculates a typical value of these distances from the mean. It is conventionally denoted *s*, and defined as:

$$s = \sqrt{\left[\frac{\sum (Y_i - \bar{Y})^2}{(N-1)} \right]}$$

The deviations from the mean are squared, summed and divided by the sample size (well, $N-1$ actually, for technical reasons), and then the square root is taken to return to the original units. The order in which the calculations are performed is very important. As always, calculations within brackets are performed first, then multiplication and division, then addition (including summation) and subtraction. Without the square root, the measure is called the **variance**, s^2.

The layout for a worksheet to calculate the standard deviation of the hours worked by this small sample of men is shown in figure 2.4.

Figure 2.4   Worksheet for standard deviation of men's weekly working hours.

Y	$Y - \bar{Y}$	$(Y - \bar{Y})^2$
54	3	9
30	−21	441
47	−4	16
39	−12	144
50	−1	1
48	−3	9
45	−6	36
40	−11	121
37	−14	196
48	−3	9
67	16	256
55	4	16
55	4	16
80	29	841
70	19	361
Sum = 765		Sum of squared residuals = 2472

Source: As figure 2.3A.

The original data values are written in the first column, and the sum and mean calculated at the bottom. The residuals are calculated and displayed in column 2, and their squared values are placed in column 3. The sum of these squared values is shown at the foot of column 3, and from it the standard deviation is calculated.

$$s = \sqrt{\left[\frac{\sum(Y_1 - \bar{Y})^2}{(N-1)}\right]}$$

$$= \sqrt{2472/14}$$

$$= 13.29$$

In most distributions, the standard deviation is smaller than the midspread. In this case, it is very slightly larger.

When working by hand, it takes much longer to calculate the standard deviation than it does to find the dQ. Quicker 'computational formulae' exist which make the task somewhat less burdensome. You may come across them in older textbooks. However, in the day of the computer and calculator, computational speed is better obtained by programmed instructions. Your calculator may have a function key to obtain the standard deviation directly. Excel also allows easy computation of the standard deviation of a column of figures using the statistical function STDEV.

The point of working through the above example using the definitional formula is to obtain insight into the composition of the standard deviation, and to show that, like the mean, it is more influenced by more extreme numbers. The second man in the dataset, whose working hours are 30 hours per week, is 21 hours below the mean, which becomes 441 when squared; that individual alone is contributing a substantial part of the standard deviation.

You will sometimes come across a formula for the standard deviation with N rather than $N-1$ in the denominator. You may even have a calculator which offers you the choice between a standard deviation using N and one using $N-1$. (It may not offer you the choice. You should then experiment to find out which formula it uses.) The formula given above using $N-1$ is preferable when using sample data to estimate variation in a population. The difference made by the adjustment, however, is trivial unless N is very small.

2.4 Other locational statistics

The information about the value of the median and the quartiles tells us quite a lot about a distribution. For some applications, we may want more detail, and wish to calculate summaries for points at other depths of the distribution. The **extremes** – the values of the top and bottom data point – are easy to find. Other commonly calculated points are **deciles**, which divide the distribution into ten, and **percentiles**, which divide the distribution into one hundred. These measures are regularly used by those studying the distribution of income and wealth, as we will see in chapter 4. In fact, the distribution can be divided into equal parts at any number of depths. The general word given to such dividing points is **quantiles**. Deciles are the quantiles at depth $N/10$, the percentiles are the quantiles at depth $N/100$, and so on.

Interpreting locational summaries

In the examples discussed above the locational statistics for only a very small sub-sample of data of 15 cases from the GHS 2005 have been calculated by hand. It is useful to experiment with calculating locational statistics in this way in order to reach a better understanding of the meaning of these summary statistics. However, with larger batches of data the median, quartiles (and deciles) can be calculated very easily using a package such as Excel or SPSS.

Total work hours (Men)

N	Valid	6392
	Missing	8188
Median		39.0000
Minimum		.00
Maximum		97.00
Percentiles	25	37.0000
	50	39.0000
	75	42.8750

Total work hours (Women)

N	Valid	6127
	Missing	9362
Median		35.0000
Minimum		.00
Maximum		97.00
Percentiles	25	20.0000
	50	35.0000
	75	37.5000

Source: Analysis of GHS 2005 data.

Figure 2.5   Numerical summaries of hours worked per week.

The numerical summaries allow us to compare all men and women in the GHS quite succinctly. In this dataset containing 6,392 men and 6,127 women, by comparing the medians we can see that the men are typically working 4 hours more per week than the women. The dQ among men is 5.9 and the dQ among women is 17.5 suggesting that the distribution of women's hours is considerably more spread out than the distribution of men's hours. In both sets of data there is a wide range from 0 to 97 hours per week. Figure 2.6 is based on exactly the same sets of data displayed in the histograms in figures 2.1 and 2.2. The locational statistics shown above thus provide an alternative method for summarizing the level and spread of the distribution.

Computers have also made it very easy to calculate the alternative measures of level and spread discussed above, namely the mean and the standard deviation. Figure 2.6 displays these alternative measures as a way of comparing the distribution of the hours worked by men and women in Britain. Once again we can see that on average men tend to work more hours per week than women (39.2 hours vs 29.6 hours) and also the higher standard deviation for women, 12.3 vs 11.6 for men indicates that there is more variation among women in terms of the hours they usually work per week. It should also be noted that the figures for the means and standard deviations in figure 2.6 are pasted directly from the SPSS output. We can see that in each case the number of decimal places provided is four for the mean and five for the standard deviation. This is clearly inappropriate when we consider the likely level of precision with which number of hours per week is measured, or recalled in a survey.

Total work hours (Men)

N	Valid	6392
	Missing	8188
Mean		39.2268
Std. Deviation		11.64234

Source Analysis of GHS 2005 data.

Total work hours (Women)

N	Valid	6127
	Missing	9362
Mean		29.5977
Std. Deviation		12.31122

Source: Analysis of GHS 2005 data.

Figure 2.6 Alternative numerical summaries of hours worked per week.

2.5 Choosing between measures

How do we decide between the median and mean to summarize a typical value, or between the range, the midspread and the standard deviation to summarize spread?

One important consideration is the intuitive intelligibility of the measure. On this count, locational statistics such as the range, median and midspread generally fare better than the more abstract means and standard deviations. If someone asks about the distribution of men's working hours, a reply that the standard deviation is 11.6 might not convey much. On the other hand, the answer that the middle 50 per cent of the population of men work between 37 and 42.9 hours per week might be more intelligible, and almost everyone would understand the statement that the range was between 0 and 97 hours. However, intelligibility is partly a product of familiarity. It is therefore not a good sole criterion. What other grounds might there be for choice?

We have already noted that means and standard deviations are more influenced by unusual data values than medians and midspreads. In fact, the former measures are usually more influenced by a change in *any* individual data point than the latter. Should we therefore prefer them for this reason? Should we be happy that a measure gives greater weight to particularly unusual data values?

If we were entirely confident that the numbers collected were accurate, we might prefer measures that used more information. We might even think that a data point that was really out of line with the rest of the distribution *deserved* more attention than the similar points around the centre. But the time has come to introduce Twyman's law, perhaps the most important single law in the whole of data analysis:

> *Twyman's law* The more unusual or interesting the data, the more likely they are to have been the result of an error of one kind or another.

We must recognize that errors of all sorts creep into the very best data sources. The values found at the extremes of a distribution (which contribute disproportionately to the mean and standard deviation) are more likely to have suffered error than the values at the centre.

John Tukey (1977) has introduced an important general principle in comparing different measures. We say that one measure is more **resistant** than another if it tends to be less influenced by a change in any small part of the data. The mean and the standard deviation are less resistant as measures than the median and midspread. For this reason, they are often preferable for much descriptive and exploratory work, especially in situations where we are worried about measurement error. We will concentrate on them in this book.

However, there are advantages which the mean and standard deviation are sometimes felt to have over the more resistant measures. The fact that they sometimes use more of the information available is viewed by some as an advantage. They also have an important relationship to one particular shape of distribution which will be discussed in the next chapter. The sampling theory of the mean and standard deviation is more developed than that of the median and midspread, which makes the former measures more popular among those who want to try to make very precise statements about the likely degree of sampling error in their data.

Finally, you should notice that the range has all of the disadvantages discussed above and none of the advantages. It only uses information from two data points, and these are drawn from the most unreliable part of the data. Therefore, despite its intuitive appeal, it cannot be recommended as a summary measure of spread.

2.6 Obtaining summaries of level and spread using SPSS and Excel

In sections 2.2 and 2.3 the procedures for calculating by hand the mean, median, midspread and standard deviation were described. Although it is important to understand how these measures of level and spread are derived, it is more usual to calculate these using a statistics package such as SPSS or Excel.

For example, in SPSS all these descriptive statistics can be obtained by selecting 'Analyze' and 'Frequencies' from the drop-down menus (see figure 2.7).

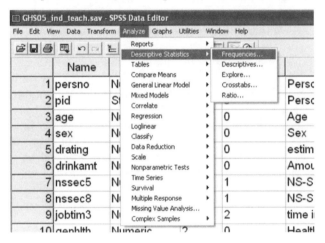

Figure 2.7   Selecting 'Analyze' and 'Frequencies' in SPSS to obtain descriptive statistics.

Next select the variable for which you want to calculate the median and midspread, mean and standard deviation. For example 'workhrs' has been selected below (in figure 2.8). It is also worth unchecking the box labelled 'Display frequency tables' for a variable such as this one, which takes many different values, because with a large dataset a very large table is produced that is unwieldy in the SPSS output.

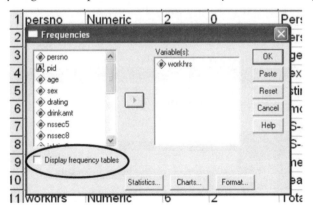

Figure 2.8   The Frequencies dialogue box in SPSS.

Figure 2.9 Selecting the descriptive statistics to calculate in SPSS.

Then click on the 'Statistics' button and select the descriptive statistics that you want SPSS to calculate (see figure 2.9).

You will notice that the mean and median are grouped together under measures of 'Central Tendency'. This is just another term for measures of 'level'. In this example we have specified that SPSS should provide the quartiles as well as the deciles (cut points for 10 equal groups). Once you have chosen the statistics you want to calculate, click on the 'Continue' button and then click on OK in the next dialogue box.

Alternatively, the syntax for this command is shown in the box.

```
FREQUENCIES
  VARIABLES=workhrs /FORMAT=NOTABLE
  /NTILES= 4
  /NTILES= 10
  /STATISTICS=STDDEV MINIMUM MAXIMUM MEAN MEDIAN
  /ORDER= ANALYSIS.
```

This syntax is automatically written to a new syntax file for you if you click on the 'Paste' button rather than the 'OK' button in the frequencies dialogue box. To 'Run' the syntax (i.e. to get the computer to obey your commands) you simply highlight the syntax with the cursor and click on the arrow button circled in the illustration below.

Figure 2.10 Running a syntax file in SPSS.

The output produced by these commands is shown below. This provides the summary statistics for hours worked per week for men and women combined (note that there are now 12,519 valid cases (6,392 men plus 6,127 women). We can see for example that the interquartile range is 12.5 and that in other words 50 per cent of the sample work for between 27.5 and 40 hours per week.

Statistics

workhrs Total work hours

N	Valid	12519
	Missing	17550
Mean		34.5142
Median		37.0000
Minimum		.00
Maximum		97.00
Percentiles	10	16.0000
	20	22.5000
	25	27.5000
	30	30.5000
	40	36.0000
	50	37.0000
	60	38.0000
	70	40.0000
	75	40.0000
	80	40.0000
	90	48.0000

Figure 2.11 Summary statistics for hours worked per week for men and women combined.

In order to produce these summary statistics separately for men and women, as shown in figures 2.5 and 2.6 the same frequencies commands can be run in SPSS but first it is necessary temporarily to select men and then temporarily to select women. Once again this can either be done using the menus or using syntax. The correct syntax is displayed in the box.

```
TEMPORARY.
SELECT IF SEX=1.
FREQUENCIES
 VARIABLES=workhrs /FORMAT=NOTABLE
 /NTILES= 4
 /NTILES= 10
 /STATISTICS=STDDEV MINIMUM MAXIMUM MEAN MEDIAN
 /ORDER= ANALYSIS.

TEMPORARY.
SELECT IF SEX=2.
FREQUENCIES
 VARIABLES=workhrs /FORMAT=NOTABLE
 /NTILES= 4
 /NTILES= 10
 /STATISTICS=STDDEV MINIMUM MAXIMUM MEAN MEDIAN
 /ORDER= ANALYSIS.
```

To use the menus to select a subset of cases, first choose 'Select cases' from the 'Data' menu (see figure 2.12).

Then select the 'If condition is satisfied' option as shown below and click on the 'If. . .' button.

Use the next dialogue box to indicate that you want to select only the men to analyse by specifying Sex = 1. Finally click on 'Continue' and then on the 'OK' button.

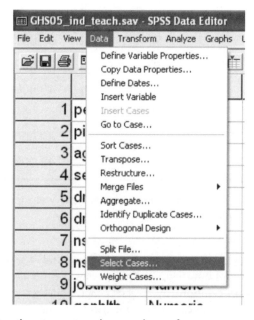

Figure 2.12 Using the menus to select a subset of cases.

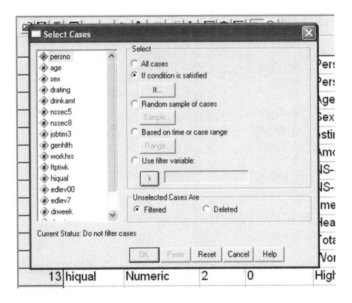

Figure 2.13 Specifying a condition for selected cases to satisfy.

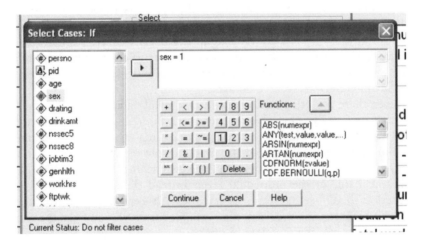

Figure 2.14 Limiting the analysis to men only.

You have now used the menus to specify that all subsequent analyses should be performed on men only, i.e. those cases for whom the variable 'Sex' has been coded as '1'. If you subsequently want to carry out analyses on women only it is necessary to follow the same process but to substitute 'Sex = 2' for 'Sex = 1' in the final dialogue box. Alternatively if you want to return to an analysis of all cases then use the 'Select cases' option on the 'Data' menu to select the 'All cases' option as shown in figure 2.15.

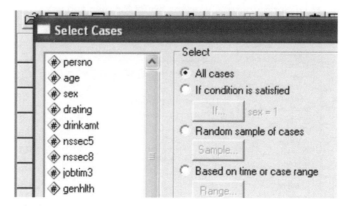

Figure 2.15 Selecting 'All cases' for analysis.

2.7 Individual and aggregate level data

So far, in both this chapter and the previous one, we have been looking at 'micro' or 'individual level' data. These are the types of data that can be analysed using SPSS or Excel, and each row of data in the data matrix would typically correspond to an individual case. As was described in the appendix to chapter 1, individual level data from surveys such as the General Household Survey are available from ESDS Government via the Data Archive in Essex. As we have seen above, it can be used to look at the distribution of working hours. Because the data are micro data it is possible to extract a small sample and examine the actual working hours of specific individuals within the dataset.

However, there are other data that are only available at aggregate level. This means that some analysis has already been carried out, and that the data are summarized in some way rather than being provided in a raw form. For example, in contrast to the General Household Survey, data from the Annual Survey of Hours and Earnings in Britain (which replaced the New Earnings Survey in 2004) are not generally available at the individual level. Instead these data are analysed by researchers at the Office for National Statistics. Although tables of summary statistics, such as means and medians, are available for download from the web, it is not possible to access the raw data in this way.

Figure 2.16 shows the distribution of working hours for men and women working full time in the UK in 2004. The Annual Survey of Hours and Earnings provides information about the distribution of hours worked in terms of deciles, and also includes the mid-spread (i.e. the difference between the values at the 25th percentile and the 75th percentile in bold in the table below). For example, from figure 2.16 we can see that 50 per cent of men, working full time, work between 37 and 42.4 hours per week, while 50 per cent of women, working full time, work between 35 and 39 hours per week. At the top end of the distribution, whereas 10 per cent of men work for 49 hours per week or more, the top 10 per cent of women in the distribution work for 41.5 hours a week or more.

Figure 2.16 Distribution of total working hours for men and women working full time in the UK in 2004.

		Men	Women
	Median	39	37
	Mean	40.8	37.5
Percentiles	10	35	33
	20	37	35
	25	37	35
	30	37.2	36
	40	37.5	37
	60	40	37.5
	70	41	37.8
	75	**42.4**	**39**
	80	44.1	40
	90	49	41.5

Source: Annual Survey of Hours and Earnings 2004, Office for National Statistics table 1.9a Hours worked - Total: United Kingdom, 2004.

2.8 Hours worked by age

The Annual Survey of Hours and Earnings also provides data on total hours of work disaggregated by age. Figure 2.17 shows the median and mean hours worked by men of different ages in the UK in 2004. Note that this includes all men whether they are working full time or part time. It can be seen that whether we focus on the mean or the median, the figures tell a similar story. It is men in their thirties and forties who work the longest hours on average, while younger men and men over the age of fifty tend to work slightly shorter average hours. For example, if we focus on median hours worked we can see that the median for men aged over 50 is 38 hours per week, which is one hour per week less than the median for men aged between 30 and 39. However, it can also be seen that the *median* hours worked vary less by age than the *mean* hours worked. In particular while the median for those aged 18–21 drops to 37 hours per week, the mean for this group drops right down to 32.2 hours per week. This illustrates the point made in section 2.5 above that the median is more resistant to a change in any small but extreme part of the data. Whereas the mean hours worked by

Figure 2.17 Hours of work by age for men in the UK (2004).

	Median	Mean
All employees	38.2	38.8
18–21	37.0	32.2
22–29	38.6	38.7
30–39	39.0	39.8
40–49	38.9	39.9
50+	38.0	38.5

Source: Annual Survey of Hours and Earnings 2004, Office for National Statistics.

men aged 18–21 is dramatically reduced by a small group of men working very short hours in part-time jobs (possibly students working part time while they are studying) the median is less affected by this small group at one extreme of the distribution.

2.9 Comparing working hours across Europe: the Working Time Directive

The aim of the 1993 European Working Time Directive was to make sure that employees are protected against any adverse effects on their health and safety caused by working excessively long hours. The Working Time Directive states that workers cannot be forced to work for more than 48 hours per week on average. It also gives workers a right to a day off each week and to four weeks paid leave per year. The Directive gives Member States of the European Union an 'opt-out' provision so that individual workers can waive the right to work no more than 48 hours per week. The opt-out has been used almost exclusively by the UK. This means that in the UK, workers can agree to work longer than the 48-hour maximum if they wish, but in this case an agreement must be put in writing and signed by the worker. As we saw in figure 2.16, in the UK in 2004 ten per cent of men were working longer than 49 hours per week.

In January 2004, the European Commission published a 10-year review of the Working Time Directive. In particular, this focused on the opt-out provision because there was some concern that workers were being coerced into 'volunteering' to work for longer hours. Although on 11 May 2005 the European parliament voted to scrap the opt-out (by 378 votes to 262, with 156 abstentions) at a Council of Ministers meeting on 3 June, no political agreement was reached to change the opt out. This meant that the arrangements for British workers to be able to opt-out of the provision remained in force.

Figure 2.18 shows the *mean* working hours for men and women working full-time in twelve of the fifteen long-standing member states of Europe (data were not available for Belgium, Germany or Luxembourg). Countries have been ranked by men's average actual weekly working hours. We can see that together with Greece, Austria and Ireland the United Kingdom is one of the countries with the longest average weekly working hours. It is also clear that in each of these countries men tend to work longer hours each week than women, even when the analysis is restricted to those describing themselves as working full time.

It should be noted that this type of clustered bar chart is very different from the histograms displayed in figure 2.1 and figure 2.2. Whereas a histogram is used to display the distribution of a single variable, this clustered bar chart is being used to compare the means of different groups of individuals. These types of graphical displays are relatively intuitive to interpret and they are often used in newspapers and other media. However, chapter 8 will provide a more thorough discussion of how we compare the means of different groups, such as the average working hours of men and women or average working hours in different countries.

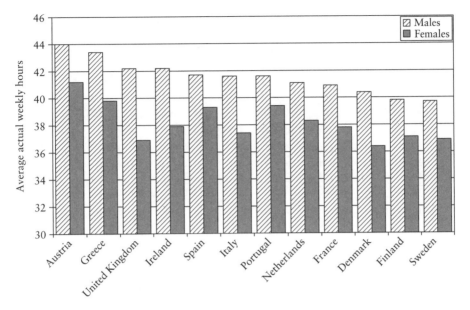

Source: Eurostat New Cronos, ESDS International, University of Manchester.

Figure 2.18 Average actual working hours for men and women working full time (2005, Q1).

2.10 Conclusion

In this chapter we have seen how aspects of a whole distribution may be reduced to single number summaries. Unless the distribution has a very simple shape, such summaries are bound to involve information loss. But the compensation is greatly enhanced power to describe important features succinctly.

Two summaries of the level of a distribution, the mean and the median, were discussed in detail. The median was seen to minimize the absolute size of residuals, whereas the mean minimized squared residuals. Two summaries of spread, the standard deviation and the midspread, were also presented. The concept of resistance was introduced as a way of comparing different summary measures; the median and midspread are more resistant than the mean and standard deviation.

Exercises

2.1 Pick any three numbers and calculate their mean and median. Calculate the residuals and squared residuals from each, and sum them. Confirm that the median produces smaller absolute residuals and the mean produces smaller squared residuals. (You are not expected to prove that this is bound to be the case.)

2.2   The dataset below shows the gross earnings in pounds per week of twenty men and twenty women drawn randomly from the 1979 New Earnings Survey (see appendix to this chapter on the accompanying website). The respondents are all full-time adult workers. Men are deemed to be adult when they reach age 21, women when they reach age 18.

Men		Women	
150	58	90	39
55	122	76	47
82	120	87	80
107	83	58	42
102	115	50	40
78	69	46	99
154	99	63	77
85	94	68	67
123	144	116	49
66	55	60	54

Calculate the median and dQ of both male and female earnings, and compare the two distributions.

2.3   Calculate the mean and standard deviation of the male earnings of the data in Exercise 2.2. Compare them with the median and midspread you calculated. Why do they differ?

2.4   Use the teaching dataset GHS05_ind_teach.sav and use SPSS to calculate the mean and median age of the sample. How similar or different are these figures and how would you explain this?

2.5   Using the teaching dataset GHS05_ind_teach.sav, and using SPSS, find out the mean and median units of alcohol that individuals report drinking each week. Which of these would you say is a better summary of the level of the data and why?

3

Scaling and Standardizing

3.1 Data are produced not given

The word 'data' must be treated with caution. Literally translated, it means 'things that are given'. However, classical scholarship must be rejected. The numbers that present themselves to us are not given naturally in that form. Any particular batch of numbers has been fashioned by human hand. The numbers did not drop from the sky ready made. The numbers usually reflect aspects of the social process which created them. Data, in short, are produced, not given.

There are often problems with using official statistics, especially those which are the by-products of some administrative process like, for example, reporting deaths to the Registrar-General or police forces recording reported crimes. Data analysts have to learn to be critical of the measures available to them, but in a constructive manner. As well as asking 'Are there any errors in this measure?' we also have to ask 'Is there anything better available?' and, if not, 'How can I improve what I've got?'

Improvements can often be made to the material at hand without resorting to the expense of collecting new data. We must feel entirely free to rework the numbers in a variety of ways to achieve the following goals:

- to make them more amenable to analysis;
- to promote comparability;
- to focus attention on differences.

The first improvement that can often be made is to change some aspect of the scale of measurement on which the data have been recorded. There is nothing sacrosanct about the particular way in which the numbers are given. The question is not which is the *right* way to express them, but rather which is the *most appropriate* way to express them for the purpose at hand. For example, we saw in chapter 1 that although income data were collected and recorded in pence, they were best displayed in a histogram in pounds (£s).

No measurement system is perfect and manages completely to represent our theoretical concepts. The numbers we work with are only indicators of the thing we are really interested in. The measures can therefore also often be improved by combining several indicators of the same underlying concept into a composite score, on the assumption that the errors in each indicator will tend to cancel each other out and leave a purer measure of the thing we are really interested in.

This chapter considers various manipulations that can be applied to the data to achieve the above goals. We start by recalling how a constant may be added to or subtracted from each data point, and then look at the effect of multiplying or dividing by a constant. Then we consider a powerful standardizing technique which makes the level and spread of any distribution identical. This allows us to return to an issue left unanswered at the end of chapter 2, namely how to summarize the shape of a distribution. It also allows us to consider the construction of composite measures. Finally, we look at the standardization of a batch of numbers using some external frame of reference.

The discussion of the shape of distributions in this chapter follows on from the discussion of their level and spread in chapter 2. Some may, however, like to read it in conjunction with chapter 10, which develops many of the ideas presented here.

3.2 Adding or subtracting a constant

One way of focusing attention on a particular feature of a dataset is to add or subtract a constant from every data value. For example, in a set of data on weekly family incomes it would be possible to subtract the median from each of the data values, thus drawing attention to which families had incomes below or above a hypothetical typical family.

The change made to the data by adding or subtracting a constant is fairly trivial. Only the level is affected; spread, shape and outliers remain unaltered. The reason for doing it is usually to force the eye to make a division above and below a particular point. A negative sign would be attached to all those incomes which were below the median in the example above. However, we sometimes add or subtract a constant to bring the data within a particular range.

3.3 Multiplying or dividing by a constant

Instead of adding a constant, we could change each data point by multiplying or dividing it by a constant. A common example of this is the re-expression of one currency in terms of another. For example, in order to convert pounds to US dollars, the pounds are multiplied by the current exchange rate. Multiplying or dividing each of the values has a more powerful effect than adding or subtracting. The result of multiplying or dividing by a constant is to **scale** the entire variable by a factor, evenly stretching or shrinking the axis like a piece of elastic. To illustrate this, let us see what happens if data from the General Household Survey on the weekly alcohol consumption of men who classify themselves as moderate or heavy drinkers are divided by seven to give the average *daily* alcohol consumption. Figures 3.1A and 3.1B show the distribution of the data before and after dividing by seven. (An extract from the raw data is shown below in figure 3.2.)

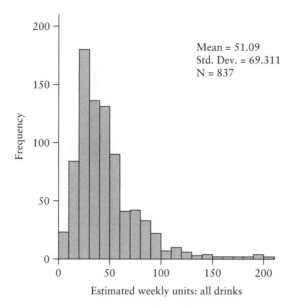

Mean = 51.09
Std. Dev. = 69.311
N = 837

Source: *GHS 2005 individual data.*

Figure 3.1A   Histogram of weekly alcohol consumption of men who describe themselves as drinking 'quite a lot' or 'heavy drinkers'.

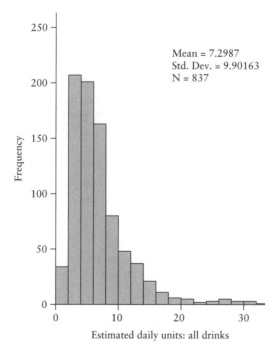

Mean = 7.2987
Std. Dev. = 9.90163
N = 837

Source: *GHS 2002–3 individual data.*

Figure 3.1B   Histogram of daily alcohol consumption of men who describe themselves as drinking 'quite a lot' or 'heavy drinkers'.

The overall shape of the distributions in figures 3.1A and 3.1B are the same. The data points are all in the same order, and the relative distances between them have not been altered apart from the effects of rounding. The whole distribution has simply been **scaled** by a constant factor. So neither the level nor the spread takes the same numeric value as previously. The original scale has been lost temporarily, but it could always be retrieved by rescaling.

	age	sex	drating	drday	d
1	27	Male	24	3.46	dri
2	27	Fem	8	1.14	dr
3	27	Fem	27	3.86	dr
4	6	Male	.	.	
5	5	Male	.	.	
6	77	Male	8	1.14	d
7	65	Fem	14	2.00	dr
8	51	Fem	3	.43	d
9	33	Male	9	1.29	dr
10	25	Male	9	1.29	d
11	49	Male	352	50.30	or
12	16	Male	2	.32	ha

GHS05_ind_teach.sav - SPSS Data Editor
File Edit View Data Transform Analyze Graphs Utilities Window
1 : age   27

Figure 3.2 Extract of data from the General Household Survey showing *weekly* alcohol consumption (drating) and *daily* alcohol consumption (drday).

In SPSS it is very straightforward to multiply or divide a set of data by a constant value. For example, using syntax, the command to create the variable drday 'Average daily alcohol consumption' from the variable drating 'Average weekly alcohol consumption' is as follows:

COMPUTE DRDAY = DRATING/7.

Alternatively, to create a new variable 'NEWVAR' by multiplying an existing variable 'OLDVAR' by seven the syntax would be:

COMPUTE NEWVAR = OLDVAR*7.

The 'Compute' command can also be used to add or subtract a constant, for example:

COMPUTE NEWVAR = OLDVAR + 100.

COMPUTE NEWVAR = OLDVAR−60.

The value of multiplying or dividing by a constant is often to promote comparability between datasets where the absolute scale values are different. For example, one way to compare the cost of a loaf of bread in Britain and the United States is to express the British price in dollars. Percentages are the result of dividing frequencies by one particular constant – the total number of cases. Their use to promote comparability between rows and columns of a table will be discussed in chapter 6. The principle of scaling variables will be an essential ingredient in the technique of variable standardization to be discussed later in this chapter.

When dividing values by a constant, we often say that each value is expressed **relative** to that constant. A common use of relatives is to examine change over time, using the value of a variable in one particular year as the base, and expressing subsequent years relative to this. For example in figure 3.3 below spending by households for a number of broad categories of expenditure are expressed in relation to expenditure in 1971. This can be interpreted to mean that for every £100 a household spent on food and non-alcoholic drink in 1971, they spent £105 in 1981 and £137 in 2001. We can see that the greatest increases in spending since 1971 are on clothing and footwear, and on communication. Increased spending on communication during the 1990s is particularly striking, which may be a result of the increase in mobile phone ownership over the decade. In contrast, spending on alcohol and tobacco has actually declined in the last three decades of the twentieth century. This may reflect the decline in smoking but also the relative decline in the cost of alcohol.

Figure 3.3 Volume of household expenditure over time (UK).

	1971	1981	1991	2001
Food and non-alcoholic drink	100	105	117	137
Alcohol and tobacco	100	99	92	88
Clothing and footwear	100	120	187	346
Housing, water and fuel	100	17	138	152
Household goods and services	100	117	160	262
Health	100	125	182	180
Transport	100	128	181	238
Communication	100	190	306	790

Source: Extract from table 6.1, *Social Trends* 35, 2005 edition.

3.4 Standardized variables

In sections 3.2 and 3.3, we saw that subtracting a constant from every data value altered the level of the distribution, and dividing by a constant scaled the values by a factor. In this section we will look at how these two ideas may be combined to produce a very powerful tool which can render any variable into a form where it can be compared with any other. The result is called a **standardized variable**.

To standardize a variable, a typical value is first subtracted from each data point, and then each point is divided by a measure of spread. It is not crucial which numerical summaries of level and spread are picked. The mean and standard deviation could be used, or the median and midspread:

$$\frac{Y_i - \overline{Y}}{s} \quad \text{or} \quad \frac{Y_i - M(Y)}{dQ}$$

A variable which has been standardized in this way is forced to have a mean or median of 0 and a standard deviation or midspread of 1.

Two different uses of variable standardization are found in social science literature. The first is in building causal models, where it is convenient to be able to compare the effect that two different variables have on a third on the same scale. This will be discussed further in chapter 12. But there is a second use which is more immediately intelligible: standardized variables are useful in the process of building complex measures based on more than one indicator. If, as we argued, the things we actually measure are often only indicators of the underlying theoretical concept which really interests us, it stands to reason that several such indicators, if added together, could tap a theoretical concept more fully.

In order to illustrate this, we will use some data drawn from the National Child Development Study (NCDS). This is a longitudinal survey of all children born in a single week of 1958. Further details about the survey can be found in the appendix to this chapter which is on the accompanying website. There is a great deal of information about children's education in this survey. Information was sought from the children's schools about their performance at state examinations, but the researchers also decided to administer their own tests of attainment.

Rather than attempt to assess knowledge and abilities across the whole range of school subjects, the researchers narrowed their concern down to verbal and mathematical abilities. Each child was given a reading comprehension test which was constructed by the National Foundation for Educational Research for use in the study, and a test of mathematics devised at the University of Manchester. The two tests were administered at the child's school and had very different methods of scoring. As a result they differed in both level and spread.

Descriptive Statistics

	N	Minimum	Maximum	Mean	Std. Deviation
Age 16 Test 1-reading comprehension	11920	0	35	25.37	7.024
Age 16 Test 2-mathematics comprehension	11920	0	31	12.75	6.997
Valid N (listwise)	11920				

Source: Analysis of National Child Development Study age 16 data.

Figure 3.4 Descriptive statistics for reading comprehension and mathematics test scores from NCDS age 16.

As can be seen from the descriptive statistics in figure 3.4, the sixteen-year-olds in the National Child Development Study apparently found the mathematics test rather more difficult than the reading comprehension test. The reading comprehension was scored out of a total of 35 and sixteen-year-olds gained a mean score of 25.37, whereas the mathematics test was scored out of a possible maximum of 31, but the 16-year-olds only gained a mean score of 12.75.

The first two columns of figure 3.5 show the scores obtained on the reading and mathematics test by fifteen respondents in this study. There is nothing inherently interesting or intelligible about the raw numbers. The first score of 31 for the reading test can only be assessed in comparison with what other children obtained. Both tests can be thought of as indicators of the child's general attainment at school. It might be useful to try to turn them into a single measure of that construct.

Figure 3.5 Scores of reading and mathematics tests at age 16.

1 Raw reading score	2 Raw maths score	3 Standardized reading score	4 Standardized maths score	5 Composite score of attainment
31	17	0.8	0.61	1.41
33	20	1.09	1.04	2.12
31	21	0.8	1.18	1.98
30	14	0.66	0.18	0.84
28	14	0.37	0.18	0.55
31	11	0.8	−0.25	0.55
29	8	0.52	−0.68	−0.16
28	17	0.37	0.61	0.98
23	8	−0.34	−0.68	−1.02
25	13	−0.05	0.04	−0.02
19	8	−0.91	−0.68	−1.59
32	25	0.94	1.75	2.69
31	22	0.80	1.32	2.12
29	8	0.52	−0.68	−0.16
30	17	0.66	0.61	1.27

Source: Extract from National Child Development Study respondents at age 16.

In order to create such a summary measure of attainment at age 16, we want to add the two scores together. But this cannot be done as they stand, because as we saw before, the scales of measurement of these two tests are different. If this is not immediately obvious try the following thought experiment. A 16-year-old who is average at reading but terrible at mathematics will perhaps score 25.4 (i.e. the mean score) on the reading comprehension test and 0 on the mathematics test. If these were summed the total is 25.4. However, a 16-year-old who is average at mathematics but can't read is likely to score 12.7 (i.e. the mean score) on the maths score and 0 on the reading comprehension. If these are summed the total would only be 12.7. If the two tests can be forced to take the same scale, then they can be summed.

This is achieved by standardizing each score. One common way of standardizing is to first subtract the mean from each data value, and then divide the result by the standard deviation. This process is summarized by the following formula, where the original variable 'Y' becomes the standardized variable 'Z':

$$Z = (Y_i - \hat{Y})/\text{St. Dev.}$$

For example, the first value of 31 in the reading test becomes:

$$(31 - 25.37)/7$$

$$\text{or } 0.8$$

In other words this individual has a reading score which is eight-tenths (or four-fifths) of a standard deviation above the mean.

The same individual's mathematics score becomes $(17 - 12.75)/7$, or 0.61. This first respondent is therefore above average in both reading and maths. To summarize, we can add these two together and arrive at a score of 1.41 for attainment in general. Similar calculations for the whole batch are shown in columns 3 and 4 of figure 3.5. We can see that the sixth person in this extract of data is above average in reading but slightly below average (by a quarter of a standard deviation) in mathematics. It should also be noted that any individual scoring close to the mean for both their reading comprehension and their mathematics test will have a total score close to zero. For example, the tenth case in figure 3.5 has a total score of −0.02.

The final column of figure 3.5 now gives a set of summary scores of school attainment, created by standardizing two component scores and summing them; so attainment in reading and maths have effectively been given equal weight. This single variable might now be used to predict occupational attainment as an adult, for example. This summary measure could also be used to compare the school attainment of 16-year-old boys and 16-year-old girls, or to compare the attainment of children from different social class backgrounds. The median and midspread could have been used just as easily to create these standardized scores.

It is very straightforward to create standardized variables using SPSS. By using the Descriptives command, the SPSS package will automatically save a standardized version of any variable. First select the menus

Analyze > Descriptive Statistics > Descriptives

The next stage is to select the variables that you wish to standardize, in this case N2928 and N2930, and check the box next to 'Save standardized values as variables.' The SPSS package will then automatically save new standardized variables with the suffix Z. In this example, two new variables ZN2928 and ZN2930 are created.

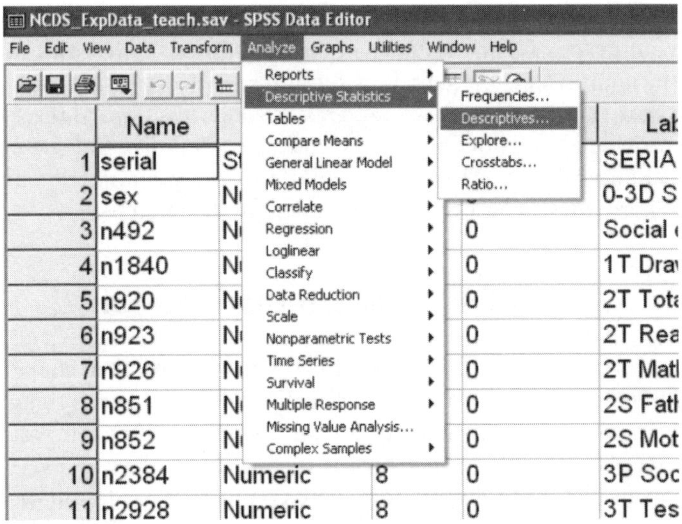

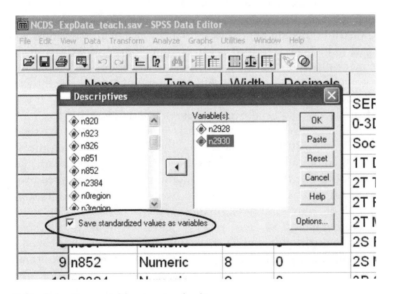

Figure 3.6 Creating standardized variables using SPSS.

Figure 3.7 Selecting variables to standardize.

The syntax to achieve this is as follows:

DESCRIPTIVES
 VARIABLES = n2928 n2930 / SAVE
 /STATISTICS = MEAN STDDEV MIN MAX.

Standardizing the variables was a necessary, but not a sufficient condition for creating a simple summary score. It is also important to have confidence that the components are both valid indicators of the underlying construct of interest. This could be gauged by inspecting the type of items included in the tests. Critics of IQ tests, for example, argue that the items selected often reflect cultural knowledge rather than underlying intelligence. It is very hard to *prove* that a test is valid. It is beyond the scope of this chapter to provide an introduction to the concept of validity and the methods for testing the validity of tests. However, for those who are interested Carmines and Zeller (1979) provides an accessible introduction to the main issues.

3.5 The Gaussian distribution

We are now ready to turn to the third feature of distributions, their shape. With level and spread taken care of, the shape of the distribution refers to everything that is left.

In order to summarize the shape of a distribution succinctly, it would need to be simple enough to be able to specify how it should be drawn in a very few statements. For example, if the distribution were completely flat (a **uniform distribution**), this would be possible. We would only need to specify the value of the extremes and the number of cases for it to be reproduced accurately, and it would be possible to say exactly what proportion of the cases fell above and below a certain level.

In fact, distributions are almost never flat. Even age distributions, which one might expect to be fairly flat, turn out to be quite lumpy, as we saw in chapter 1. However, many distributions do have a characteristic shape – a lump in the middle and tails straggling out at both ends. How convenient it would be if there was an easy way to define a more complex shape like this and to know what proportion of the distribution would lie above and below different levels.

One such shape, investigated in the early nineteenth century by the German mathematician and astronomer, Gauss, and therefore referred to as the **Gaussian distribution,** is commonly used. It is possible to define a symmetrical, bell-shaped curve which looks like those in figure 3.8, and which contains fixed proportions of the distribution at different distances from the centre. The two curves in figure 3.8 look different – (a) has a smaller spread than (b) – but in fact they only differ by a scaling factor.

Any Gaussian distribution has a very useful property: it can be defined uniquely by its mean and standard deviation. Given these two pieces of information, the exact shape of the curve can be reconstructed, and the proportion of the area under the curve falling between various points can be calculated (see figure 3.9). However, the Gaussian is not the only family of distributions with this property, you should note, but it is the one which, when used to represent a sample, involves the simplest calculations from sample values.

The Gaussian distribution is a hypothetical entity. Up to now, we have used histograms to look at empirical distributions. The Gaussian distribution is defined theoretically; you can think of it as being based on an infinitely large number of cases. For this reason it is perfectly smooth, and has infinitely long tails with infinitely small proportions of the distribution falling under them. The theoretical definition of the curve is given by an equation. You do not need to know it for most purposes, but it will be found in any set of mathematical tables.

This bell-shaped curve is often called 'the normal distribution'. Its discovery was associated with the observation of errors of measurement. If sufficient repeated measurements were made of the same object, it was discovered that most of them centred around one value (assumed to be the true measurement), quite a few were fairly near the centre, and measurements fairly wide of the mark were unusual but did occur. The distribution of these errors of measurement often approximated to the bell-shape in figure 3.8.

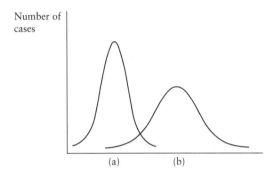

Figure 3.8   The Gaussian distribution.

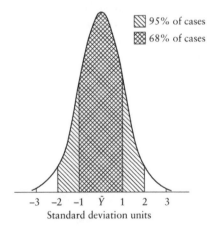

Figure 3.9   Fixed proportions under the Gaussian curve with mean 0 and standard deviation 1.

When social accounting became widespread in the nineteenth century, and crime statistics, education statistics and so on became available for the first time, early social statisticians became very excited. It seemed as though the social world yielded distributions that looked very like those of the natural world. A Belgian astronomer-cum-social-scientist, Adolphe Quetelet, hypothesized the existence of *l'homme moyen*, the average human type about whom laws as firm as those of planetary motion could be framed. The Gaussian distribution became known as the 'normal distribution', as if it were a distribution which was normally found empirically.

Some empirical distributions are reasonably well described by this shape. For example, heights and weights are approximately Gaussian in shape, as you will see from data on the heights of boys in the National Child Development Study displayed in figure 3.10. Others, such as IQ, are human constructs, carefully fashioned to make sure that they are close to Gaussian in their shape. The items are selected to ensure a reassuring bell-shaped distribution when they are scored over a large sample. But, in general, it is not all that common to find variables whose distribution approximates closely to the Gaussian shape. For this reason the term 'normal distribution' is something of a misnomer, and is not used here.

How is the distribution to be used if we are not going to define it mathematically? The answer is that tables exist to allow one to look up what proportion of the distribution falls within given distances from the mean. Now the link with the previous section becomes clear. It would be impossible to do this for every conceivable Gaussian distribution – with every possible mean and standard deviation. The tables are therefore presented for a *standardized* distribution where the mean is 0 and the standard deviation 1.

To know if the shape of a particular empirical distribution approximates to the Gaussian shape, it is first standardized, and then examined to see if the proportion of the cases which lie given distances from the mean agrees with the proportion given in the tables. If it does, the tables predict that approximately:

- 68 per cent of the cases lie within one standard deviation unit of the mean
- 95 per cent of the cases lie within two standard deviations units of the mean
- 99.7 per cent of the cases lie within three standard deviation units of the mean

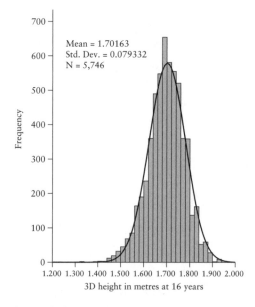

Source: National Child Development Study.

Figure 3.10   Histogram of boys' heights at age 16, with superimposed 'normal' curve.

So, for example, in the distribution of 16-year-old boys' heights in figure 3.11, which is an approximately Gaussian distribution with a mean of 170 cm and a standard deviation of 8 cm, 95 per cent of all the cases would be between 154 and 186 cm tall.

In order to discover how closely our sample of 16-year-old boys' heights fit the Gaussian distribution the height variable was standardized using SPSS and the procedure described above. This standardized variable was then recoded to create a categorical variable using the following syntax:

recode zn3height (lo thru $-3 = -3$) (-3 thru $-2 = -2$) (-2 thru $-1 = -1$)
(-1 thru $1 = 0$) (1 thru $2 = 1$) (2 thru $3 = 2$)
(3 thru hi $= 3$) into htgroup.

Figure 3.11 displays the first twenty cases and we can see that case 1 with a height of 1.71 m is just above the mean height of 1.70 cm. His standardized height is therefore 0.11 and he is in category 0 for the variable 'htgroup'. In contrast, case 11 is only 1.54 m tall and is therefore just over two standard deviations below the mean with a standardized score of -2.04 and in category -2.00 for the variable 'htgroup'.

A simple frequency table of this new categorical variable (figure 3.12) confirms that the distribution of boys' heights is very close to a Gaussian distribution. Just over 70 per cent of cases are less than a standard deviation away from the mean (compared with 68 per cent in a theoretical Gaussian distribution); 94.8 per cent

	serial	sex	dvht16	Zdvht16	htgroup
1	010001K	Male	1.71	.11	.00
2	010003P	Male	1.66	-.52	.00
3	010004R	Male	1.56	-1.79	-1.00
4	010006V	Male	1.66	-.52	.00
5	010008Z	Male	1.75	.61	.00
6	010017A	Male	1.66	-.52	.00
7	010018C	Male	1.57	-1.66	-1.00
8	010020P	Male	1.72	.23	.00
9	010024X	Male	1.72	.23	.00
10	010033Y	Male	1.59	-1.41	-1.00
11	010038K	Male	1.54	-2.04	-2.00
12	010041X	Male	1.84	1.74	1.00
13	010048N	Male	1.60	-1.28	-1.00
14	010049Q	Male	1.73	.36	.00
15	010055K	Male	1.79	1.11	1.00
16	010056M	Male	1.61	-1.15	-1.00
17	010059T	Male	1.75	.61	.00
18	010067S	Male	1.75	.61	.00
19	010068U	Male	1.70	-.02	.00
20	010069	Male	1.75	.61	.00

Source: National Child Development Study.

Figure 3.11 Extract from data on boys' heights from the National Child Development Study.

Figure 3.12   Frequency table of boy's heights recoded for comparison with the Gaussian distribution.

Boys' height grouped by standard deviations away from the mean

		Frequency	Per cent	Valid Per cent	Cumulative Per cent
Valid	-3.00	26	.5	.5	.5
	-2.00	164	2.9	2.9	3.3
	-1.00	675	11.7	11.7	15.1
	.00	4069	70.8	70.8	85.9
	1.00	710	12.4	12.4	98.2
	2.00	96	1.7	1.7	99.9
	3.00	6	.1	.1	100.0
	Total	5746	100.0	100.0	

Source: Analysis of National Child Development Study age 16 data.

Topic for discussion

The following brief article by Gavyn Davies, published in the *Guardian* on 10 November 2005, uses the concepts of the average (mean) score, the standard deviation and the Gaussian distribution to underpin an argument about whether selection tests such as the 11+ are fair. The article is interesting for two reasons; firstly it provides a practical illustration of the use of the concepts introduced in this chapter and secondly it uses the rhetoric of statistics to add credibility to an argument against selection tests.

Why school-selection exams are unfair

Gavyn Davies does the Maths
Thursday, 10 November 2005
Guardian
http://guardian.co.uk/politics/2005/nov/10/publicservices.schools

---

of cases are within two standard deviations of the mean; and 99.4 per cent of cases are within three standard deviations of the mean.

Exercise 3.4 at the end of this chapter suggests that you follow a similar procedure to see how closely girls' heights fit a Gaussian distribution.

The Gaussian distribution may not be 'normal', in the sense of commonly occurring as an empirical distribution, but this does not stop it being useful. It acts as a benchmark for comparison, a standard shape against which to compare the particular shape in hand. Although few empirical distributions start life with a Gaussian shape, we will discover in chapter 10 that they can often be transformed to help them approximate to it. Once this has been achieved, their approximate shape can be described succinctly. Moreover, distributions which started out with different shapes can, once they have been transformed into similar characteristic shapes, be better compared.

The Gaussian curve also has an important role to play in statistical inference, which is covered in chapter 7. You will come across this shape again as you acquire more experience with data analysis.

3.6 Standardizing with respect to an appropriate base

In the scaling and standardizing techniques considered up to now, the same *numerical* adjustment has been made to each of the values in a batch of data. Sometimes, however, it can be useful to make the same *conceptual* adjustment to each data value, which may involve a different number in each case.

A batch of numbers may be reworked in several different ways in order to reveal different aspects of the story they contain. A dataset which can be viewed from several angles is shown in figure 3.13: the value of the lower quartile, the median and the upper quartile of male and female earnings in the period between 1990 and 2000. The data are drawn from the New Earnings Survey that collects information about earnings in a fixed period each year from the employers of a large sample of employees. More information about this survey is given in the appendix to chapter 2 on the accompanying website.

As the figures stand, the most dominant feature of the dataset is a rather uninteresting one: the change in the value of the pound. While the median and midspreads of the money incomes each year have increased substantially in this period, real incomes and differentials almost certainly have not. How could we present the data in order to focus on the trend in real income differentials over time?

Figure 3.13 Male and female earnings 1990–2000: gross earnings in pounds per week for full-time workers on adult rates whose pay was not affected by absence.

Year	Male earnings			Female earnings		
	QL	M	Qu	Ql	M	Qu
1990	193.4	258.2	347.5	136.2	177.5	244.7
1991	206.9	277.5	376.5	150.6	195.7	271.6
1992	219.3	295.9	401.9	161.4	211.3	295.9
1993	226.0	304.6	417.3	168.2	221.6	309.1
1994	231.1	312.8	427.3	174.6	229.4	320.1
1995	237.1	323.2	442.7	179.5	237.2	332.5
1996	245.2	334.9	460.7	186.8	248.1	347.3
1997	256.4	349.7	480.0	196.1	260.5	364.7
1998	265.3	362.8	499.0	203.6	270.0	379.1
1999	274.5	374.3	517.3	213.3	284.0	398.2
2000	284.7	389.7	537.7	223.6	296.7	417.6

Source: Extract from New Earnings Survey 2000 tables A28.1 and A28.2.

Figure 3.14   Male and female earnings relative to medians for each sex.

Year	Male earnings			Female earnings		
	QL	M	Qu	Ql	M	Qu
1990	75	100	135	77	100	138
1991	75	100	136	77	100	139
1992	74	100	136	76	100	140
1993	74	100	137	76	100	139
1994	74	100	137	76	100	140
1995	73	100	137	76	100	140
1996	73	100	138	75	100	140
1997	73	100	137	75	100	140
1998	73	100	138	75	100	140
1999	73	100	138	75	100	140
2000	73	100	138	75	100	141

Source: Re-expression of data in figure 3.13.

One approach would be to treat the distribution of incomes for each sex in each year as a separate distribution, and express each of the quartiles relative to the median. The result of doing this is given in figure 3.14. The figure of 75 for the Q_L for men in 1990, for example, was obtained by dividing £193 by £258 and multiplying the result by 100. All of the results have been rounded to the nearest pound (£).

The internal differentials within each income distribution in each year can now be compared, although any overall growth or decline in the purchasing power of the incomes has been lost. The gradual widening of both male and female earnings differentials over time is quite apparent. Interested readers might like to explore this further by consulting the New Earnings Survey to obtain information on other quantiles of the distribution (and see also Exercise 3.4 at the end of this chapter).

3.7 Has the Equal Pay Act worked?

In re-expressing the male earnings relative to the male median and the female earnings relative to the female median, we lost the ability to compare male and female earnings. One way to facilitate such a comparison with the original money earnings would be to correct the money incomes in each year for inflation, thus to express them all in real terms. But if we were concerned to focus on the relativities between male and female earnings, irrespective of the value of real earnings, the female earnings could be expressed relative to the male earnings at the same point in the distribution.

Figure 3.15 shows the value of the female earnings each year at the three points on the distribution relative to male earnings at the same point. For example, the value of 70 for Q_L in 1990 was obtained from figure 3.13 by dividing £136 by £193 and multiplying the result by 100.

In 1970 the British Labour Party passed an Equal Pay Act, which aimed to promote equality of earnings between men and women. The Act came into force

Figure 3.15 Female earnings relative to male earnings at the same quantile.

	QL	M	QU
1990	70	69	70
1991	73	71	72
1992	74	71	74
1993	74	73	74
1994	76	73	75
1995	76	73	75
1996	76	74	75
1997	76	74	76
1998	77	74	76
1999	78	76	77
2000	79	76	78

Source: Re-expression of data in figure 3.13.

in 1975, so employers had five years to make any adjustments necessary to bring the pay of their male and female employees into line. The Act was amended with effect from the beginning of January 1984, to bring Britain in line with European law, and to specify equality of pay for 'work of equal value'. Analysis of data from the 1970s and 1980s suggests that the Equal Pay Act had some impact, albeit only raising women's earnings to around two-thirds of male earnings (Marsh, 1988). The data in figure 3.15 suggest that during the 1990s, women's earnings continued to increase relative to those of men but that women's earnings were still only about three-quarters of their male counterparts.

One explanation for this continued inequality in earnings is that the earnings in figure 3.13 include earnings from overtime. Since men work much more overtime than women, it could be argued the differential in pay *rates* would not be as great as this. Indeed, if a similar analysis is carried out comparing male and female *hourly* earnings, the differential is found to be less. However, the major problem with equal pay legislation is that men and women in all societies tend to be found in very different jobs. Decreeing that *'there shall be the same pay for the same work'* fails to address this problem. For women who do 'women's work', there is often no male comparison, especially if we want to focus on individuals who are working for the same employer.

3.8 Conclusion

The important lesson of this chapter is that numbers are not given in any divine and unchangeable form. One of the most fruitful things for the data analyst to do before searching for any associations between variables is to see if some re-expression would make the numbers more suitable for the problems in hand.

Subtracting a constant from each value in a dataset alters the level of the distribution. Multiplying or dividing by a constant alters the spread. Standardized scores are constructed by altering both the level and the spread to a norm of zero and one respectively. Each value in a dataset can often usefully be expressed relative to some appropriate base for comparison and the effect of this on the distribution varies. You should routinely think if any of these re-expressions would help in analysing data in exercises from now on.

The aim of the data analysis game is comparison. The Gaussian shape is a useful hypothetical distribution with which the shape of particular empirical distributions can be compared. Gaussian distributions are bell-shaped, and have the convenient property of being reproducible from their mean and standard deviation. If the Gaussian distribution is expressed in standardized form (with a mean of zero and a standard deviation of one), tables exist to establish how much of the distribution falls a given number of standard deviation units from the mean.

Exercises

3.1 If you were told that the distribution of a test of ability on a set of children was Gaussian, with a mean of 75 and a standard deviation of 12,
   (a) What proportion of children would have scores over 75?
   (b) What proportion of children would have got scores between 51 and 99?
   (c) What proportion of children would you expect to have scores of less than 39?

3.2 The data below have been extracted from the National Child Development Study, and shows the scores obtained by nine respondents on three different tests which claim to be measuring general intelligence.
   The first test was administered at age 7. The children were asked to draw a

Figure 3.16 Scores obtained by nine respondents on three different tests.

Draw-a-man test	Verbal ability	Non-verbal ability
18	25	23
25	16	12
27	38	31
1	8	15
26	30	20
19	19	12
26	16	15
24	24	24
16	11	17

Source: National Child Development Study.

picture of a man, and the result was scored for indications of the child's general mental and perceptual ability (Goodenough, 1926). The second and third are tests of verbal and non-verbal abilities respectively, administered at age 11 (Douglas, 1964). Convert these three scores into one general IQ score, using Excel or SPSS if you wish.

3.3 Read (i.e. load) the NCDS teaching dataset NCDS_ExpData_teach.sav into SPSS, and standardize the heights of girls at age 16 using means and standard deviations as demonstrated in section 3.4, and present the result as a histogram. How would you describe the shape of the distribution? Recode the standardized measure as described in section 3.4 and ascertain how close the distribution is to a Gaussian distribution.

3.4 Using data from tables A28.1 and A28.2 from the 2000 edition of the New Earnings Survey, examine how the gross weekly earnings of the lowest decile and highest decile of full-time males and females changed relative to median earnings between 1990 and 2000.

3.5 Using data from tables A29.1 and A29.2 from the 2000 edition of the New Earnings Survey, examine how the median *hourly* earnings of women compared with the median *hourly* earnings of men between 1990 and 2000. Repeat this analysis focusing first on men and women in manual occupations and then on men and women in non-manual occupations. Where are the gender disparities greatest?

4

Inequality

How true is the old proverb that the rich get richer and the poor get poorer? What evidence can we use to look at how the gap between the richest and the poorest in society is shifting over time? Does the way that we measure inequality impact on our conclusions? Those who are interested in income inequality have traditionally used techniques of displaying income distributions and summarizing their degree of spread. These are rather different methods from those outlined in chapters 1 and 2. This chapter provides an introduction to these techniques, so is somewhat separate from the cumulative structure of the book. The chapter does, however, build on the discussion of quantiles in chapter 2 and of re-expressing data relative to a particular quantile in chapter 3.

4.1 Prosperity and inequality

Over the past three decades or so, the British economy has grown and this has made a real difference to people's lives. Household disposable income per head, adjusted for inflation, increased more than one and a third times between 1971 and 2003 so that for every £100 a household had to spend in 1971, by 2003 they had to spend £234 (Summerfield and Gill, 2005). During the 1970s and early 1980s, growth in household income was somewhat erratic, and in some years there were small year on year falls, such as in 1974, 1976, 1977, 1981 and 1982. However, since then there has been growth each year, with the exception of 1996 when there was a very small fall. Data from the British Social Attitudes Survey (Park et al., 2004) show that whereas in 1983, 24 per cent of people said they were living comfortably and 25 per cent said they found it difficult or very difficult to cope, by the early 1990s, 40 per cent said they were comfortable while 16 per cent said they were finding it hard to cope.

However, despite this general increase in prosperity there is widespread agreement among the public that levels of inequality in British society are too high. The British Social Attitudes Survey 2003 found that over three-quarters of people said that the gap between the richest and poorest is too large and this proportion is little changed from when the question was first asked in 1984 (Summerfield and

Gill, 2005). There are a number of reasons why we might want to reduce inequality in society. For example, as Layard (2005) argues, if we accept that extra income has a bigger impact on increasing the happiness of the poor than the rich, this means that if some money is transferred from the rich to the poor this will increase the happiness of the poor more than it diminishes the happiness of the rich. This in turn suggests that the overall happiness rating of a country will go up if income is distributed more equally. Of course, as Layard acknowledges, the problem with this argument is that it only works if it is possible to reduce inequality without raising taxes to such an extent that there is no longer an incentive for individuals to strive to make money so that the total income is reduced as a result of policies aimed at redistribution. Although this chapter cannot provide a detailed discussion of these types of arguments it is clearly important to understand the principal ways of *measuring* inequality if we are to monitor the consequences of changing levels of inequality in society. This chapter will focus on how we can measure inequality in such a way as to make it possible to compare levels of inequality in different societies and to look at changes in levels of inequality over time.

4.2 Income and wealth

Considered at the most abstract level, income and wealth are two different ways of looking at the same thing. Both concepts try to capture ways in which members of society have different access to the goods and services that are valued in that society. Wealth is measured simply in pounds, and is a snapshot of the **stock** of such valued goods that any person owns, regardless of whether this is growing or declining. Income is measured in pounds per given period, and gives a moving picture, telling us about the **flow** of revenue over time.

In this chapter, for the sake of simplicity, we restrict our focus to the distribution of income. We will look in detail at the problems of measuring income and then consider some of the distinctive techniques for describing and summarizing inequality that have evolved in the literature on economic inequality.

There are four major methodological problems encountered when studying the distribution of income:

1. How should income be defined?
2. What should be the unit of measurement?
3. What should be the time period considered?
4. What sources of data are available?

Definition of income

To say that income is a flow of revenue is fine in theory, but we have to choose between two approaches to making this operational. One is to follow accounting and tax practices, and make a clear distinction between income and additions to wealth. With this approach, capital gains in a given period, even though they might be used in the same way as income, would be excluded from the definition. This is the approach of the Inland Revenue, which has separate taxes for income and capital gains. In this context a capital gain is defined as the profit obtained by selling an asset that has increased in value since it was obtained. However, interestingly, in most cases this definition (for the purposes of taxation) does not include any profit made when you sell your main home.

The second approach is to treat income as the value of goods and services consumed in a given period plus net changes in personal wealth during that period. This approach involves constantly monitoring the value of assets even when they do not come to the market. That is a very hard task. So, although the second approach is theoretically superior, it is not very practical and the first is usually adopted.

The phrase 'the value of goods and services' rather than 'money' was used above, to indicate that incomes both in cash and in kind should be considered. If an employee gets the free use of a company car, this has an important bearing on his or her standard of living, freeing income for other goods. It is, however, hard to get good data on non-cash benefits.

The definition of income usually only includes money spent on goods and services that are consumed privately. But many things of great value to different people are organized at a collective level: health services, education, libraries, parks, museums, even nuclear warheads. The benefits which accrue from these are not spread evenly across all members of society. If education were not provided free, only families with children would need to use their money income to buy schooling.

Sources of income are often grouped into three types:

- **earned income**, from either employment or self-employment;
- **unearned income** which accrues from ownership of investments, property, rent and so on;
- **transfer income**, that is benefits and pensions transferred on the basis of entitlement, not on the basis of work or ownership, mainly by the government but occasionally by individuals (e.g. alimony).

The first two sources are sometimes added together and referred to as **original income**. While earnings form some three-quarters of the total income in the UK, they form a much higher proportion among higher quantiles of the income distribution. Conversely, transfer payments constitute a very large proportion of the income of those at the bottom of the income distribution.

Deciding what to count as income for current consumption has proved problematic, especially in the area of National Insurance and pension contributions. If people use part of their current income to purchase an insurance of income in the future, should their current income be considered before or after that outlay? If income is measured before deductions, the savings element will eventually be counted twice – now while it is being bought and later when it is being used as income. But if it is ignored, two individuals who have the same income after deductions will be considered to be in the same boat. This may not seem sensible when one has some guaranteed income in the future and the other has none.

There are a large number of other detailed difficulties in the fine grain definition of income. For example, how are benefits in kind, such as access to company clubs, to be valued, or what should be done about the value of living in a house that is owned outright?

Measuring income: the unit of analysis

In many of the reports that examine inequality (such as 'The effect of taxes and benefits on household income' (Jones, 2007)) the basic unit of analysis used is the household, and not the family or the individual. This chapter will also use the household as the main unit of analysis. For these purposes, a household is defined in precise terms based on a harmonized definition as used in the Census and nearly all other government household surveys since 1981. This is one person, or a group of persons, who have the accommodation as their only or main residence and (for a group) share the living accommodation, that is a living or sitting room, or share meals together or have common housekeeping. Up until 1999–2000, the definition was based on the pre-1981 Census definition. This required a group of persons to share eating and budgeting arrangements as well as shared living accommodation in order to be considered as a household. The effect of the change was fairly small, but not negligible.

While most income is paid to individuals, the benefits of that income are generally shared across broader units. Spending on many items, particularly on food, housing, fuel and electricity, is largely joint spending by the members of the household. While there are many individuals who receive little or no income of their own, many of these will live with other people who do receive an income. This makes the household a good unit to study for those who are interested in inequality. This approach means that total household income is understood as representing the (potential) standard of living of each of its members. However, the assumption of equal sharing of resources between each member of the household is very difficult to test and is likely to be problematic in some cases.

Clearly households can have very different numbers of people living within them. Therefore it would be wrong to suggest that household A, with a disposable income of £30,000 per year, is less well off than household B with a disposable income of £40,000 per year if household A comprises a single person living alone and household B comprises a couple with a 6-year-old child. In order to adjust household incomes, so that it is possible to compare households of different sizes, an **equivalence scale** is used (for further details see the appendix on the accompanying website). An equivalence scale assigns a value to each individual based on their age and circumstances. The values for each household member are then summed to give the total equivalence number for that household. This number is then divided into the disposable income for that household to give **equivalized disposable income**. For example, a household with a married couple and one child aged six would have an **equivalence number of 1.0 + 0.21 = 1.21** (these figures are found in the appendix to this chapter). In the example above the household's disposable income (for Household B) is £40,000, and so its equivalized disposable income is £33,058 (i.e. £40,000/1.21). The equivalence number for Household A is 0.61 for a single head of household and therefore the equivalized disposable income would be £49,180.

The time period

It is difficult to decide what the appropriate period should be for the assessment of income. It is usually important to distinguish inequalities between the same people over the course of their life-cycle and inequalities between different people. If a short period, like a week, is chosen, two people may appear to have identical incomes even though they are on very different lifetime career paths; conversely, two individuals who appear to have very different incomes may be on identical lifetime career paths but just be at different ages. In general, income inequality will appear greater the shorter the time period considered.

The solution might be to take a longer period – ideally a lifetime, perhaps. However, either guesses will have to be made about what people will earn in the future, or definitive statements will only be possible about the degree of inequality pertaining in society many decades previously. For most purposes, one tax year is used as the period over which information about income is collected.

Sources of data on income

There are now many large-scale, regular surveys of individuals and households in Britain that include questions about income from employment and benefits. For example, to mention just three, there are the General Household Survey discussed in the appendix to chapter 1, the British Household Panel Study (which will be discussed in more detail in chapter 13) and the Labour Force Survey. However, there are two main sources of information about income that Government departments use to produce regular annual publications on income inequalities. The Department for Work and Pensions uses the Family Resources Survey (FRS) to produce its publication 'Households Below Average Income', while the Office for National Statistics uses the 'Expenditure and Food Survey' (EFS) to produce a series on the redistribution of income published annually as 'The effects of taxes and benefits on household incomes'.

The FRS is a large-scale survey that collects data from approximately 27,000 households through household interview. In comparison the Expenditure and Food Survey is a much smaller survey that collects more detailed information by asking household members to keep a diary of expenditure over a two-week period. Whereas the FRS collects data only from households in Great Britain the Expenditure and Food Survey includes data from households in Northern Ireland, so the figures it reports cover the whole of the United Kingdom. Further information about the Expenditure and Food Survey is provided in the appendix to this chapter on the accompanying website.

Although there are a great many large-scale surveys in Britain that collect data on income, in contrast to the US Census the British Census has historically not included a question on income. However, this is regularly reviewed as many researchers believe that information about income from the census would be an important resource.

In addition to analysing survey data to build up a picture of income inequality in Britain, government departments such as ONS and DWP use other data sources to validate their findings. For example, comparisons between the data collected by the FRS and the Inland Revenue's Survey of Personal Incomes (SPI) (drawn from tax records) suggest that the FRS is likely to understate the incomes of individuals with very high incomes and is also likely to under report the number of individuals at this end of the income distribution. The SPI data are therefore used to adjust for this under-representation of the very rich to avoid biases in the estimation of mean income based on the survey data. Comparisons between data from the Expenditure and Food Survey and the Family Resources Survey and the National Accounts suggest that the surveys' estimates of gross income are in line with the figures in the National Accounts.

4.3 Measuring inequality: quantiles and quantile shares

Figure 4.1 illustrates one method for summarizing data on the income received by households. It displays the gross income of different deciles of the distribution (gross income is defined as income from employment, self-employment, investments, pensions, etc. plus any cash benefits or tax credits). For example, figure 4.1 shows that in 2003–4 the poorest ten per cent of households had a gross income of less than £124 per week, while the richest ten per cent of households had a gross income of over £1,092 per week. The median gross income is £445 per week.

An alternative technique for examining the distribution of incomes is to adopt the **quantile shares** approach. This is illustrated in figure 4.2, which is a modified version of a table produced as part of the annual report from the Office for National Statistics '*The effects of taxes and benefits on household income*'. The income of all units falling in a particular **quantile group** – for example, all those

Figure 4.1   Lower boundaries of each gross income decile group.

Lower boundary of group (£ per week gross income)	2003/4
2nd decile	£124
3rd decile	£193
4th decile	£263
5th decile	£351
6th decile	£445
7th decile	£558
8th decile	£673
9th decile	£828
10th decile	£1092

Source: Data extracted from table A54 Appendix A, Family Spending 2004 edition, based on the Expenditure and Food Survey.

with income above the top decile, is summed and expressed as a proportion of the total income received by everyone. In contrast to the focus on gross income in figure 4.1, four different types of income are displayed in this table. **Original income** is defined as the income in cash of all members of the household before the deduction of taxes or the addition of any state benefits. It therefore includes income from employment and self-employment as well as investment income, occupational pensions and annuities. **Gross income** is then calculated by adding cash benefits and tax credits to original income. Cash benefits and tax credits include contributory benefits such as retirement pension, incapacity benefit and statutory maternity pay and non-contributory benefits such as income support, child benefit, housing benefit and working families tax credit. Income tax, Council tax and National Insurance contributions are then deducted to give **disposable income**. The final stage is to deduct indirect taxes to give **post-tax income**.

The amount spent by households on indirect taxes such as VAT, TV licences and stamp duty is calculated using the household's expenditure record in the Expenditure and Food Survey. From figure 4.2 we can see that, as might be expected, the largest inequalities exist if we focus on *original income*. For example, the bottom quintile group (i.e. the poorest 20 per cent of households) only receives 3 per cent of the share of total income, whereas the top quintile receives just over a half of the total income for all households. It is also clear that while adding benefits to original income has an impact on the levels of inequality, the impact of taxation is negligible.

This quantile share technique can also be useful for tracing trends in inequality by considering changes over time in the share of total income received by particular quantile groups. However, it is important to remember that the individuals who make up the top ten per cent of the income distribution may have changed over time. This quantile share approach is regularly used by the Office for National Statistics in the figures they report.

Figure 4.2   Percentage shares of household income, 2003–4.

	Percentage shares of equivalized income for ALL households[1]			
	Original income	Gross income	Disposable income	Post-tax income
Quintile group[1]				
Bottom	3	7	8	7
2nd	7	11	12	12
3rd	15	16	17	16
4th	24	22	22	22
Top	51	44	42	44
All households	100	100	100	100
Decile group[1]				
Bottom	1	3	3	2
Top	33	29	27	29

1 Households are ranked by equivalized disposable income.

Source: Table 2 of 'The effects of taxes and benefits on household incomes', 2003–4.

Governments can affect the distribution of income in two ways – they can alter pre-tax income through macro-economic policies, and they can alter post-tax income through fiscal policies. As the last two rows of the first column of figure 4.2 show, the Labour administration of 2001–5 did not manage to eradicate inequality in original or 'pre-tax' incomes. For example, the top 10 per cent of income units had over thirty times as much income as the bottom 10 per cent of units.

Perhaps it is fairer to judge the record of the administration by the extent to which it managed to alter the distribution of income through its fiscal policies. However, the information in the post-tax column of figure 4.2 is not much more impressive. Even after tax, the differences between top and bottom are almost as large. The overall distribution of incomes does not change dramatically before and after tax. The question of change over time during the Labour administration is postponed for the moment.

It should also be noted that although a careful attempt has been made in these figures to assess the total effect of government policy by taking account of benefits, direct taxes and indirect taxes, the redistributive effect of non-cash benefits such as health services and education has not been taken into account.

4.4 Cumulative income shares and Lorenz curves

Neither quantiles nor quantile shares lend themselves to an appealing way of presenting the distribution of income in a graphical form. This is usually achieved by making use of **cumulative distributions**. The income distribution is displayed by plotting cumulative income shares against the cumulative percentage of the population.

The cumulative distribution is obtained by counting in from one end only. Income distributions are traditionally cumulated from the lowest to the highest incomes. To see how this is done, consider the worksheet in figure 4.3. The bottom 5 per cent receive 0.47 per cent of the total original income, and the next 5 per cent receive 0.51 per cent. In summing these, we can say that the bottom 10 per cent receive 0.98 per cent of the total original income. We work our way up through the incomes in this fashion. It can be noted that the first two columns of this table are simply a more detailed version of the data presented in figure 4.2. For example, from figure 4.2 we can see that the top quintile group receives 51 per cent of original income; this figure is also obtained if you sum the first three numbers in the first column of figure 4.3.

The cumulative percentage of the population is then plotted against the cumulative share of total income. The resulting graphical display is known as a **Lorenz curve**. It was first introduced in 1905 and has been repeatedly used for visual communication of income and wealth inequality. The Lorenz curve for pre-tax income in 2003–4 in the UK is shown in figure 4.4.

Lorenz curves have visual appeal because they portray how near total equality or total inequality a particular distribution falls. If everyone in society had the same income, then the share received by each decile group, for example, would be 10 per cent, and the Lorenz curve would be completely straight, described by the

Figure 4.3 Cumulative income shares: 2003–4.

	Percentage of total income received by the quantile		Cumulative share of total income	
Cumulative share of population	Original income	Post-tax income	Original income	Post-tax income
100	21.6	18.9	100	100
95	11.8	9.8	78.4	81.1
90	17.6	15	66.6	71.3
80	13.5	12.1	49	56.3
70	10.5	10	35.5	44.2
60	8.5	8.6	25	34.2
50	6.3	7.4	16.5	25.6
40	4.6	6.3	10.2	18.2
30	2.9	5.3	5.6	11.9
20	1.72	4.3	2.7	6.6
10	0.51	1.76	0.98	2.3
5	0.47	0.54	0.47	0.54

Source: Figure 4.3 (data from Expenditure and Food Survey 2003–4).

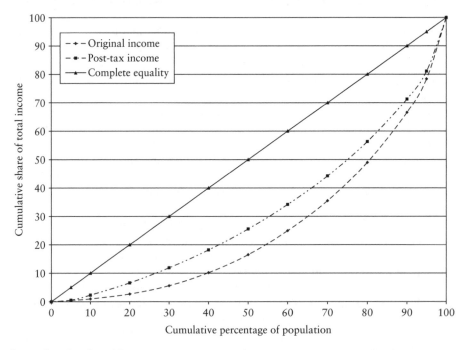

Source: Data from figure 4.3.

Figure 4.4 Lorenz curves of income: 2003–4.

diagonal line in figure 4.4. If, on the other hand, one person received all the income and no one else got anything, the curve would be the L-shape described by the two axes. The nearer the empirical line comes to the diagonal, the more equally distributed income in society is.

The degree of inequality in two distributions can be compared by superimposing their Lorenz curves, as in figure 4.4. The fact that the post-tax curve lies nearer the diagonal than the original income curve shows that benefits and income tax do have some effect in redistributing income from the rich to the poor in society. If the two lines represented income inequality in two different societies, it is quite possible that the two lines would intersect; one society might have more equality at the lower ends of the distribution, and another more at the higher ends.

4.5 Desirable properties in a summary measure of inequality

In the previous section, we saw how the whole of an income distribution is conventionally presented in both numerical and graphical form. In order to trace trends in income inequality over time, or in order to make comparisons across nations, or in order to compare inequalities in income with inequalities in wealth or housing or health, however, a single numerical summary is desirable. Very many different measures have been proposed. Before we consider any of them in detail, it is useful to ask what properties we would want such a measure to have.

Scale independence

We have already come across two measures of the spread of a distribution – the standard deviation and the midspread. Unfortunately, if money incomes change because they are expressed in yen rather than pounds, or, less obviously, if they increase simply to keep pace with inflation, the standard deviation and midspread of the distribution will also change. As we saw in chapter 3, the dominant source of variation in income over time is usually the purchasing power of the currency. We want a measure of inequality that is insensitive to such scaling factors.

However, it is important that the measure be sensitive to the level of the distribution. Imagine a hypothetical society containing three individuals who earned £5,000, £10,000 and £15,000 respectively. If they all had an increase in their incomes of £1 million, we would expect a measure of inequality to decline, since the differences between these individuals would have become trivial. The standard deviation and midspread would, however, be unaffected. A popular approach is to log income data before calculating the numerical summaries of spread. If two distributions differ by a scaling factor, the logged distributions will differ only in level. However, if they differ by an arithmetic constant (£1,000,000 in this example), they will have different spreads when logged. The existence of units with zero incomes leads to problems, since the log of zero cannot be defined mathematically. An easy technical solution to this problem is to add a very small number (for example £0.50p) to each of the zeros. If a numerical summary of spread in a logged distribution met the other desirable features of a measure of inequality, we could stop here. Unfortunately, it does not.

The principle of transfers

It makes intuitive sense to require that a numerical summary of inequality should decline whenever money is given by a rich person to a poor person, regardless of how poor or how rich, and regardless of how much money is transferred (provided of course that the amount is not so big that the previously poor person becomes even richer than the previously rich person).

One numerical summary – the income share of a selected quantile group – fails to meet this principle. By focusing on one part of the distribution only, perhaps the top 5 per cent, it would fail to record a change if a transfer occurred elsewhere in the distribution. Similar objections apply to another commonly used summary, the **decile ratio**, which simply expresses the ratio of the upper decile to the lower decile.

Other inequality measures meet this principle, and so are to be preferred. However, they unfortunately still fail to agree on an unambiguous ranking of different societies in terms of income inequality, because they are sensitive in different ways to transfers of varying amounts and at different points in the income scale. Cowell (1977) argues that the principle of transfers should be strengthened to specify that the measure of inequality should be sensitive only to the distance on the income scale over which the transfer is made, not to the amount transferred. He also adds a third principle to the two considered here, that of **decomposition**: a decline in inequality in part of a distribution should lead to a decline in inequality overall. We shall return to these more stringent criteria below.

4.6 The Gini coefficient

A measure that summarizes what is happening across all the distribution is the **Gini coefficient**. An intuitive explanation of the Gini coefficient can be given by looking back at figure 4.4. The Gini coefficient expresses the ratio between the area between the Lorenz curve and the line of total equality and the total area in the triangle formed between the perfect equality and perfect inequality lines. It therefore varies between 0 (on the line of perfect equality) and 1 (on the L-shaped line of perfect inequality), although it is sometimes multiplied by 100 to express the coefficient in percentage form.

The Lorenz curve of original income in figure 4.4 represents a Gini coefficient of 52. Is this a large or small amount of inequality? It is certainly greater than 0, the value it would take if incomes were equally distributed. But beyond that, we have to compare it with something before we can decide whether it is high or low. For example, it is considerably larger than the post-tax Gini coefficient of 38, as one would expect.

These Gini coefficients were not calculated from the data as given in figure 4.3, but from the original ungrouped distribution of income not shown here. There is a measure of spread (which was alluded to but not developed in chapter 2) which is the average absolute difference between the value of every individual compared with every other individual. The Gini coefficient is this amount divided by twice the mean.

As you might expect, a measure which requires you to look at every possible pair of incomes is tremendously laborious to calculate, although relatively straightforward when a computer takes the strain. Because income distributions are so often presented in grouped form, the intuitive definition based on the Lorenz curve is usually sufficient. A rough guide to the numerical value of the Gini coefficient can always be obtained by plotting the Lorenz curve on to squared paper and counting the proportion of squares that fall in the shaded area.

However, since we live in an era where we now have ready access to computers, and since a computationally convenient version of the formula for the Gini coefficient exists (Cowell, 1977), the formula is presented here:

$$\text{Gini coefficient} = \frac{2}{YN^2}\sum iY_i - \frac{N+1}{N}$$

These symbols were introduced in chapter 2. Notice that the key term $(\Sigma i\,Y_i)$ involves a weighted sum of the data values, where the weight is the unit's rank order in the income distribution. You are not expected to be able to manipulate this formula or calculate the Gini coefficient by hand, but for completeness it is included here.

One approach to evaluating Labour's success in reducing inequality is to see if Gini coefficients have reduced since its landslide victory over the Conservatives in 1997. Figure 4.5 shows the trends in inequality as measured by the Gini coefficient of original, gross, disposable and post-tax income from 1981 to 2003–4.

The first thing to note about the graph is that, as noted in section 4.3, levels of inequality are much higher for original income than for either gross, disposable or post-tax income. In other words throughout the period from 1981 to the mid 2000s, the benefit and tax systems have had a major impact on overall levels of inequality in British society. Focusing on trends over time, there seems to be something of an increase in inequality during the 1980s and particularly the late 1980s, but from 1990 onwards, levels of inequality appear to have remained relatively stable.

The gap between the measure of inequality for original and for post-tax income indicates the effectiveness of the government in using the tax and benefit system to combat inequality. However, from figure 4.5 it is clear that from the time that the Labour Government was first elected in 1997, the impact of taxes and the welfare state on levels of inequality has remained almost constant. As Dixon and Paxton (2005) have argued, this is particularly puzzling because original income inequality has remained reasonably constant and the more progressive tax and benefit policies of the Labour government would be expected to raise the incomes of the poorest households while having little impact on the wealthiest sections of the population. Dixon and Paxton suggest that there are two possible explanations for this. One is that means-tested benefits, targeted at the poorest groups in society, are not always claimed by those who are entitled to them. The second is that the Labour Government has focused its policies very explicitly on two main groups, namely children and the elderly, with a pledge to reduce child poverty by a quarter between 1999 and 2004/5. This has meant that some other groups, such as unemployed adults of working age without children, have been left relatively

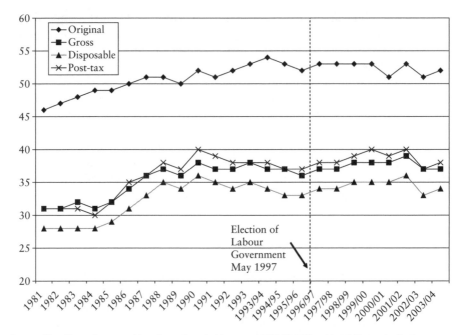

Source: The effects of taxes and benefits on household income (2003/4) ONS, table 27 (Appendix 1): Gini coefficients for the distribution of income at each stage of the tax-benefit system.

Figure 4.5   Trends in income inequality using the Gini coefficient: 1981–2003–4.

unaffected by the changes in the tax and welfare system. Indeed, the fact that benefit rates have not kept pace with average income means that between 1994–5 and 2003–4 the absolute number of working age adults without children, who are living in poverty, has increased from 3.3 million to 3.6 million (DWP, 2004).

4.7   Alternative measures of inequality

The Gini coefficient does meet the criteria of scale independence and the principle of transfers discussed above. It does not, however, meet the principle of decomposition. It is also more sensitive to transfers that displace the rank orders of more individuals. It is therefore more sensitive to changes in the middle of the distribution than to changes at either the top or the bottom.

Furthermore, it is now generally recognized that the Gini coefficient is not a technical, value-free measure of inequality. It should be clear from the discussion of Lorenz curves that two different income distributions could yield two identical Gini coefficients. It may well be that a society would care more about gross income inequalities in the lower half of the income distribution than about inequalities higher up. The Gini coefficient implicitly treats inequality the same wherever it occurs, thus applying one particular set of values to the discussion of inequality.

Atkinson has proposed a set of measures which allows researchers and policy-makers to make their social value judgements explicit and to give increased weight to inequality at the bottom end of the distribution if they wish. These indices of

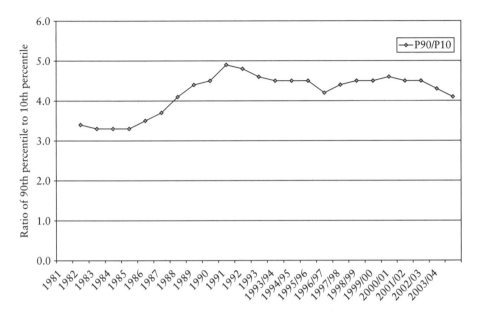

Source: The effects of taxes and benefits on household income (2003/4) ONS, table 27 (appendix 1): Gini coefficients for the distribution of income at each stage of the tax-benefit system.

Figure 4.6 Trends in income inequality using P90/P10: 1981–2003/4.

inequality, while far less widely used than Gini coefficients, meet all the criteria for numerical summaries discussed above. A clear and non-technical discussion is given in Atkinson (1983, pp. 56–9).

An alternative measure of inequality that is better at highlighting change in inequality at the extremes of the distribution (i.e. the gap between the very rich and the very poor) is the ratio of the income of the 90th percentile to the income of the 10th percentile. This measure is also routinely presented in annual government publications such as 'The effects of taxes and benefits on household income'. Figure 4.6 uses this alternative measure to chart trends in income inequality between 1981 and 2003–4 and focuses on disposable income. Following a dramatic increase in inequality during the 1980s, this does show a moderate decline in inequality from a ratio of 4.9 in 1990 to 4.4 in 1996–7 and 4.1 in 2003–4.

A very clear and detailed discussion of changes in inequality over the 1990s and the first half of the 2000s is provided by Goodman and Oldfield (2004). They stress that judgements about whether inequality rose or fell during the 1990s depends on the exact measure of inequality chosen. Measures such as the Gini coefficient, which focus on differences in income across the whole population, including the very richest and very poorest, tend to suggest a widening in the income distribution and an increase in inequality. These have been driven by rapidly rising incomes at the very top of the income scale, particularly the top 1 per cent of households (approximately the top half-a-million people in Britain). The increasing share of income earned by the top 1 per cent of the population has also been a feature of changes in inequality in other countries including the USA and Canada (Piketty and Saez, 2003; Saez and Veall, 2003).

In contrast, measures in inequality that do not consider the far extremes of the income scale, such as the 90/10 ratio shown in figure 4.6, suggest a pattern of falling inequality in incomes over the first half of the 1990s followed by relatively stable levels of inequality. In addition, Goodman and Oldfield (2004) argue that these trends can be placed in the wider historical context of changes in income inequality over the twentieth century. The rise in inequality during the 1980s brings levels of inequality back to those seen in Britain during the 1950s, but these are still lower than those seen before the Second World War.

4.8 Conclusion

In this chapter, special attention has been given to ways of conceptualizing, displaying and summarizing inequalities in the distribution of personal incomes. It has only been possible to provide a brief introduction to some of the most commonly used measures of inequality. For further discussion of the major new directions in the analysis of inequality over the last three to four decades, Jenkins and Micklewright provide a very accessible summary and numerous additional references to current research (Jenkins and Micklewright, 2007).

In terms of techniques, the chapter followed on from those presented in chapter 3, building especially on the analysis of different quantiles of a distribution. The share of income received by a quantile group is the primary way in which information about the distribution of incomes is usually presented. When these income shares are cumulated, they can be presented effectively as Lorenz curves, and summarized by Gini coefficients.

Lorenz curves and Gini coefficients have been most widely applied to the study of inequality in income and wealth. But they have not been restricted to that field. They have been used to describe inequalities in other areas – in the allocation of housing (Robinson et al., 1985), and in health (Le Grand, 1985), and occupational segregation (Siltanen et al., 1995) for example.

However, inequalities have far from disappeared in any of these areas. The depressing conclusion of most studies is that Tawney's verdict from 1931 (1964, p. 73) still holds true today:

> Not only are there the oft-cited disparities of financial resources, which are susceptible of statistical measurement, but, what is more fundamental, education, health, the opportunities for personal culture and even decency, and sometimes, it would seem, life itself, seem to be meted out on a graduated scale.

Exercises

4.1 Construct a cumulative income distribution for *gross* income based on the figures in the table below and check that your answers are consistent with figure 4.2. From these figures, plot the data as a Lorenz curve, either using paper and pencil or Excel. If this curve was superimposed on figure 4.4, where would you expect it to lie in relation to the Lorenz curve for original and post-tax income? (N.B. the definition of gross income is given in section 4.3.)

Cumulative share of population	Percentage of total gross income received by the quantile
100	28.5
90	15.4
80	12.3
70	10.1
60	8.6
50	7.3
40	6
30	4.9
20	4.2
10	2.7
0	0

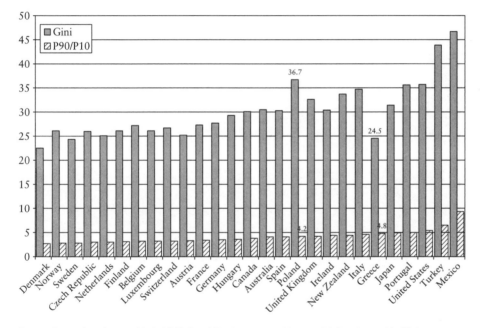

Source: Extract from Annex table 3, OECD Social, Employment and Migration Working Papers No. 22, Income Distribution and Poverty in OECD Countries in the second half of the 1990s, Michael Förster and Marco Mira d'Ercole.

Figure 4.7 Two income inequality indicators for OECD countries for 2000 (or 1995 for Belgium and Spain).

4.2 The bar chart in figure 4.7 shows the Gini coefficients and the ratio of the 90th percentile to the 10th percentile (P90/P10) for twenty-seven OECD countries. The countries have been ranked according to the P90/P10 measure of inequality.

(a) Focusing on P90/P10, which countries have low, medium and high levels of inequality? Is this what you would expect?

(b) The bar chart also illustrates the fact that the Gini coefficient and P90/P10 measure slightly different aspects of inequality. This is demonstrated by the figures for Poland which has a relatively high Gini coefficient given its value of P90/P10 and Greece which has a low Gini coefficient compared with the measure of P90/P10. How would you interpret this?

5

Smoothing Time Series

5.1 Time series

Economists are held to treat one month's figures as a freak, two months' as a fact and three months' as a trend. In this chapter we will look at ways of smoothing the edges off the initial jagged appearance of data plotted over time. We will look at the observations three at a time, taking seriously the spirit of this somewhat sarcastic remark, to get indications of the trend. This chapter is relatively free-standing, and could be read at any point after chapter 2.

The aim of this chapter is to introduce a method for presenting time series data that brings out the underlying major trends and removes any fluctuations that are simply an artefact of the ways the data have been collected. In addition the chapter will highlight the importance of examining how statistics such as the number of recorded crimes are produced. Governments, and other producers of statistics, frequently revise the way that statistics are calculated and this can lead to apparent change (or stability) over time that is no more than a reflection of the changing way in which a statistic is derived. For example, the change in the numbers of unemployed over time is of great political significance. In the early 1980s, when unemployment was particularly high in Britain, many changes were made either to the benefit system or in the method of counting the unemployed. Critics of the then Conservative government claimed that almost all these changes served the purpose of keeping the monthly unemployed claimant count down.

The total number of crimes recorded every year from 1965 to 1994, as shown in figure 5.1, is an example of a **time series**. Other examples might be the monthly Retail Price Index over a period of ten years, the monthly unemployment rate or the quarterly balance of payment figures during the last Conservative government. These examples all have the same structure: **a well-defined quantity is recorded at successive equally spaced time points over a specific period**. But problems can occur when any one of these features is not met – for example if the recording interval is not equally spaced.

5.2 Smoothing

Time series such as that shown in the second column of figure 5.1 are displayed by plotting them against time, as shown in figure 5.2. When such trend lines are smoothed, the jagged edges are sawn off. A smoothed version of the total numbers of recorded crimes over the thirty years from the mid 1960s to the mid 1990s is displayed in figure 5.3.

Figure 5.1   Total numbers of recorded crimes: 1965–94.

Year	Total recorded crimes	Year	Total recorded crimes
1965	1,133,882	1980	2,688,235
1966	1,199,859	1981	2,963,764
1967	1,207,354	1982	3,262,422
1968	1,289,090	1983	3,247,030
1969	1,488,638	1984	3,499,107
1970	1,555,995	1985	3,611,883
1971	1,646,081	1986	3,847,410
1972	1,690,219	1987	3,892,201
1973	1,657,669	1988	3,715,767
1974	1,963,360	1989	3,870,748
1975	2,105,631	1990	4,543,611
1976	2,135,713	1991	5,276,173
1977	2,636,517	1992	5,591,717
1978	2,561,499	1993	5,526,255
1979	2,536,737	1994	5,252,980

Source: Home Office RECORDED CRIME STATISTICS 1898–2002/3 from: www.homeoffice.gov.uk/rds/pdfs/100years.xls

Most people, if asked to smooth the data by eye, would probably produce a curve similar to that in figure 5.3, which has been derived using a well-defined arithmetic procedure described later in the chapter. However, smoothing by an arithmetic procedure can sometimes reveal patterns not immediately obvious to the naked eye.

5.3 The aim of smoothing

Figure 5.2 was constructed by joining points together with straight lines. Only the points contain real information of course. The lines merely help the reader to see the points. The result has a somewhat jagged appearance. The sharp edges do not occur because very sudden changes really occur in numbers of recorded crimes. They are an artefact of the method of constructing the plot, and it is justifiable to want to remove them. According to Tukey (1977, p. 205), the value of smoothing is 'the clearer view of the general, once it is unencumbered by detail'. The aim of smoothing is to remove any upward or downward movement in the series that is not part of a sustained trend.

Sharp variations in a time series can occur for many reasons. Part of the variation across time may be error. For example, it could be sampling error. The

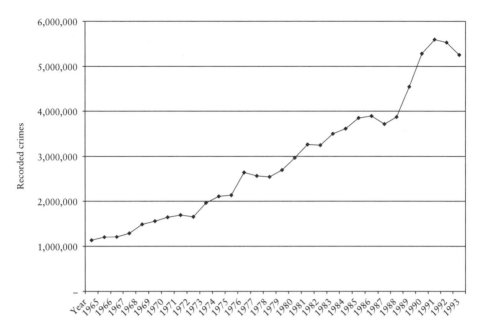

Source: Column 2 of figure 5.1.

Figure 5.2 Total number of recorded crimes: unsmoothed.

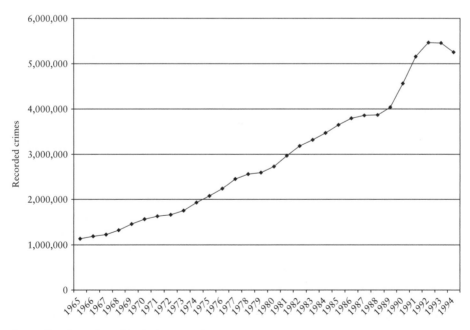

Source: Raw data in figure 5.1: calculations not shown.

Figure 5.3 Total recorded crimes 1965–94: smoothed.

opinion-poll data used later in this chapter were collected in monthly sample surveys, each of which aimed to interview a cross-section of the general public, but each of which will have deviated from the parent population to some extent. Similarly, repeated measures may each contain a degree of measurement error. In such situations, smoothing aims to remove the error component and reveal the underlying true trend.

But the variable of interest may of course genuinely swing around abruptly. For example, the monthly count of unemployed people rises very sharply when school-leavers come on to the register. In these cases, we may want to smooth to remove the effect of events which are unique, or which are simply not the main trend in which we are interested. It is good practice to plot the rough as well as the smooth values, to inspect exactly what has been discarded.

In engineering terms we want to recover the signal from a message by filtering out the noise. The process of smoothing time series also produces such a decomposition of the data. In other words, what we might understand in engineering as

$$\text{Message} = \text{Signal} + \text{Noise}$$

becomes

$$\text{Data} = \text{Smooth} + \text{Rough}$$

This choice of words helps to emphasize that we impose no *a priori* structure on the form of the fit. The smoothing procedure may be determined in advance, but this is not the case for the shape and form of the final result: the data are allowed to speak for themselves. Put in another way, the same smoothing recipe applied to different time series will produce different resulting shapes for the smooth, which, as we will see in chapter 9, is not the case when fitting straight lines.

As so often, this greater freedom brings with it increased responsibility. The choice of how much to smooth will depend on judgement and needs. If we smooth too much, the resulting rough will itself exhibit a trend. Of course, more work is required to obtain smoother results, and this is an important consideration when doing calculations by hand. The smoothing recipe described later in the chapter generally gives satisfactory results and involves only a limited amount of computational effort.

Most time series have a past, a present and a future. For example, the rising crime figures plotted in figure 5.2 and figure 5.3 are part of a story that begins well before the 1960s and continues to the present day. However, the goal of the smoothing recipes explained in this chapter is not the extrapolation of a given series into the future. The following section provides the next instalment in this story and discusses what happened after the very dramatic increases in total recorded crime in the early 1990s.

5.4 Tough on crime, tough on the causes of crime?

After the 1992 election, when the Conservative Party narrowly won its fourth consecutive victory, Labour's new leader, John Smith, promoted Tony Blair to

Shadow Home Secretary. It was in this post that Blair made his famous pledge that Labour would be 'tough on crime, tough on the causes of crime'. This soundbite quickly became part of the 'New Labour' lexicon and was used as a campaign slogan in the 1997 election, which Blair won with a landslide majority of 179 seats. It is now over ten years since Blair first promised that a Labour government would use both punishment *and* prevention to tackle the rising crime rates. Tony Blair first used the famous phrase 'Tough on crime and tough on the causes of crime' in the Radio 4 programme 'The World This Weekend' on 10 January 1993. So it should therefore now be possible to examine whether the Labour strategy has managed to curb the dramatic increases in recorded crime shown in figure 5.3.

Figure 5.4A shows the unsmoothed recorded crime rates for the fifteen years between 1990 and 2004, while figure 5.4B shows the same figures smoothed. We can see that after the rapid increase in crime during the early 1990s, there was a corresponding decrease in recorded crime between the last quarter of 1992 and the third quarter of 1997. However, in the first few years of the new Labour administration, in 1997 to 1999 there appears to be a further sharp increase in recorded crime followed by another dramatic rise between the end of 2000 and the middle of 2002. Although the process of smoothing helps us to see these patterns more easily, it cannot explain what lies behind the observed rises and falls in recorded crime.

Before jumping to the conclusion that Tony Blair failed in his promise to reduce crime rates, it is necessary to do some further research into how these statistics for the total number of recorded crimes are calculated.

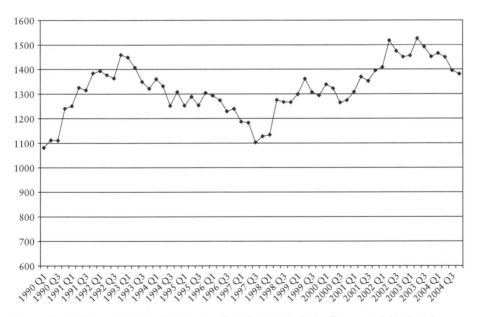

Source: Monthly Digest of Statistics: 5.1 – Recorded Crime Statistics Notifiable offences recorded by the police: Total: Thousands: NSA: England and Wales. www.statistics.gov.uk/StatBase/TSDtables1.asp.

Figure 5.4A Total quarterly recorded crimes 1990–2004: unsmoothed.

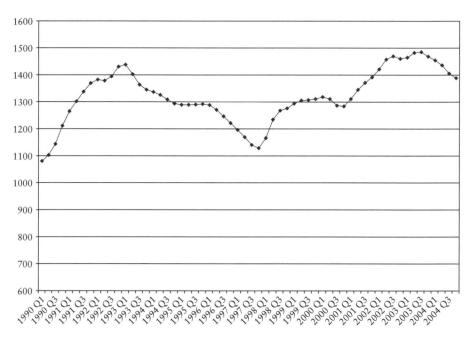

Source: Monthly Digest of Statistics: 5.1 – Recorded Crime Statistics Notifiable offences recorded by the police: Total:Thousands: NSA: England and Wales. www.statistics.gov.uk/StatBase/TSDtables1.asp.

Figure 5.4B   Total quarterly recorded crimes 1990–2004: smoothed.

Over the years, police recorded crime figures have been susceptible both to changes in the public's willingness to report crime, and variations in recording practices among police forces. In the seven years between 1997 and 2004 there were two major changes in the way that crimes were recorded. So it is very difficult to draw any firm conclusions about underlying trends from recorded crime statistics. The first major change to recording procedures occurred in 1998. There were changes both to the 'counting rules' and to the scope of notifiable offences. The counting rules lay down procedures about the ways in which incidents involving multiple offenders and multiple victims should be recorded, and the ways in which series of linked incidents should be recorded. The basic principle followed by the new rules was that there should be one crime recorded for each time that any single person fell victim to a crime. This served to inflate the count of crimes committed, since previously many group offences were recorded as a single incident. At the same time, twenty-four offences were added to the list of notifiable offences by the new rules. The Home Office estimated that these changes resulted in an artificial increase in recorded crime of 14 per cent in 1998–9 (Povey and Prime, 1999). We might expect that these changes to the counting rules would result in a single dramatic shift in the figures. In reality, the changes are likely to have taken several years to be implemented fully at a local level. In other words, the changes will have artificially inflated the count of crimes each year, as officers across the country became more aware of, and compliant with, the new procedures.

In April 2002 a further change occurred when the National Crime Recording Standard (NCRS) was introduced across police forces in England and Wales. Its purpose was to promote greater consistency in how police record crime and to take a more victim-led approach in recording crime – by recording alleged offences, as well as evidence-based ones. Previously, the police were not required to record an alleged offence if there was no evidence to support that it had occurred. The Home Office argued that in many cases, the NCRS has led to a further *increase* in police recorded crime figures, making it look like more crimes were committed, when that might not be the case. They estimate that the total figure for **all crime** in 2002–3 was 10 per cent higher than it would have been under pre-NCRS recording, reflecting a change in recording practice, not a real increase in crime.

The foregoing discussion highlights the fact that statistics can rarely be left to speak for themselves and even when they appear to tell a clear story about change, it is important to examine how they have been constructed. Now that so many statistics are readily available on the world wide web, with many time series available through the National Statistics Time Series data website (this can be found at www.statistics.gov.uk/statbase/tsdintro.asp), it is tempting to take them at face value. However, as has been demonstrated above, it is always important to check who is responsible for producing statistics and how they have been calculated.

At a more fundamental level, it is important to remember that the criminal statistics remain solely a list of reported offences and can never become a list which also includes the crimes which people face, but which are never discovered. It has therefore been argued that the British Crime Survey, which focuses on individuals' experience of crime rather than on crimes reported to the police, provides a more accurate representation of the amount of crime in Britain. Further details about this annual survey are given in the appendix to chapter 7, which can be found on the website that accompanies this book (www.polity.co.uk/exploringdata).

5.5 Opinion polls

We now turn to a rather different set of statistics that are frequently displayed as time series. That is, the results of opinion polls which aim to capture individuals' political allegiances and voting intentions. The purpose of the following discussion is to highlight that just as crime statistics do not simply reflect the numbers of crimes committed, opinion polls do not provide a direct window onto individuals' voting intentions. The data reported by polling companies are a product of the methodologies used, in just the same way that information about the number of crimes committed can be described as 'constructed'.

Opinion polls represent only a small fraction of all the social research that is conducted in Britain, but they have become the public face of social research because they are so heavily reported. Predicting who is going to win an election makes good newspaper copy. The newspaper industry was therefore among the first to make use of the development of scientific surveys for measuring opinion. In all general elections in Britain since the Second World War, polls have been conducted to estimate the state of the parties at the time, and the number of such polls continues to grow. By-elections and local elections are now also the subject of such investigations.

Opinion polls in Britain have historically almost always been conducted on **quota samples**. In such a sample, the researcher specifies what type of people he or she wants in the sample, within broad categories (quotas), and it is then left up to the interviewer to find such people to interview. In a national quota sample, fifty constituencies might be selected at random, and then quotas set within each constituency on age, sex and employment status. Interviewers would then have to find so many women, so many unemployed and so many young people, etc. In the better quota samples, such quotas are **interlocked**: the interviewer is told how many young housewives, how many male unemployed and so on to interview. The idea is that when all these quotas are added together, the researcher will be sure that the national profile on age, sex and employment status will have been faithfully reproduced.

Many people have doubts about such sampling methods. Interviewers are bound to seek out co-operative people, those who are not very busy and so on, thus inevitably leading to biases. It is not always easy to get up-to-date information on which to set the quotas, especially in a small area sample. The result is only representative on those variables selected for the quota, and may be quite unrepresentative on other factors.

Before the 1992 General Election, all the main UK polling companies used very similar methods and had always been remarkably accurate. However, in 1992 the pollsters produced their worst collective performance ever. The average error in party lead was 8.7 per cent and in levels of party support 2.7 per cent. The only pollsters who managed to show a Conservative lead were Gallup – and even then it was only half a percentage point. In the event, the Conservatives won by 8 per cent. After the election, an inquiry held by the Market Research Society suggested there were three main explanations for the failure of the 1992 polls. A late swing to the Conservatives, errors in quota sampling leading to pollsters not recruiting enough people from the higher social classes, and differential response rates amongst different parties' supporters.

After 1992, both Gallup and the market research company ICM decided to switch from quota sampling and interviewing face-to-face to some form of random or quasi-random sampling together with interviewing by telephone. In contrast, the remaining companies continued to use the same mode and sampling method as they used in 1992, albeit with modifications designed to overcome the problems they experienced on that occasion (Curtice, 1997).

The final voting figures reported by polling companies are not only influenced by the sampling method used, but also by a process of 'filtering' because the percentages reported are not based on the whole sample. First, individuals are excluded if they are undecided how they will vote, if they state that they do not intend to vote at all, or if they are not prepared to say how they will vote. In recent years a second stage of filtering has become common, to cope with the problem of low election turnouts. For example, since 2002, MORI's 'headline' voting intention figure has been calculated by excluding all those who are not 'absolutely certain to vote'. This is measured by asking respondents to rate their certainty to vote on a scale from 1 to 10, where '1' means absolutely certain not to vote and

Figure 5.5　Voting intention in Britain: recent trends.

(Figures are based on all those absolutely certain to vote)

	Conservative %	Labour %	Lib. Dem. %
Feb-03	29	41	22
Mar-03	29	43	21
Apr-03	29	43	21
May-03	31	39	22
Jun-03	32	41	19
Jul-03	38	35	21
Aug-03	34	36	24
Sep-03	31	40	21
Oct-03	35	38	21
Nov-03	35	36	22
Dec-03	31	40	22
Jan-04	35	37	21
Feb-04	35	36	21
Mar-04	35	35	23
Apr-04	34	36	22
May-04	34	35	18
Jun-04	31	34	19
Jul-04	31	32	24
Aug-04	32	36	21
Sep-04	33	32	25
Oct-04	29	39	22
Nov-04	31	35	23
Dec-04	30	35	26
Jan-05	32	38	22
Feb-05	37	39	18
Mar-05	37	37	20

Source: MORI – www.mori.com/polls/trends/voting-cert-trends.shtml.

'10' means absolutely certain to vote, and only those rating their likelihood of voting at '10' are included. Figure 5.5 shows MORI's data on trends in voting intention leading up to the 2005 General Election, held on 5 May.

5.6 Techniques

Figure 5.6 shows the percentage of those who said they were certain to vote, and who intended to vote Labour, plotted over time without being smoothed. The curve is jagged because the values of raw time series data at adjacent points can be very different. On a smooth curve, both the values and the slopes at neighbouring time points are close together.

To smooth a time series we replace each data value by a smoothed value that is determined by the value itself and its neighbours. The smoothed value should be close to each of the values which determine it except those which seem atypical. We therefore want some form of resistant numerical summary – some local typical value.

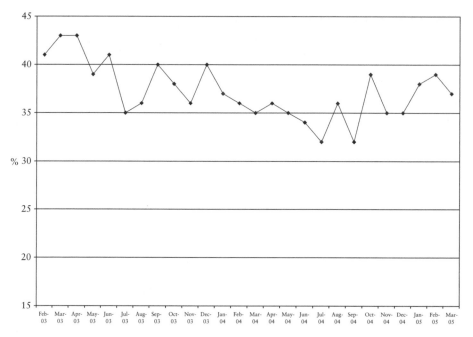

Source: Column 2 of figure 5.5.

Figure 5.6 Percentage stating they will vote Labour: unsmoothed.

This involves two decisions: which neighbouring points are to be considered local and which changes are atypical? The answers to these questions must depend in part on the particular problem, but this chapter presents some multipurpose procedures which give generally satisfactory results. These procedures answer the two questions as follows: take one point either side as local and treat as real an upward or downward change of direction which is sustained for at least two successive points.

Summaries of three

The simplest such resistant average is to replace each data value by the median of three values: the value itself, and the two values immediately adjacent in time. Consider, again, the percentage of respondents who intended to vote Labour (column 2 of data in figure 5.5). To smooth this column, we take the monthly figures in groups of three, and replace the value of the middle month by the median of all three months.

In March, April and May 2003, the median is 43 per cent, so April's value is unchanged. In April, May and June 2003, the median is 41 per cent, so the value for May is altered to 41 as shown in figure 5.7. The process is repeated down the entire column of figures.

Since, for the purpose of this exercise, we are supposing that the January 2003 and April 2005 rates are unknown, we simply **copy on** the first and last values, 41

Figure 5.7   Smoothing numbers by replacing the value of the middle month by the median of all three months.

	Raw data	Median of 3 months
Mar-03	43 ⎫	
Apr-03	43 ⎬ ⎫	43
May-03	39 ⎬	41
Jun-03	41	

Figure 5.8   Worksheet: running medians and means of three.

	1 Data	2 Medians of 3	3 Residuals	4 Means of 3	5 Residuals
Feb-03	41	41	0	41.0	0.0
Mar-03	43	43	0	42.3	0.7
Apr-03	43	43	0	41.7	1.3
May-03	39	41	−2	41.0	−2.0
Jun-03	41	39	2	38.3	2.7
Jul-03	35	36	−1	37.3	−2.3
Aug-03	36	36	0	37.0	−1.0
Sep-03	40	38	2	38.0	2.0
Oct-03	38	38	0	38.0	0.0
Nov-03	36	38	−2	38.0	−2.0
Dec-03	40	37	3	37.7	2.3
Jan-04	37	37	0	37.7	−0.7
Feb-04	36	36	0	36.0	0.0
Mar-04	35	36	−1	35.7	−0.7
Apr-04	36	35	1	35.3	0.7
May-04	35	35	0	35.0	0.0
Jun-04	34	34	0	33.7	0.3
Jul-04	32	34	−2	34.0	−2.0
Aug-04	36	32	4	33.3	2.7
Sep-04	32	36	−4	35.7	−3.7
Oct-04	39	35	4	35.3	3.7
Nov-04	35	35	0	36.3	−1.3
Dec-04	35	35	0	36.0	−1.0
Jan-05	38	38	0	37.3	0.7
Feb-05	39	38	1	38.0	1.0
Mar-05	37	37	0	37.0	0.0

Source: Figure 5.5, column 2: from MORI.

and 37, for February 2003 and March 2005. More sophisticated rules for smoothing these **end values** are available, but discussion of them is postponed for the present.

The data, the smoothed values and the residuals are shown in the first three columns of data in figure 5.8. (In this chapter, we will adopt the convention that all numbers that change when they are smoothed are shown in bold print.) Notice the large residuals for the somewhat atypical results in August, September and

October 2004. The effect of median smoothing is usually to exchange the jagged peaks for flat lines.

One other possible method of smoothing would be to use means rather than medians. The result of using the mean of each triple instead of the median is shown in columns 4 and 5 of figure 5.8. As with the median smoothing, the residuals in the seemingly atypical months are large, but the sharp contrast between the typical and atypical months has been lost. Close inspection reveals that mean smoothing creates relatively large residuals in months adjacent to the strikingly atypical months, where perhaps common sense would suggest otherwise. If the slightly high percentage saying they will vote Labour in December 2003 represents some kind of error, for example, then the less resistant mean has spread this error over into the adjacent months.

However, as we might expect, the median smooth is more jagged than the mean smooth (shown in figure 5.9). A sensible compromise would be first to use medians to set aside atypical behaviour, and then to apply some form of mean analysis to the median smooth to round off the corners. We will return to the details of how to do this later in this chapter.

We could stop after one pass through the data, but we can also repeat the running three-median procedure on the values just smoothed to produce a

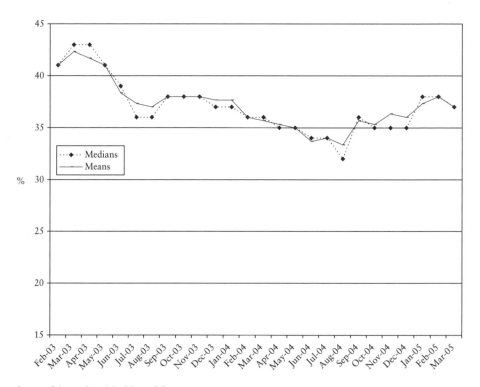

Source: Columns 2 and 4 of figure 5.7.

Figure 5.9   Percentage intending to vote Labour: comparison of median and mean smoothing.

smoother result. If we do this, most values will not change. In this case, only the values for August and September 2004 change on the second pass through. This procedure is repeated until it produces no change; usually two or three passes through the data (**iterations**) are sufficient. The worksheet for repeated median smoothing is shown in figure 5.10. Column 3 is headed '3R', a shorthand to denote repeated medians of three. When working by hand, it is only necessary to record those values that change upon iteration. In this text the values that change are denoted by bold print, but the other numbers are copied over for clarity.

To sum up, the recommended procedure so far is:

1. Plot the data first, as arithmetic smoothing may not be required.
2. List the times and data in two adjacent columns, rescaling and relocating to minimize writing and computational effort. Judicious cutting or rounding can reduce work considerably.
3. Record the median of three consecutive data values alongside the middle value. With a little practice, this can be done quickly and with very little effort.
4. Pass through the data, recording medians of three as many times as required.
5. Copy on the two endpoint values.

Hanning

Although smoothing by repeated medians of three is adequate for most purposes and successfully dealt with seemingly atypical values, the results still have a somewhat jagged appearance. One way to smooth off the corners would be to use running means of three on the 3R smooth. However, we can do better than taking simple means of three. This would give equal weight, one-third, to each value. As the data have already been smoothed, it would seem sensible to give more weight to the middle value.

A procedure called **hanning**, named after its protagonist, a nineteenth-century Austrian meteorologist called Julius von Hann, goes some way to meeting these criticisms. Given any three consecutive data values, the adjacent values are each given weight one-quarter, whereas the middle value, the value being smoothed, is given weight one-half. This is achieved in the following way: first calculate the mean of the two adjacent values – the **skip mean** – thus skipping the middle value; then calculate the mean of the value to be smoothed and the skip mean. It is easy to show that these two steps combine to give the required result.

In practice, we first form a column of skip means alongside the values to be smoothed and then form a column of the required smoothed values.

$$
\begin{array}{llll}
41 & & & \\
43 & 42 & \mathbf{42.5} \\
43 & & &
\end{array}
$$

This procedure is depicted above for the first three values of the repeated median smooth, shown in full in figure 5.10.

Figure 5.10   Worksheet for repeated median smoothing and hanning (3RH).

	1 Data	2 Medians of 3	3 3R	4 Skip mean	5 Hanned	6 Residuals
Feb-03	41	41	41	41	41	0
Mar-03	43	43	43	42	42.5	0.5
Apr-03	43	43	43	42	42.5	0.5
May-03	39	41	41	41	41	−2
Jun-03	41	39	39	38.5	38.75	2.25
Jul-03	35	36	36	37.5	36.75	−1.75
Aug-03	36	36	36	37	36.5	−0.5
Sep-03	40	38	38	37	37.5	2.5
Oct-03	38	38	38	38	38	0
Nov-03	36	38	38	37.5	37.75	−1.75
Dec-03	40	37	37	37.5	37.25	2.75
Jan-04	37	37	37	36.5	36.75	0.25
Feb-04	36	36	36	36.5	36.25	−0.25
Mar-04	35	36	36	35.5	35.75	−0.75
Apr-04	36	35	35	35.5	35.25	0.75
May-04	35	35	35	34.5	34.75	0.25
Jun-04	34	34	34	34.5	34.25	−0.25
Jul-04	32	34	34	34	34	−2
Aug-04	36	32	34	34.5	34.25	1.75
Sep-04	32	36	35	34.5	34.75	−2.75
Oct-04	39	35	35	35	35	4
Nov-04	35	35	35	35	35	0
Dec-04	35	35	35	36.5	35.75	−0.75
Jan-05	38	38	38	36.5	37.25	0.75
Feb-05	39	38	38	37.5	37.75	1.25
Mar-05	37	37	37	37	37	0

Source: Figure 5.5, column 2: from MORI.

Thus 43 is the value to be smoothed, the skip mean 42 is the mean of 41 and 43 and the smoothed value 42.5 is the mean of 43 and 42.

A new element of notation has been introduced into figure 5.10: the column of *hanned* data values is sometimes labelled 'H'. We can now summarize the smoothing recipe used in this figure as '3RH'.

The results are plotted in figure 5.11 and this also displays the percentage of individuals saying they would vote Conservative and Liberal Democrat over the same period. Hanning has produced a smoother result than repeated medians alone. Whether the extra computational effort is worthwhile depends on the final purpose of the analysis. Repeated medians are usually sufficient for exploratory purposes but, if the results are to be presented to a wider audience, the more pleasing appearance that can be achieved by hanning may well repay the extra effort.

Figure 5.11 now tells a much clearer story. The proportion of people reporting that they would vote Labour declined from early 2003 to a low point around July 2004, but then revived somewhat. The Tory revival seems to have taken place in two stages, during the second half of 2003 and at the very beginning of 2005. In

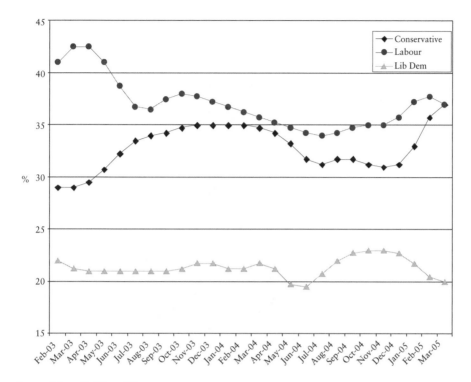

Source: *Column 5 of figure 5.9.*

Figure 5.11   Voting intentions for the three major parties: median smoothed and hanned.

March 2005, based on evidence from the opinion polls, the Tories could have been forgiven for thinking that they stood a good chance of winning the May 2005 General Election.

It is also interesting to note that despite the Liberal Democrats' opposition to the 2003 Iraq war, the lack of popular support for Tony Blair's decision to fight shoulder to shoulder with the United States did not translate into an increase in the percentage saying that they would vote for the Liberal Democrats.

5.7 Residuals

Having smoothed time series data, much can be gained by examining the residuals between the original data and the smoothed values, here called the rough. Residuals can tell us about the general level of variability of data over and above that accounted for by the fit provided by the smoothed line. We can judge atypical behaviour against this variability, as measured, for example, by the midspread of the residuals.

Ideally we want residuals to be small, centred around zero and patternless, and, if possible, symmetrical in shape with a smooth and bell-shaped appearance. These properties will indicate that the residuals represent little more than negligible

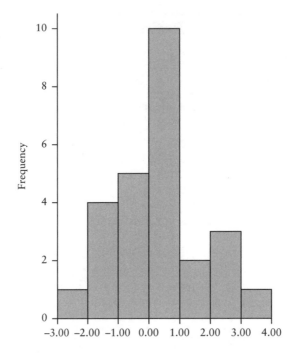

Source: Column 6 of figure 5.10.

Figure 5.12 Residuals from the 3RH smooth.

random error and that we are not distorting the main patterns in the data by removing them. Displaying residuals as a histogram will reveal their typical magnitude and the shape of their distribution. Figure 5.12 shows the histogram of the residuals from the repeat median and hanning smooth (the 3RH for short). This shows that the residuals are small in relation to the original data, fairly symmetrical, centred on zero and devoid of outliers.

Pattern in the residuals

There are two generally useful ways to examine residuals for pattern. They can be plotted against the explanatory variable (in this case, time) once more, to see if all of the trend has indeed been extracted. Or they can be plotted against the fitted (here smoothed) values, to look for indications of non-constant variability. If the residuals get bigger as the smoothed values get bigger, this usually means that the analysis would be better carried out on another scale. As we will see in chapter 10, such non-constant variability is usually dealt with by a power transformation of the scale of measurement. If we are smoothing with repeated medians, the appropriate transformation can simply be applied to the smoothed values and new residuals calculated. However, this cannot be done after hanning. It is necessary to repeat the hanning on the transformed repeated median smooth.

5.8 Refinements

There are a number of refinements designed to produce even better smooths. We can only give cursory attention to these here but more details are given in books by Tukey (1977) and Velleman and Hoaglin (1981). Before discussing how the first and last values in a time series might also be smoothed it is helpful to introduce a convenient special notation $y_1, y_2, \ldots, y_N$, or y_t in general; y_t refers to the value of the quantity, y, recorded at time t. It is conventional to code t from 1 to N, the total period of observation. For example, in figure 5.10 the months February 2003 to March 2005 would be coded from 1 to 26.

Endpoint smoothing

So far we have been content to copy on the initial and final values for February 2003 and March 2005 (y_1 and y_N), but we can do better. Instead of copying on y_1, we first create a *new* value to represent y at time 0, January 2003. This will give us a value on either side of y_1 so that it can be smoothed. This value is found by extrapolating the smoothed values for times 2 and 3, which we will call z_2 and z_3 and this is shown graphically in figure 5.13.

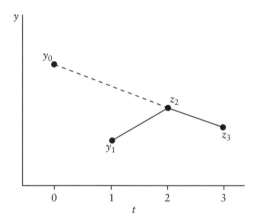

Figure 5.13 Creating a value for t_0.

To compute this new value without recourse to graph paper, the following formula can be used:

$$y_0 = 3z_2 - 2z_3$$

For example, a hypothetical value for January 2003 is given by $(3 \times 42.5) - (2 \times 42.5)$ or 42.5 (data derived from figure 5.10). To provide a smooth endpoint value, we replace y_1 by z_1, the median of y_0, y_1 and z_2. In this case, the median of 42.5, 42.5 and 42.5 is simply 42.5, so this becomes the new, smoothed endpoint value.

A similar rule is used to smooth y_N, by creating a new value, y_{N+1}. The letter E is added to the recipe formula to indicate that the endpoints have been smoothed; the total smooth is now '3RHE'.

Breaking the smooth

Sometimes time series exhibit an obvious change in level and it may be sensible to analyse the two parts separately, producing two roughs and two smooths. In such cases, the two sections often exhibit markedly different levels of variability. Breaks in time series also occur when the method for collecting data changes. For example, the crime figures plotted in figures 5.4A and 5.4B could helpfully be displayed with a break in 1998 and 2002 to highlight that significant changes have occurred in the way that crimes are recorded.

5.9 Conclusion

In this chapter, techniques have been presented for smoothing time series data. They can be performed relatively easily and effectively by hand. For longer series of data Excel is invaluable for helping with the calculations. In most of the examples discussed in this chapter, the finished product is a smooth curve which resembles what we might have drawn if we had smoothed the raw data by eye. Looking from the smooth back to the rough, we could usually see the trend in the raw data. Why bother smoothing? Well, it can sometimes reveal patterns not immediately obvious to the naked eye; it can make a story line clearer, which is always an advantage.

All powerful tools can be misused, of course. It is always worth having a look at the roughs plotted over time, and thinking hard about what has been discarded in the smoothing operation. Moreover, there is a danger that data that presented very little pattern originally can be smoothed into an artefactually interesting story. But, for the data analyst who is prepared to use judgement as well as arithmetic, smoothing can clarify many otherwise ragged situations.

Exercises

5.1 Smooth the data on violent crime presented in figure 5.14. What are the advantages and disadvantages of smoothing the data in this example? For further discussion of changes in recording of violent crime and changes in trends over time see chapter 5 of the Home Office Statistical Bulletin 'Crime in England and Wales 2005–6', www.homeoffice.gov.uk/rds/pdfs06/hosb 1206.pdf

5.2 Most of the evidence about whether industrialism raised or diminished the living standards of the working class has centred on the wages and prices prevalent at different periods, data which are patchy and hard to interpret. In an inspired contribution to this debate, Floud and Wachter (1982) ask what happened to the heights of working class people in this period.

Figure 5.14 Quarterly crime statistics: violent crime 1990–2006.

Violent crime (Thousands)		Violent crime (Thousands)	
1990 Q1	41	1998 Q3	127.1
1990 Q2	47	1998 Q4	122.7
1990 Q3	49.5	1999 Q1	129.8
1990 Q4	47.2	1999 Q2	146.9
1991 Q1	41.6	1999 Q3	151.8
1991 Q2	48.1	1999 Q4	142.5
1991 Q3	52.3	2000 Q1	139.9
1991 Q4	48.3	2000 Q2	152.8
1992 Q1	45.5	2000 Q3	153.2
1992 Q2	53.4	2000 Q4	148.1
1992 Q3	53.1	2001 Q1	146.8
1992 Q4	49.8	2001 Q2	163.5
1993 Q1	47.2	2001 Q3	166.3
1993 Q2	53.2	2001 Q4	162.4
1993 Q3	54.1	2002 Q1	158.1
1993 Q4	50.6	2002 Q2	210.6
1994 Q1	51.4	2002 Q3	216.5
1994 Q2	58.1	2002 Q4	210.2
1994 Q3	57.8	2003 Q1	207.8
1994 Q4	51	2003 Q2	236.3
1995 Q1	45.2	2003 Q3	253
1995 Q2	53.2	2003 Q4	236.9
1995 Q3	59.5	2004 Q1	241
1995 Q4	54.8	2004 Q2	266.3
1996 Q1	51.9	2004 Q3	269.2
1996 Q2	62.6	2004 Q4	262
1996 Q3	63.3	2005 Q1	250.7
1996 Q4	61.5	2005 Q2	277.6
1997 Q1	56.2	2005 Q3	278.2
1997 Q2	63.2	2005 Q4	262.4
1997 Q3	66.6	2006 Q1	241.5
1997 Q4	64.8	2006 Q2	278.2
1998 Q1	61.4	2006 Q3	276.8
1998 Q2	123.1	2006 Q4	257.7

Source: Monthly Digest of Statistics: 5.1 – Recorded Crime Statistics Notifiable offences recorded by the police: Total: Thousands: NSA: England and Wales. www.statistics.gov.uk/StatBase/TSDtables1.asp

A complete set of records has survived which shows the heights of recruits to the Marine Society, a charity which trained young boys for the navy. The authors wanted to estimate the mean height of the population from which recruits were drawn. Unfortunately, the Society would not accept boys below a certain minimum height, and this minimum varied over time. They therefore estimated the missing lower end of the distribution of heights on the assumption that the whole distribution was Gaussian in shape (see Wachter, 1981). The values for 15-year-olds are given in figure 5.15.

Figure 5.15 Heights of recruits to the Marine Society.

Year of birth of recruits	Number of cases	Estimated mean height (inches)
1756–60	216	56.0
1761–63	338	55.1
1764–66	339	55.9
1767–69	253	55.8
1770–76	860	56.9
1777–78	386	57.7
1779–81	309	56.3
1782–85	382	56.6
1786–88	350	56.3
1789–94	848	54.9
1795–99	731	55.0
1800–03	341	54.3
1804–09	766	58.5
1810–14	809	57.3
1815–16	216	57.6
1817–18	227	58.9
1819–20	439	58.8
1821–22	486	57.9
1823–24	579	57.1
1825–26	363	58.1
1827–29	473	58.1
1830–31	388	57.7
1832–35	623	57.0
1836–37	385	57.0
1838–39	547	58.8
1840–42	584	59.0
1843–44	414	56.9
1845–47	458	56.9
1848–49	325	57.0
1850–51	298	57.0
1852–53	296	57.3
1854–55	407	57.6
1856–57	403	57.5
1858–59	151	59.1

Source: Data kindly supplied by Floud to the original author (Cathie Marsh).

Ignoring the problem that the time intervals are not equal, smooth and plot the series. What can you say from the result about the effects of early industrialism on the physical health of the working class?

Part II

Relationships between Two Variables

In the first five chapters of this book we looked in detail at how single variables could be measured, displayed and summarized. Most of the interesting questions about those variables, however, involved bringing another variable into the picture. How does the pay of men compare with the pay of women? What has been happening to the distribution of incomes over time?

Relationships between two variables (**bivariate** relationships) are of interest because they can suggest hypotheses about the way in which the world works. In particular, they are interesting when one variable can be considered a cause and the other an effect. It is customary to call these variables by different names. We shall call the variable that is presumed to be the cause the **explanatory** variable (and denote it X) and the one that is presumed to be the effect the **response** variable (denoted Y); they are termed independent and dependent variables respectively in some textbooks. A more detailed discussion of causality is provided in chapter 11 at the beginning of the third part of this book.

In different chapters in this part of the book we shall look at a variety of techniques for examining bivariate relationships, to see if the explanatory variable seems to have an effect on the response. In order to do this, it will be helpful to introduce some terms and graphical devices used by social scientists analysing relationships between variables.

Causal reasoning is often assisted by the construction of a schematic model of the hypothesized causes and effects: a **causal path model**. If we believe that the social class a child comes from is likely to have an effect on its school performance, we could model the relationship as in the sketch.

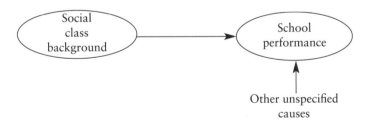

Such models are drawn up according to a set of conventions:

1. The variables are represented inside boxes or circles and labelled; in this example the variables are class background and performance at school.
2. Arrows run from the variables which we consider to be causes to those we consider to be effects; class background is assumed to have a causal effect on school performance.
3. Positive effects are drawn as unbroken lines and negative effects are drawn as dashed lines.
4. A number is placed on the arrow to denote how strong the effect of the explanatory variable is.
5. An extra arrow is included as an effect on the response variable, often unlabelled, to act as a reminder that not all the causes have been specified in the model.

There is no arrow running into class background because it is the explanatory variable, and we are not interested, in this instance, in causal factors affecting it. The general model is therefore as shown in the accompanying diagram.

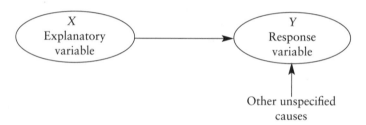

It is good to get into the habit of constructing hypothetical causal path models before turning to examine data; it nearly always clarifies one's analytic strategy to think through the relationships one would expect to be present before seeing if they exist as predicted. In non-experimental research, when many variables may be operating simultaneously, such models can prove invaluable in helping the researcher keep a clear head.

The task in this part of the book is to learn how the effects of an explanatory variable on a response variable may be quantified and summarized. The next two chapters deal with the relationship between two nominal scale variables. Chapter 8 deals with situations where the explanatory variable is a nominal scale and the response variable is an interval. Chapter 9 deals with situations where both explanatory and response variables are measured on interval scales, and linear models can be fitted. Finally, chapter 10 discusses the use of power transformations to change the scale of a variable.

Throughout this part of the book, it is important to remember that statistical effects need not be true causal effects. The birth rate in different counties in Sweden can be predicted moderately well from the number of storks observed in that county. Is this because storks cause babies? Clearly not. What, then, is the point of looking at statistical effects, especially when they produce such seemingly nonsensical links as that between storks and babies? The answer is that, by making a set of careful judgements about the operation of other variables, we can reason about likely patterns of causation. How that is done is the subject of the third part of this book. Previewing the argument, it turns out that, if we control for how rural a particular county in Sweden is, the association between storks and babies disappears; the bivariate association exists because there are both more babies and more storks in rural communities.

6

Percentage Tables

6.1 Introduction

In this chapter and the next we will consider ways of dealing with the relationship between two variables when both of them may only be measured at the nominal level. There has been some controversy in recent years about the techniques of analysis best suited to these types of data. Inferential techniques based on log-linear models have become very fashionable, but humble old percentages survive because of their intuitive intelligibility. In this chapter we will take a close look at percentage tables, their construction and their interpretation. In the next we will look at how percentages may be used to summarize the effect of one variable upon another, and at how we can test whether the relationship between two variables in a table can be understood to be **significant**. The two chapters should be read together sometime after chapter 3 and before chapter 12.

The relationship which forms the subject matter of this chapter is that between an individual's social class background and their educational attainment. In particular the focus is on the relationship between an individual's social class background and their propensity to participate in higher education. This chapter also provides an introduction to the National Statistics Socio-Economic Classification (NS-SEC). It is debatable whether social class is nominal or ordinal. If one views it as a classification of people according to their conditions of employment (the method of classification favoured by theorists such as Goldthorpe), then it should arguably be treated as a nominal scale variable. However, many view these class divisions as ranked divisions on a dimension of social status, and treat class as measured on an ordinal scale. Since the techniques of analysis to be discussed in these two chapters are suitable for both nominal and ordinal variables, the distinction is not of practical importance here.

6.2 Higher education: a question of access?

There are two views of the function of education. Reformers from John Stuart Mill to the present day have viewed it as a mechanism capable of promoting social equality; if there was equal access to education, they argue, individuals would be able to move out of the social class in which they were born. Others have been less sanguine, viewing education as a mechanism for transmitting social inequalities rather than reducing them.

In January 2003, Charles Clarke, who was then the Secretary of State for Education and Skills, announced the publication of the Labour Government's White Paper 'The Future of Higher Education'. This document set out the government's plans for major reforms and investment in universities and HE colleges including plans for making higher education more accessible to more young people. The foreword to the White Paper acknowledged that although participation in higher education in Britain had risen from only around 6 per cent of under 21s in the 1960s, to over 40 per cent of those aged 18 to 30 in 2002, participation rates were still much higher for those children with parents in the higher social classes than for those with parents in unskilled and semi-skilled occupations. As Charles Clarke wrote: 'In Britain today too many of those born into less advantaged families still see a university place as being beyond their reach, whatever their ability' (The Future of Higher Education: Foreword, 2003). In order to promote wider participation in higher education among those from all social classes, the government pledged to support those from disadvantaged backgrounds by restoring grants, helping with fee costs, and abolishing up-front tuition fees for all students. The White Paper was followed in April 2003 by the publication of 'Widening participation in higher education'.

The Youth Cohort Study

One important source of information about the proportions of young people entering higher education in England and Wales is the Youth Cohort Study (YCS). This is a series of longitudinal surveys, begun in 1985, designed to monitor the behaviour and decisions of representative samples of young people aged 16 upwards as they make the transition from compulsory education to further or higher education, or to the labour market. It tries to identify and explain the factors which influence post-16 transitions, for example, educational attainment, training opportunities, and young people's experiences at school. The study first contacts a sample of an academic year-group or 'cohort' of young people in the spring following completion of compulsory education and usually again one and two years later. The survey collects longitudinal data about young people's education and labour market experience, their training and qualifications and a range of other issues, including their family background in terms of parental education and socio-economic status. A brief history of the first ten years of the YCS can be found in Courtenay (1996). In this chapter we will use data from the Youth Cohort Study to examine the relationship between an individual's social class background and their propensity to participate in higher education at age 19.

6.3 Proportions, percentages and probabilities

How is information about the distribution of social class in the population to be presented? Bar charts were introduced in chapter 1 as a way of displaying the distribution of a nominal scale variable. The height or length of the bar was used to represent the number of cases in a category, thus making the relative size of categories clear. The same effect can be achieved numerically by means of proportions or percentages. To express a variable in proportional terms, the number in each category is divided by the total number of cases N. Percentages are proportions multiplied by 100.

Figure 6.1 shows the proportions of young people aged 19 from different social class backgrounds, measured using family's socio-economic classification. The data were collected in 2005 and from the eleventh cohort of the Youth Cohort Study, which is discussed in the appendix to this chapter, which can be accessed from the companion website at www.polity.co.uk/exploringdata

Since proportions and percentages can only be converted back to raw frequencies if we know the total number of cases (the **base** N), the reader should always be given at least this figure. A spurious air of scientific precision can be created by presenting results in proportional terms, perhaps even correct to several decimal places, when the total sample size is very small. It is good practice to draw the reader's attention to proportions based on a sample of less than 50, and not to calculate them at all on a sample of less than 20.

Proportions and percentages are **bounded numbers**, in that they have a floor of zero, below which they cannot go, and a ceiling of 1.0 and 100 respectively. (People do sometimes talk of '300 per cent', but this is just a shorthand way of saying that one value is three times another. Percentages over 100 are called 'relatives' in this book.) Distributions which are effectively bounded at the bottom by the zero point, such as income, tend to straggle up. When numbers are bounded at the top and the bottom, as percentages are, this can cause problems in an analysis based on very small or large percentages, which may need to be taken into account.

Proportions can be used descriptively as in figure 6.1 to represent the relative size of different subgroups in a population. But they can also be thought of as probabilities. For example, we can say that the probability of an individual aged 19 in 2005 having a parent in a 'Higher professional' occupation is 0.168.

Figure 6.1   Social class (NS-SEC) background of individuals aged 19 in 2005.

Parental occupation (NS-SEC)	Number of cases	Proportion	Percentage
Higher professional	1036	0.168	16.8
Lower professional	1708	0.276	27.6
Intermediate	1384	0.224	22.4
Lower supervisory	687	0.111	11.1
Routine	900	0.146	14.6
Other/unclassified	465	0.075	7.5
Total	6180	1.000	100.0

Source: Extract from Table A 19-year-olds in 2005: Main activity by characteristics Youth Cohort Study: The Activities and Experiences of 19-Year-Olds: England and Wales 2005.

Probabilities are not the only way of giving numerical expression to the idea of chance. As well as saying that there is a 0.168 probability that something will happen, we could also say that the odds of it happening are approximately 1 to 5. In the first case, the number of cases in one category is divided by the total, in the second it is divided by the number of cases not in the category. If proportions are denoted p, then odds are $p/(1-p)$. We will take up the idea of odds in chapter 12.

6.4 NS-SEC: a new measure of social class?

In figure 6.1, parental occupations were classified according to the National Statistics Socio-Economic Classification (NS-SEC) which has been developed to replace the old social class and socio-economic group classifications. Since the 1960s, two different socio-economic classifications have been widely used by both academic researchers and in the presentation of official statistics. These were social class based on occupation (which was formerly known as the Registrar General's Social Class) and Socio-economic Groups (SEG). As a result of a review of Government Social Classifications, the Economic and Social Research Council (ESRC) recommended that these two socio-economic classifications be replaced by a single classification. The NS-SEC is based on the 'Goldthorpe schema' (see Goldthorpe, 1980 and 1997; Goldthorpe et al., 1987; Erikson and Goldthorpe, 1992) and has been constructed to measure employment relations and the conditions of occupations i.e. aspects of work and market situations and the labour contract. These are understood as central to delineating the structure of socio-economic positions in modern societies and therefore as crucial for explaining variations in social behaviour and other social phenomena.

The NS-SEC aims to classify occupations in terms of the typical 'employment relations' attached to them. Among employees, there are quite diverse employment relations and conditions, that is they occupy different labour market situations and work situations. Source of income, economic security and prospects of economic advancement are all related to an individual's labour market situation, while work situation refers primarily to location in systems of authority and control at work.

The NS-SEC categories therefore distinguish between different positions (not persons) as defined by social relationships in the workplace – i.e. by how employees are regulated by employers through employment contracts. Three main forms of employment regulation are distinguished.

1. In a 'service relationship' the employee renders 'service' to the employer in return for 'compensation' in terms of both immediate rewards (e.g. salary) and long-term or prospective benefits (e.g. assurances of security and career opportunities). The service relationship typifies Class 1 and is present in a weaker form in Class 2.
2. In a 'labour contract' employees give discrete amounts of labour in return for a wage calculated on amount of work done or by time worked. The labour contract is typical for Class 7 and in weaker forms for Classes 5 and 6.
3. Intermediate forms of employment regulation that combine aspects from both forms (1) and (2) are typical in Class 3.

6.5 Contingency tables

The distribution of a single variable can, as we saw in chapter 1, be represented graphically as a bar chart. The separate univariate distributions of the social class background of individuals as measured by NS-SEC and their main activity at age 19 is shown in figure 6.2.

Parental occupation (NS-SEC)

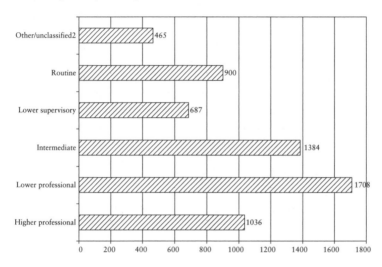

Main activity at age 19

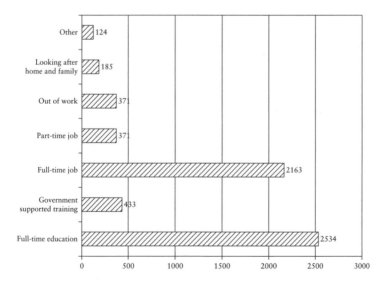

Source: Extract from table A 19-year-olds in 2005: Main activity by characteristics Youth Cohort Study: The Activities and Experiences of 19-Year-Olds: England and Wales 2005.

Figure 6.2   Social class background and main activity of those aged 19 in 2005.

These two distributions, then, describe two separate features of a sample of young people aged 19 in 2005. These two distributions must be interpreted with a little care. For example, the class distribution tells us about the socio-economic status of parents with 19-year-old children in 2005. It does not strictly represent the whole occupational structure at a fixed point in the past, since any individuals who did not have children would be excluded from the analysis. By looking at both the bar chart of main activity and the bar chart of class background, however, nothing can be inferred about the *relationship* between the two. For that purpose, we need some kind of three-dimensional bar chart, showing the joint distribution of the two variables, as shown in figure 6.3.

A **contingency table** does numerically what the three-dimensional bar chart does graphically. The *Concise Oxford Dictionary* defines contingent as 'true only under existing or specified conditions'. A contingency table shows the distribution of each variable conditional upon each category of the other. The categories of one of the variables form the **rows**, and the categories of the other variable form the **columns**. Each individual case is then tallied in the appropriate pigeonhole depending on its

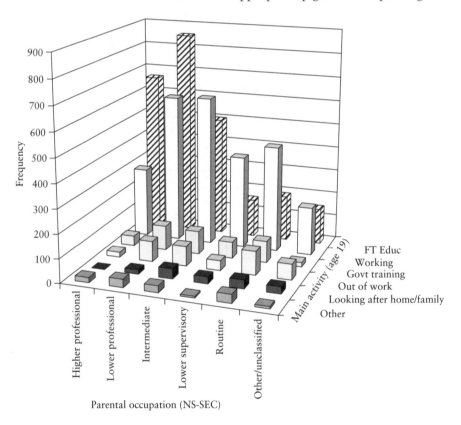

Source: Data extracted from table A 19-year-olds in 2005: Main activity by characteristics Youth Cohort Study: The Activities and Experiences of 19-Year-Olds: England and Wales 2005.

Figure 6.3 Three-dimensional bar chart: main activity by class background, young people aged 19 in 2005.

value on both variables. The pigeonholes are given the more scientific name **cells,** and the number of cases in each cell is called the **cell frequency.** Each row and column can have a total presented at the right-hand end and at the bottom respectively; these are called the **marginals,** and the univariate distributions can be obtained from the **marginal distributions.** Figure 6.4 shows a schematic contingency table with four rows and four columns (a four-by-four table).

Let us now look at a real contingency table. Figure 6.5 shows the joint distribution of class background and main activity depicted graphically in figure 6.3. The

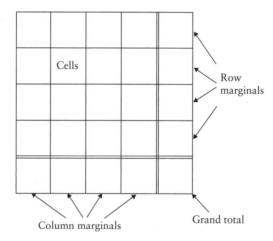

Figure 6.4 Anatomy of a contingency table.

Figure 6.5 Main activity by class background (frequencies).

Parental occupation (NS-SEC)	Main activity at age 19							
	Full-time education	Govt. supported training	Full-time job	Part-time job	Out of work	Looking after home/ family	Other	Total
Higher professional	663	41	249	41	21	0	21	1036
Lower professional	854	102	529	85	85	17	34	1706
Intermediate	498	97	554	69	83	42	28	1371
Lower supervisory	158	69	330	55	41	27	7	687
Routine	189	90	369	72	99	36	36	891
Other/ unclassified[2]	149	19	144	56	65	28	9	470
Total	2511	418	2175	378	394	150	135	6161

Source: Extract from table A 19-year-olds in 2005: Main activity by characteristics Youth Cohort Study: The Activities and Experiences of 19-Year-Olds: England and Wales 2005.

contingency table in figure 6.5 depicts the bivariate relationship between the two variables, but it is hard to grasp.

Gaze as you will, it is extremely difficult to decide, on the basis of raw numbers such as these, whether class background has an effect on educational destination. Something further is called for.

6.6 Percentage tables

The commonest way to make contingency tables readable is to cast them in percentage form. There are three different ways in which this can be done, as shown in the three panels of figure 6.6.

The first table, shown in panel (a) of figure 6.6, was constructed by dividing each cell frequency by the grand total. We now know that the 663 respondents with higher professional parents who were in full-time education at age 19 represented 10.8 per cent of the total population aged 19 in 2005. But the table as a whole is scarcely more readable than the raw frequencies were, because there is nothing we can compare this 19 per cent with. For this reason, total percentage tables are not often constructed.

Panel (b) of figure 6.6 shows the percentage of young people within each category of social class background who are in each main activity grouping at age 19. The table was constructed by dividing each cell frequency by its appropriate row total. We can see that whereas nearly two-thirds of those with a parent in a higher professional occupation are still in full-time education at age 19, less than a quarter of those with parents in Lower supervisory or Routine occupations are still in full-time education by this age. Tables that are constructed by percentaging

Figure 6.6 Main activity at age 19 by class background.

(a) Total percentages

Parental occupation (NS-SEC)	Main activity at age 19							
	Full-time education	Govt. supported training	Full-time job	Part-time job	Out of work	Looking after home/ family	Other	Total
Higher professional	10.8	0.7	4.0	0.7	0.3	0.0	0.3	16.8
Lower professional	13.9	1.7	8.6	1.4	1.4	0.3	0.6	27.7
Intermediate	8.1	1.6	9.0	1.1	1.3	0.7	0.5	22.3
Lower supervisory	2.6	1.1	5.4	0.9	0.7	0.4	0.1	11.2
Routine	3.1	1.5	6.0	1.2	1.6	0.6	0.6	14.5
Other/ unclassified[2]	2.4	0.3	2.3	0.9	1.1	0.5	0.1	7.6
Total	40.8	6.8	35.3	6.1	6.4	2.4	2.2	100.0

Figure 6.6 (continued)

(b)   Row percentages

Parental occupation (NS-SEC)	Main activity at age 19							
	Full-time education	Govt. supported training	Full-time job	Part-time job	Out of work	Looking after home/ family	Other	Total
Higher professional	64	4	24	4	2	-	2	100.0
Lower professional	50	6	31	5	5	1	2	100.0
Intermediate	36	7	40	5	6	3	2	100.0
Lower supervisory	23	10	48	8	6	4	1	100.0
Routine	21	10	41	8	11	4	4	100.0
Other/ unclassified[2]	32	4	31	12	14	6	2	100.0

(c)   Column percentages

Parental occupation (NS-SEC)	Main activity at age 19							
	Full-time education	Govt. supported training	Full-time job	Part-time job	Out of work	Looking after home/ family	Other	Total
Higher professional	26.4	9.8	11.4	10.8	5.3	0.0	15.6	16.8
Lower professional	34.0	24.4	24.3	22.5	21.6	11.3	25.2	27.7
Intermediate	19.8	23.2	25.5	18.3	21.1	28.0	20.7	22.3
Lower supervisory	6.3	16.5	15.2	14.6	10.4	18.0	5.2	11.2
Routine	7.5	21.5	17.0	19.0	25.1	24.0	26.7	14.5
Other/ unclassified[2]	5.9	4.5	6.6	14.8	16.5	18.7	6.7	7.6
Total	100.0	100.0	100.0	100.0	100.0	100.0	100.0	100.0

Source: As figure 6.5.

the rows are usually read down the columns (reading along the rows would probably only confirm two things we already know: the broad profile of the marginal distribution and the fact that the percentages sum to 100). This is sometimes called an 'outflow' table. The row percentages show the different outcomes for individuals with a particular social class background.

It is also possible to tell the story in a rather different way, and look at where people who ended up doing the same main activity at age 19 came from: the 'inflow table'. This is shown in panel (c) of figure 6.6. For example, the fifth column of data shows that of all those who are 'out of work', only 5.3 per cent i.e. just over five in every hundred or one in twenty, are from backgrounds where one of the parents was a higher professional, whereas approximately a quarter (25.1 per cent) of those who were 'out of work' had parents with routine occupations. Inflow tables describe the class composition of each of the main activity groupings. The inflow and outflow tables focus attention on the data in rather different ways, and the researcher would have to be clear about what questions were being addressed in the analysis to inform which way the percentages were calculated.

Running the percentages the other way round can cast a table in a different light, and there are many considerations that might be taken into account before deciding which percentages to construct. However, there is a firm rule when we have a causal hypothesis about the relationship between the two variables. Tables of the outflow variety are better suited for exploring causal ideas. This will be fully discussed in the next chapter and also in chapter 11.

6.7 Good table manners

A well-designed table is easy to read, but takes effort, time and perhaps many drafts to perfect. Clear display of data not only aids the final consumer of the research but also helps the data analyst. It pays to take care over the presentation of your own working and calculations, however preliminary. This can help reveal patterns in the data, and can save time at a later stage. Here are some guidelines on how to construct a lucid table of numerical data. Some of the hints, those about labelling for example, apply to all illustrations, whether tabular or pictorial.

Reproducibility versus clarity

We are often trying to do two jobs at once when we present data: to tell a story while also allowing readers to check the conclusions by inspecting the data for themselves. These two jobs tend to work against one another, although the techniques of exploratory data analysis allow the researcher to pursue both at once to a much greater extent than more traditional techniques. For clarity we prefer visual displays, and we leave out extraneous detail to focus attention on the story line. To allow others to inspect and possibly reinterpret the results we want to leave as much of the original data as possible in numerical form. Think hard about which job any particular table is aiming to achieve. Dilemmas can often be solved by simplifying a table in the text and placing fuller details in an appendix, although in general it is desirable to place a table as near as possible to the text which discusses it. There are some elementary details which must always appear.

Labelling

The title of a table should be the first thing the reader looks at (although many readers of data often neglect this obvious first step). A clear title should summarize the contents. It should be as short as possible, while at the same time making clear when the data were collected, the geographical unit covered, and the unit of analysis. You may find it helpful to number figures so that you can refer to them more succinctly in the text. Other parts of a table also need clear, informative labels. The variables included in the rows and columns must be clearly identified. Don't be tempted to use mnemonics in '*computerese*'. You may have called household income 'HHINC' so many times you think everyone will know what it means – they won't.

Sources

The reader needs to be told the source of the data. It is not good enough to say that it was from *Social Trends*. The volume and year, and either the table or page, and sometimes even the column in a complex table must be included. When the data are first collected from a published source, all these things should be recorded, or a return trip to the library will be needed.

Sample data

If data are based on a sample drawn from a wider population, it always needs special referencing. The reader must be given enough information to assess the adequacy of the sample. The following details should be available somewhere: the method of sampling (for example 'stratified random sample' or 'sample based on interlocking age and sex quotas'), the achieved sample size, the response rate or refusal rate, the geographical area which the sample covers and the frame from which it was drawn.

Missing data

It is important to try to present the whole of a picture. One of the commonest ways in which data can mislead people is for some unstated principle of selection to have been used. Don't exclude cases from analysis, miss out particular categories of a variable or ignore particular attitudinal items in a set without good reason and without telling the reader what you are doing and why.

Providing details of the overall response rate in a survey does not usually tell the whole story about missing information. Many particular items in a survey attract refusals or responses that cannot be coded, and the extent of such **item non-response** should be reported.

Definitions

There can be no hard and fast rule about how much definitional information to include in your tables. They could become unreadable if too much were included. Err on the side of repeating definitions in a table when in doubt. If complex terms are explained elsewhere in the text, include a precise section or page reference.

Opinion data

When presenting opinion data, always give the exact wording of the question put to respondents, including the response categories if these were read out. There can be big differences in replies to open questions such as: 'Who do you think is the most powerful person in Britain today?' and forced choice questions such as 'Which of the people on this card do you think is the most powerful person in Britain today?'

Ensuring frequencies can be reconstructed

It should always be possible to convert a percentage table back into the raw cell frequencies. To retain the clarity of a percentage table, present the minimum number of base Ns needed for the entire frequency table to be reconstructed.

Showing which way the percentages run

Proportions add up to 1 and percentages add up to 100, at least they do in theory. In practice, rounding may mean that they are slightly out. In a table where it is not clear whether the percentages have been calculated on rows or columns, it can be infuriating not to be able to make either rows or columns sum exactly to the expected figure. One solution is to point out every time the total comes to something other than the expected figure because of rounding error. It is usually helpful to include an explicit total of 100 as in figures 6.6(b) and 6.6(c).

However you achieve it, check that frequencies and proportions or percentages can be clearly differentiated.

Layout

The effective use of space and grid lines can make the difference between a table that is easy to read and one which is not. In general, white space is preferable, but grid lines can help indicate how far a heading or subheading extends in a complex table. Tables of monthly data can be broken up by spaces between every December and January, for example. Labels must not be allowed to get in the way of the data. Set variable headings off from the table, and further set off the category headings. Avoid underlining words or numbers.

Clarity is often increased by reordering either the rows or the columns. It can be helpful to arrange them in increasing order of size, or size of effect on another variable. Make a decision about which variable to put in the rows and which in the columns by combining the following considerations:

1. closer figures are easier to compare;
2. comparisons are more easily made down a column;
3. a variable with more than three categories is best put in the rows so that there is plenty of room for category labels.

6.8 Producing contingency tables using SPSS

It is straightforward to produce contingency tables such as those in figures 6.5 and 6.6 using SPSS. Once you have opened the appropriate data file within SPSS, select 'Analyze', 'Descriptive statistics', and then 'Crosstabs' from the drop-down menus as shown below.

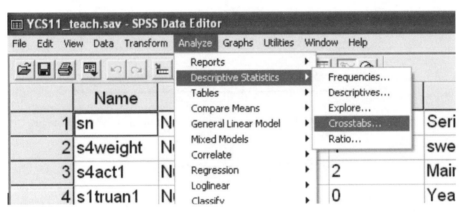

Figure 6.7   Using SPSS to produce contingency tables.

You will then be presented with a list of all the variables available in the dataset and can select which variable will form the rows of the table and which variable will form the columns. Note that it is important to remember to select nominal or ordinal variables with not too many categories for both the rows and the columns, otherwise you will be presented with a very large and unwieldy table that is difficult to interpret.

By default, SPSS will produce a table with just the observed frequencies in each cell i.e. similar to the kind of table shown in figure 6.5. Calculating row or column percentages will make the table much easier to interpret.

By clicking on the Cells . . . button (circled on the screenshot in figure 6.8) it is possible to specify whether you want Row percentages (as shown in figure 6.6b); Column percentages (as shown in figure 6.6c) or Total percentages (as shown in figure 6.6a).

In the current example, if famsec (Family grouped ns-sec) is chosen as the row variable and s4act1 (Main activity at age 19) is chosen as the column variable it makes more sense to specify that SPSS should calculate row percentages. This produces a table very similar to that in panel b of figure 6.6. Note that to produce exactly the table shown here it is necessary to 'weight' the data from the Youth Cohort Study using the command 'Weight by s4weight'.

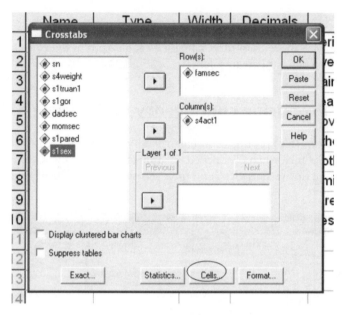

Figure 6.8 Using the 'Cells' button to specify row, column or total percentages.

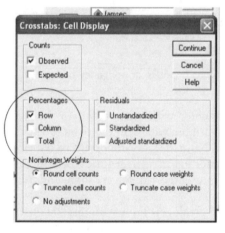

Figure 6.9 Selecting just row percentages.

6.9 Simplifying tables by recoding variables and collapsing categories

To examine the relationship between class background and young people's decision to stay on in full-time education after age 18 in more detail, it would be helpful to further subdivide the table in figure 6.10 by sex. However, splitting a six-by-eight category table into two separate tables, one for men and one for women, makes it even more fussy and complicated to follow. It would be better if we could distil the story line first.

Figure 6.10 SPSS output of contingency table family ns-sec by individual's main activity at age 19.

famsec family grouped ns-sec * s4act1 Main activity at sweep 4 Crosstabulation

| | | | | | | s4act1 Main activity at sweep 4 | | | | |
		1.00 GST	2.00 FT Education	3.00 FT job	4.00 Part-time job	5.00 Looking after home or family	6.00 Looking for work/ Unemployed	7.00 Taking a break	8.00 Doing something else	Total
famsec family grouped ns-sec	1.00 Large employers and higher professionals									
	Count	43	663	248	37	5	23	14	3	1036
	% within famsec family grouped ns-sec	4.2	64.0	23.9	3.6	.5	2.2	1.4	.3	100.0
	2.00 Lower professional and higher technical occupations									
	Count	103	847	536	90	20	78	17	17	1708
	% within famsec family grouped ns-sec	6.0	49.6	31.4	5.3	1.2	4.6	1.0	1.0	100.0
	3.00 Intermediate									
	Count	96	500	558	75	44	80	16	16	1385
	% within famsec family grouped ns-sec	6.9	36.1	40.3	5.4	3.2	5.8	1.2	1.2	100.0
	4.00 Lower supervisory occupations									
	Count	69	157	332	56	28	38	5	2	687
	% within famsec family grouped ns-sec	10.0	22.9	48.3	8.2	4.1	5.5	.7	.3	100.0
	5.00 Semi routine and routine occupations									
	Count	92	192	371	68	38	103	20	17	901
	% within famsec family grouped ns-sec	10.2	21.3	41.2	7.5	4.2	11.4	2.2	1.9	100.0
	6.00 Other									
	Count	17	149	143	55	28	63	3	6	464
	% within famsec family grouped ns-sec	3.7	32.1	30.8	11.9	6.0	13.6	.6	1.3	100.0
Total	Count	420	2508	2188	381	163	385	75	61	6181
	% within famsec family grouped ns-sec	6.8	40.6	35.4	6.2	2.6	6.2	1.2	1.0	100.0

Source: Analysis of Youth Cohort Study, cohort 11.

Cutting down the number of categories would reduce the complexity of the table considerably. There are several factors to consider when deciding how to **collapse** the number of categories in a variable. Most importantly, a substantive judgement must be made that categories are similar. Obviously, if a variable is ordinal, it only makes sense to collapse adjacent categories. With a variable like NS-SEC the six-category version (i.e. five main categories and other/unclassified as the sixth category) presented in figure 6.10 is already a simplified version of the most detailed version of NS-SEC. However, as was discussed above, the concepts behind the creation of the classification suggest that even with NS-SEC5 there are close similarities between categories 1 and 2 and between categories 4 and 5 in terms of their labour contract. One possible way to simplify the table still further would therefore be to combine categories 1 and 2 and to combine categories 4 and 5, so that the six categories are replaced by four categories.

Since one aim of collapsing tables is to produce cells with adequate frequencies for analysis, a second, more technical, consideration must be the size of the marginals (i.e. the row totals and the column totals). This is less relevant here, since all of the cells have adequate numbers of cases, but when sample sizes are small it may well be important to combine small categories.

In SPSS, the recode command in the 'Transform' drop-down menu can be used to reduce the number of categories in a variable in order to produce a simplified table. From the menus select 'Transform', 'Recode' and 'Into Different Variables'. Note that by choosing to recode a variable into a new variable you are effectively creating a new simplified variable with fewer categories rather than replacing the existing variable with your new variable (see figure 6.11).

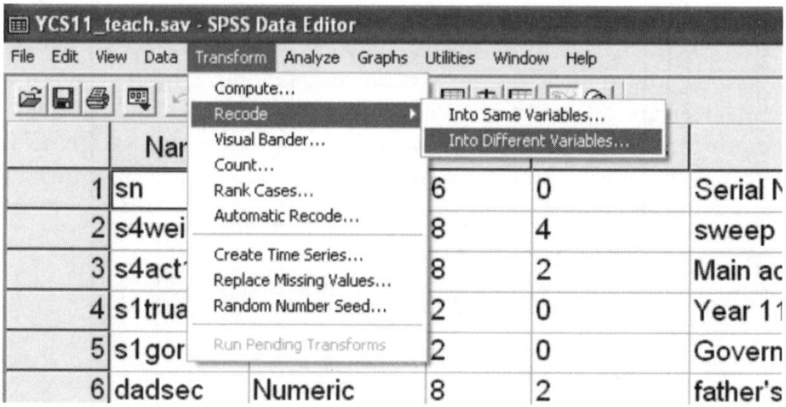

Figure 6.11   Screenshot demonstrating how to recode a variable into a different variable.

Next select the variable which you want to recode into fewer categories, and send it to the 'Numeric Variable' box. As we are recoding the original values into a different variable our new variable will need to have a name and label assigned to it. We therefore provide a name for the 'Output variable', in this case 'FAMSECR'. This command will allow you to create a new variable based on the categories of the old variable rather than over-writing the original variable. Click on 'Change'. This will replace the question mark following the arrow with our new variable name 'FAMSECR'. Next click on the 'Old and New Values' button in order to define the categories in your new variable. This is where we specify the boundaries of our groups (see figure 6.12).

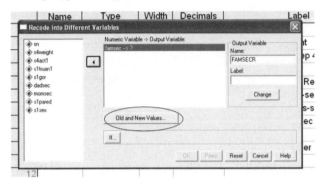

Figure 6.12 Specifying a name for the new variable in the process of recoding an existing variable.

The next step is to use the dialogue box to define the new categories in relation to the old values as shown in figure 6.13.

The default selection is for single values to be recoded. In this example we are specifying a range of values for some new groups. For example, we want categories 1 and 2 of the old variable to be replaced by 1 in the new variable. We therefore select the 'Range' option. The lowest value is entered into the first box and the highest value into the second box. A new value for our first group now needs to be entered. Once this is complete, click on the 'Add' button. The 'Old → New' box summarizes the way we are recoding a variable and it can be seen that categories 1 and 2 will become the new category 1 and category 3 will become category 2 in the new variable. Once all the recoding specifications are complete, clicking on the 'Continue' and then the 'OK' button will finish the creation of the new recoded variable. This can then be used to create a simpler table.

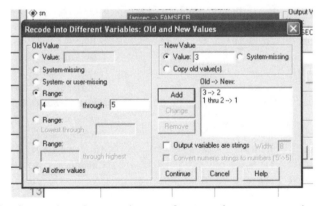

Figure 6.13 Screenshot showing the specification of new groups when recoding a variable.

It is quite time consuming, and can be confusing, to use the menus for recoding variables, as described above. An alternative method, that many researchers find preferable, is to use syntax to carry out the Recode command. For example, the syntax for the recoding of 'Famsec' described above is shown in the box below:

```
RECODE
  famsec
  (3 = 2) (6 = 4) (1 thru 2 = 1) (4 thru 5 = 3) INTO FAMSECR.
EXECUTE.
```

The logic of the syntax is that you first give SPSS the command that you want to recode a variable 'RECODE' and then specify which variable is to be recoded – in this case 'FAMSEC'. A series of brackets are then used to specify the value of the old variable and the value of the new variable. For example, in this case those coded with a 3 on the original 'FAMSEC' variable will be assigned a code of 2 on the new variable. Finally the syntax specifies that the variable will be recoded 'INTO' a new variable and the name of the new variable is given, in this case 'FAMSECR'.

Adding variable labels and value labels

Once a new variable has been created, it is helpful to give it a variable label and also provide a label for each value. These labels will then appear as labels on the table created using the Crosstabs command. There are two ways of adding these labels in SPSS.

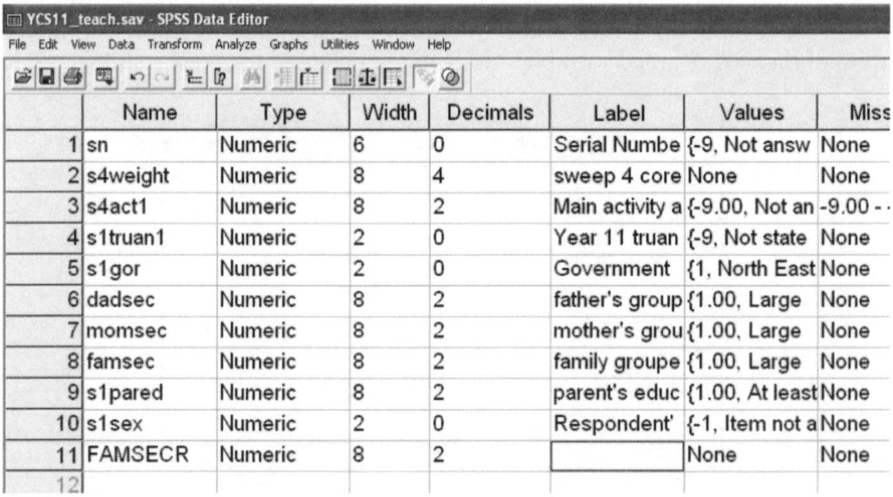

YCS11_teach.sav - SPSS Data Editor

File Edit View Data Transform Analyze Graphs Utilities Window Help

	Name	Type	Width	Decimals	Label	Values	Miss
1	sn	Numeric	6	0	Serial Numbe	{-9, Not answ	None
2	s4weight	Numeric	8	4	sweep 4 core	None	None
3	s4act1	Numeric	8	2	Main activity a	{-9.00, Not an	-9.00 -
4	s1truan1	Numeric	2	0	Year 11 truan	{-9, Not state	None
5	s1gor	Numeric	2	0	Government	{1, North East	None
6	dadsec	Numeric	8	2	father's group	{1.00, Large	None
7	momsec	Numeric	8	2	mother's grou	{1.00, Large	None
8	famsec	Numeric	8	2	family groupe	{1.00, Large	None
9	s1pared	Numeric	8	2	parent's educ	{1.00, At least	None
10	s1sex	Numeric	2	0	Respondent'	{-1, Item not a	None
11	FAMSECR	Numeric	8	2		None	None
12							

Figure 6.14 Adding variable label and labels for each value.

One method is to use the 'Variable View' toggle on the Data Editor screen in SPSS and simply type in the label for the new variable as shown in figure 6.14. In addition, using the same screen, clicking in the right hand corner of the relevant box in the Values column opens a dialogue box that allows for the specification of the value labels (see figure 6.15).

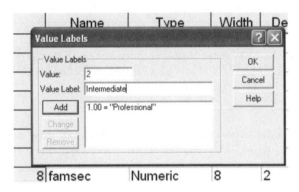

Figure 6.15 Adding value labels.

An alternative method for providing a new variable with a variable label and value labels is to use syntax. The syntax to label our new variable FAMSECR is given in the box.

> VARIABLE LABELS FAMSECR 'Family grouped ns-sec recoded'.
> VALUE LABELS FAMSECR 1 'Professional' 2 'Intermediate' 3 'Lower supervisory' 4 'Routine and other'.
>
> EXECUTE.

Recoding main activity at age 19.

The same process can be used to simplify the variable describing the individual's main activity at age 19. For example we could simplify the original eight-category variable into a six-category variable as shown in figure 6.16.

Figure 6.16 Reducing the numbers of values.

Old categories	New categories
1 Government training	1 Government training
2 FT-education	2 FT-education
3 FT-job	3 Working
4 Part-time job	
5 Looking after home or family	4 Looking after home or family
6 Looking for work/unemployed	5 Looking for work
7 Taking a break	6 Other
8 Doing something else	

The syntax to recode the variable and provide variable and value labels is as follows:

```
RECODE
  s4act1
  (1 = 1) (2 = 2) (3 4 = 3) (5 = 4) (6 = 5) (7 8 = 6) INTO s4act1r

EXECUTE.

VARIABLE LABELS s4act1r 'Main activity at age 19 recoded'.
VALUE LABELS s4act1r 1 'Govt. training' 2 'FT education' 3 'Working' 4
'Looking after home' 5 'Unemployed' 6 'Other'.
```

Having simplified the two variables, Family NS-SEC and main activity at age 19, it is now possible to examine the relationship between them in more detail by looking at the relationship separately for young men and women. This can be done by selecting 'Analyze', 'Descriptive statistics' and then 'Crosstabs' from the drop-down menus as described previously. Then in the dialogue box sex can be specified as a third 'Layer' variable as shown in figure 6.17, so that a separate table is produced for young men and women.

Figure 6.18 clearly shows that for both men and women there is a strong association between family social position and the likelihood of a young person going into higher education so that those from families with a professional mother or father are more likely to stay on into higher education than other groups. However, it also shows some differences between the sexes. For example, none of the men in the survey classified themselves as looking after home and family. Allied to this, the percentages of young women who are classified as unemployed are substantially lower than the percentages of young men classified as unemployed in three of the four social groupings. We can also see

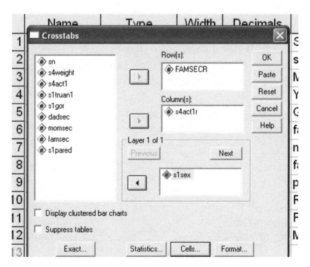

Figure 6.17 Specifying a third 'layer' variable.

Figure 6.18 Separate tables for young men and women.

FAMSECR Family grouped ns-sec recoded * s4act1r Main activity at age 19 recoded * s1sex Respondent's gender Crosstabulation

s1sex Respondent's gender				s4act1r Main activity at age 19 recoded						Total
				1.00 Govt. training	2.00 FT education	3.00 Working	4.00 Looking after home	5.00 Unemployed	6.00 Other	
1 Male	FAMSECR Family grouped ns-sec recoded	1.00 Professional	Count	110	684	475		60	18	1347
			% within FAMSECR Family grouped ns-sec recoded	8.2	50.8	35.3		4.5	1.3	100.0
		2.00 Intermediate	Count	66	230	299		38	14	647
			% within FAMSECR Family grouped ns-sec recoded	10.2	35.5	46.2		5.9	2.2	100.0
		3.00 Lower supervisory	Count	114	160	430		89	26	819
			% within FAMSECR Family grouped ns-sec recoded	13.9	19.5	52.5		10.9	3.2	100.0
		4.00 Routine and other	Count	11	70	88		36	2	207
			% within FAMSECR Family grouped ns-sec recoded	5.3	33.8	42.5		17.4	1.0	100.0
	Total		Count	301	1144	1292		223	60	3020
			% within FAMSECR Family grouped ns-sec recoded	10.0	37.9	42.8		7.4	2.0	100.0
2 Female	FAMSECR Family grouped ns-sec recoded	1.00 Professional	Count	37	827	436	26	40	33	1399
			% within FAMSECR Family grouped ns-sec recoded	2.6	59.1	31.2	1.9	2.9	2.4	100.0
		2.00 Intermediate	Count	29	269	334	44	42	19	737
			% within FAMSECR Family grouped ns-sec recoded	3.9	36.5	45.3	6.0	5.7	2.6	100.0
		3.00 Lower supervisory	Count	47	189	397	65	52	18	768
			% within FAMSECR Family grouped ns-sec recoded	6.1	24.6	51.7	8.5	6.8	2.3	100.0
		4.00 Routine and other	Count	6	79	110	28	27	7	257
			% within FAMSECR Family grouped ns-sec recoded	2.3	30.7	42.8	10.9	10.5	2.7	100.0
	Total		Count	119	1364	1277	163	161	77	3161
			% within FAMSECR Family grouped ns-sec recoded	3.8	43.2	40.4	5.2	5.1	2.4	100.0

that in each social group women are more likely than men to be in higher education but men are correspondingly more likely than women to be in Government supported training. Overall this suggests that similar proportions of young men and women are either in education or training or not in work. However, there are subtle gender differences, with women being more likely to be classified as in higher education than men and less likely than men to be classified as unemployed.

6.10 Conclusion

In this chapter we have looked at the basic apparatus for constructing contingency tables and casting them into probabilistic or percentage terms. Further aspects of layout and presentation of tables were also discussed. We have seen that the same frequencies can be expressed in many different ways, and that the data analyst must judge which is required to answer the question at hand.

It can be useful to collapse the number of categories in a variable. There are several factors to take into consideration when collapsing a variable: categories that are substantively similar, categories with small marginal frequencies, and categories which behave in a similar fashion with respect to a second variable are all good candidates for combining. It is usually bad practice to leave categories out completely when collapsing a variable. We have not yet shown how to quantify the effect of one variable upon another, but that is the subject of the next chapter.

Exercises

6.1   The teaching dataset YCS11_teach.sav includes a variable s1truan1 which describes truanting behaviour in year 11 (i.e. age 15–16).
   (a) Use SPSS to produce a simple frequency table and bar chart to display the distribution of this nominal variable.
   (b) Use SPSS to produce a contingency table (using the Crosstabs command) to discover whether there is any association between gender and truanting behaviour. Put sex in the rows of the table and truanting behaviour in the columns of the table – what type of percentages is it most sensible to calculate using SPSS?

6.2   The teaching dataset YCS11_teach.sav also includes a separate variable for mother and father's social position measured using NS-SEC. Figure 6.19 shows a contingency table of mother's social position by father's social position.
   (a) What percentage of mothers and fathers are in the same category of NS-SEC?
   (b) What percentage of fathers are in a higher social class position than their wives/partners and what percentage of mothers are in a higher social class position than their husbands/partners?
   (c) Check that you can replicate the table using SPSS.

Figure 6.19 SPSS output showing contingency table of mother's social position by father's social position.

		momsec mother's grouped ns-sec						
		1.00 Large employers and higher professionals	2.00 Lower professional and higher technical occupations	3.00 Intermediate occupations	4.00 Lower supervisory occupations	5.00 Semi routine and routine occupations	6.00 Other	Total
dadsec father's grouped ns-sec	1.00 Large employers and higher professionals — Count	90	298	184	38	157	106	873
	% of Total	1.5	4.8	3.0	.6	2.5	1.7	14.1
	2.00 Lower professional and higher technical occupations — Count	61	380	235	63	210	129	1078
	% of Total	1.0	6.1	3.8	1.0	3.4	2.1	17.4
	3.00 Intermediate — Count	37	215	383	99	292	212	1238
	% of Total	.6	3.5	6.2	1.6	4.7	3.4	20.0
	4.00 Lower supervisory occupations — Count	23	168	138	132	270	128	859
	% of Total	.4	2.7	2.2	2.1	4.4	2.1	13.9
	5.00 Semi routine and routine occupations — Count	13	107	122	95	392	206	935
	% of Total	.2	1.7	2.0	1.5	6.3	3.3	15.1
	6.00 Other — Count	31	202	139	62	302	465	1201
	% of Total	.5	3.3	2.2	1.0	4.9	7.5	19.4
Total	Count	255	1370	1201	489	1623	1246	6184
	% of Total	4.1	22.2	19.4	7.9	26.2	20.1	100.0

Figure 6.20   Household size by numbers in poverty.

Number in household	In poverty	Not in poverty	Total
1	259	991	1250
2	148	2159	2307
3	45	1319	1364
4	21	1272	1293
5	16	573	589
6 or more	21	324	345
Total	510	6638	7148

6.3   Figure 6.20 is adapted from Fiegehan et al. (1977); the authors set out to investigate both the causes of poverty and the type of social policy that would best alleviate it. In order to discover whether household size had any effect on poverty, they re-analysed some data originally collected for the Family Expenditure Survey, and got a table something like that shown in figure 6.20.

Construct two tables running the percentages both ways and say how each table might contribute to understanding the relationship between poverty and household size. What advice would you give to a policy-maker about where to concentrate resources to alleviate poverty on the basis of these figures?

6.4   The NCDS teaching dataset NCDS_ExpData_teach.sav contains information on the social class of cohort members at age 46 and the social class of their father when they were aged 16. Construct both an inflow and an outflow mobility table and discuss the results.

7

Analysing Contingency Tables

In the previous chapter, we introduced percentage tables as a way of making contingency data more readable. This chapter follows on directly. The properties of percentages and proportions will be scrutinized more closely, and other ways of analysing contingency data considered in the quest for a summary measure of the effect of one variable upon another. First, however, we must come back to the question of how to read a contingency table when one variable can be considered a likely cause of the other i.e. when one variable is interpreted as the explanatory variable and the other as the response or outcome variable. (We will shift from percentages to proportions from now on, since we need measures of effect which can be multiplied together.)

7.1 Which way should proportions run?

When we have a hypothesis about the possible causal relationship between variables, this can be conveyed by the choice of which proportions one uses in the analysis. Over the last two decades researchers have consistently found age to be associated with whether individuals feel safe walking alone after dark: older people, and particularly older women, are more likely to feel unsafe than younger individuals (Hough and Mayhew, 1983; Mirlees-Black, Mayhew, and Percy, 1996; Allen, 2006). In this example, the explanatory variable must be old age and the response or outcome variable is feeling unsafe, we would not suggest that feeling unsafe causes people to be old (although perhaps fear and anxiety may make a few individuals prematurely grey?). This means that in a cross-tabulation of age by feeling unsafe, it is more natural to examine the proportion of each age group who feel unsafe, rather than the proportion of each category of a 'feeling safe walking alone after dark' variable who are old. This can be formalized into a rule when dealing with contingency data:

> Construct the proportions so that they sum to one *within* the categories of the *explanatory* variable.

The rule is illustrated by the following diagram.

Response variable

		⟶	1.00
Explanatory variable		⟶	1.00
		⟶	1.00
		⟶	1.00

Note that it cannot be formulated as 'always calculate proportions along the rows'. This would only work if the explanatory variable was always put in the rows, and no such convention has been established. This rule is worth memorizing. The idea is directly analogous to the treatment of interval level variables which we will discuss in the next chapter. The response variable thus provides the proportions, and the explanatory variable the categories.

7.2 The base for comparison

In the previous chapter, tables and the association between variables were discussed without reference to any causal hypothesis or to causal path diagrams. However, it is often plausible to imagine that one variable in a table has a likely causal effect on the other variable and this can help us to interpret the figures in a meaningful way. For example, in figure 7.1 the explanatory variable is age group, a three-category variable while the response or outcome variable is feelings of safety walking alone after dark. In accordance with the rule provided in the previous section, the proportions expressing fear of walking alone after dark should be calculated within each age group. In figure 7.1 the full raw frequencies have been included as they will be helpful in the following discussion. The data are from the British Crime Survey 2004–5 which was introduced in chapter 5. This survey is described in the appendix to this chapter, which can be found on the accompanying website.

Figure 7.1 How safe do you feel walking alone after dark? 2004–5.

	Very safe / fairly safe / a bit unsafe		Very unsafe		Total	
Age group	p	N	p	N	p	N
16–39	0.93	13,589	0.07	1083	1	14,672
40–59	0.93	13,861	0.07	1099	1	14,960
60+	0.84	12,722	0.16	2432	1	15,154
Total		40,172		4614		44,786

Source: Analysis of data from the 2004–5 British Crime Survey (unweighted). The British Crime Survey is not a completely random sample of the population. Data from the study should therefore be 'weighted' to take account of the design effects of the survey and to provide the best possible estimates of summary statistics from the survey. However, for simplicity in this chapter the analyses are carried out on unweighted data. This means that some figures will be very slightly different from those published in reports based on the British Crime Survey data.

Numbers only have meaning in comparison with other numbers. To decide whether 0.07 of individuals aged 16–39 reporting feeling 'very unsafe' when walking alone after dark is high or low, it can be compared with the 0.07 of individuals aged 40–59 and 0.16 of individuals aged 60 or over. One category is picked to act as the **base** for comparison with all other categories.

By making comparisons with this base, quantitative estimates of the likely causal effect of one variable on another can be made, and positive and negative relationships between nominal level variables can be distinguished, as we will see shortly.

Which category should be selected as the base for comparison? The decision is to some extent arbitrary, but there are several relevant considerations. Since the base category will be used in every comparison, it is desirable that there should be a substantial number of cases in it. We do not want comparisons to be made with an unreliable figure. For the same reason, it should be a category that is of substantive interest. Moreover, if there is one category that is markedly different from others, this is a good one to choose as the base, since it will focus attention on the difference. Finally, when picking the base categories for several variables whose interrelationships are to be examined, an attempt should be made to keep negative relationships between variables to a minimum: double negatives are as confusing in data analysis as they are in prose.

Which categories, then, should be selected as bases for comparison among age groups feeling unsafe walking alone after dark? An important rule of thumb is to choose a category with a relatively large number of individuals within it. In this case, since the age-groups are all of similar size, any one of them could be used as the base category for the age-group variable. If we select the youngest age group as the base and then pick feeling very unsafe as the base for comparison in the fear of walking alone after dark variable, we will almost certainly avoid too many negative relationships. In summary, each age group can be compared with those aged 16–39 in their feeling very unsafe when walking alone after dark.

In order to represent one three-category variable, like age group, in a causal path model, we have to present it as two dichotomous variables. Instead of coding the age of respondents as 1, 2 or 3 to denote 60 and over, 40–59, or 16–39, for example, the information is effectively presented as two dichotomous variables – whether someone is aged 60 and over or not, and aged 40–59 or not. Someone who was in neither of these age groups would, by elimination, be in the youngest age group.

Age group as a three-category variable		Age group as two dichotomies	
		Aged 60+ or not	Aged 40–59 or not
60+	1	1	0
40–59	2	0	1
16–39	3	0	0

Choosing one category as a base effectively turns any polytomous variable into a series of dichotomous variables known as **dummy variables**.

Figure 7.2 shows how the effect of a three-category explanatory variable on a dichotomous response variable can be portrayed in a causal path model. Age group is represented by two dummy variables. The effect of the first is denoted b_1

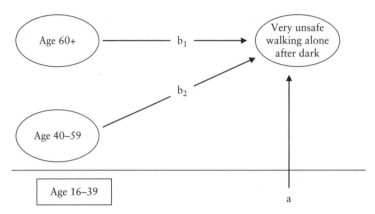

Figure 7.2 Causal path model of age group and feeling unsafe walking alone after dark.

and the effect of the second b_2. A line is drawn under which the base category of the explanatory variable is noted; the fact that some young people are afraid of walking alone after dark (path a) reminds us that there are some factors influencing feeling very unsafe that this particular model does not set out to explain.

7.3 Summarizing effects by subtracting proportions

In figure 7.2, the effect of being in the oldest age group on feeling unsafe when walking alone after dark is denoted b_1, and the effect of being in the middle age group is denoted b_2. How are these to be quantified? There is no answer to this question that commands universal acceptance. In this section we will consider d, the difference in proportions (Davis, 1976). This measure of effect has two virtues: it is simple and intuitively appealing. In later sections we will look at alternatives.

As long as we keep cool when deciding which proportion to subtract from which, the procedure is simple. Attention is restricted to the non-base category of the response variable. In this example, it is the proportion of people who feel very unsafe that is at issue, and the shadow proportion, i.e. those who feel 'very safe', 'fairly safe' or 'a bit unsafe', is ignored.

> The effect, d, is calculated by subtracting this proportion in the base category of the explanatory variable from this proportion in the non-base category of the explanatory variable.

In this particular example, path b_1 represents the effect of being in the oldest age group as opposed to being in the youngest age group on the chances of feeling very unsafe walking alone after dark. It is found by subtracting the proportion of the youngest age group feeling very unsafe from the proportion of the oldest age group class giving the same response. If we look back at figure 7.1, in this case, $d = 0.16 - 0.07$, or $+0.09$. The result is positive, as we expected: older people are more likely to be afraid of walking alone after dark than are the youngest age group.

If we had selected different base categories, we could have ended up with negative values of d. For example, if we were trying to explain feeling **safe** when walking alone after dark, the d for the oldest age group would have been $0.84 - 0.93$, or -0.09. The magnitude of effect would not have altered but the sign would have been reversed.

Path b_2 represents the effect of being in the middle age group on feeling very unsafe walking alone after dark. We might expect this to be lower than the effect of being in the oldest age group. It is. In fact, $d = 0.07 - 0.07$, or 0; the younger two age groups are extremely similar in their fear of walking alone after dark.

While the paths b_1 and b_2 are the focus of our attention, it is also important to remember the other factors which lead to people being afraid to walk alone after dark: age group is not a complete determinant of who is fearful, since some in the youngest age group report feeling very unsafe about walking alone after dark. Path a reminds us of this.

The value of path a is given by the proportion of cases in the base category of the explanatory variable who fall in the non-base category of the response variable.

In fact, 7 per cent of those in the youngest age group reported feeling very unsafe walking alone after dark. The value of this path is therefore 0.07. This figure represents the starting point, the fitted value to which the other path values should be added. For this reason it does not have a sign attached.

The quantified model is shown in figure 7.3. The model allows us to decompose the proportion of older people who are fearful of walking alone after dark (0.16) into a fitted component (0.07) and an effect ($+0.09$).

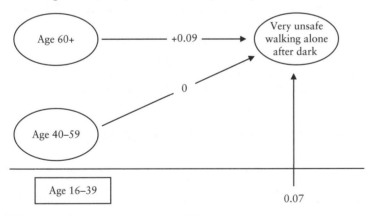

Figure 7.3   Quantifying model in figure 7.2.

Some readers will have come across the idea of expressing a simple relationship between an explanatory variable X and a response variable Y as $Y = a + bX$. If the idea is familiar to you, you may like to note here that proportions can also be expressed in this way. The overall proportion Y who feel very unsafe when walking alone after dark is 4,614/44,786, or 0.103 (figure 7.1). This can be decomposed as:

$$Y = a + b_1 X_1 + b_2 X_2$$

where X_1 and X_2 are the proportions of the sample in the oldest and middle age groups (0.338 and 0.334) respectively.

We will consider equations like this for interval level variables later in the book. You may find it useful to come back to this paragraph after you have read chapter 9.

Measuring the fear of crime?

The focus in this chapter so far has been on how age is associated with individuals' responses to the question 'How safe do you feel walking alone after dark?' This question has been asked repeatedly within the British Crime Survey which means that it is possible to look at how answers to this question have changed over time. The proportion reporting that they feel very unsafe has remained relatively constant at between 10 per cent and 13 per cent since 1984 (Allen, 2006). However, it is now widely recognized that this question itself does not provide an appropriate measure of the fear of crime (Hollway and Jefferson, 2000; Allen, 2006). As is explained in the most recent annual reports on crime in England and Wales the question 'How safe do you feel walking alone after dark?' makes no explicit reference to crime and there could be other reasons why individuals would feel unsafe, for example fear of a fall. In addition for many people the question will be purely hypothetical as they may never go out after dark or may always go out with another member of the family. The British Crime Survey includes several questions which ask about individuals' levels of worry about specific types of crime. An example is provided in Exercise 7.1. The focus of this chapter is primarily on how we analyse the relationships between categorical variables. However, it is also important that we pay close attention to what is being measured by the variables we are using. A further discussion of this that specifically focuses on understanding the fear of crime is provided by chapter 2 in Hollway and Jefferson (2000).

7.4 Properties of *d* as a measure of effect

The difference in proportions, *d*, has been used to summarize the effect of being in a category of one variable upon the chances of being in a category of another. This measure has several advantages. People understand it intuitively (Hunter, 1973). It retains the same numerical value (while changing its sign) if the other category in a dichotomy is chosen as the base for comparison. Furthermore, it can be used to decompose overall proportions, as shown in the previous section, and it can be decomposed itself when other variables are brought into the picture. However, it does have some properties which are less well understood, and which, in the view of some data analysts, can make it unsuitable for analysing some contingency tables.

If the proportions were run in the opposite direction, the value of *d* would change. Some statisticians dislike this property: they prefer **symmetric** measures of association which take the same value whichever way round the causal effect is presumed to run. Quantitative summaries of causal effects such as *d*, however, are nearly all **asymmetric**, taking different values depending on which variable is presumed to be the cause of the other. One advantage of this is that these measures force us to be explicit about our hypotheses as to which variable is the explanatory variable and which is the response.

Secondly, because proportions are bounded numbers, we may wish to distinguish differences between proportions in the middle of the range from those between extreme proportions. In the above example, the proportions stating that they felt very unsafe walking alone after dark were all relatively small. This means that although the size of the effect *d* for the oldest age group is relatively small (0.09), older people are more than twice as likely as the younger age groups to say that they feel very unsafe. For proportions in the middle of the range e.g. 0.51 compared with 0.60 the difference '*d*' would be identical to that calculated above. However, intuitively the differences between the groups would not appear as marked.

There are other strategies we might adopt to solve this problem. We could look at ratios between proportions rather than differences. Or we could apply some kind of transformation which would stretch out the tails of the distribution, which would let us stick with arithmetic procedures and avoid multiplicative models. Transformations are discussed in chapter 10.

7.5 How large a difference in proportions is a 'significant' difference?

In the example in figure 7.1, the analysis was based on data from the British Crime Survey 2004–5 and the sample size was extremely large at nearly 45,000 individuals and is designed to represent the adult population. This makes us reasonably confident that the observed difference between the oldest age group and the two younger age groups in their feeling very unsafe walking alone after dark is a 'real' one. That is, we expect that the results we have found in our very large sample will be extremely similar to the results we would obtain if we had asked another large sample, or even the whole population, about their feeling safe or unsafe walking alone after dark. Using the same logic, because of the large sample covered by the British Crime Survey, if we look at the data in figure 7.4 we would conclude that women are more likely than men to feel very unsafe walking alone after dark (0.16 vs 0.03, with men as the base category d = 0.13). Provided a sample is of sufficient size (above around 30 cases) then we know that the distribution of sample means (or any other sample parameter) for all samples of that size drawn from the population will have a normal distribution (bell-shaped curve). This is the case regardless of the shape of the distribution of the original variable of interest in the population. For example, even though we know weekly income is positively skewed, if we took repeated random samples of 30 individuals and then plotted the mean of each of the samples as a histogram the distribution of these means would have a normal or Gaussian shape. This is important because it enables us to calculate estimates of population parameters from sample

Figure 7.4   Feeling safe walking alone after dark by gender.

	Very safe, fairly safe or a bit unsafe		Very unsafe		Total	
	p	N	p	N	p	N
Male	0.97	19,388	0.03	697	1	20,085
Female	0.84	20,827	0.16	3,924	1	24,751
Total		40,215		4,621		44,836

Source: Analysis of British Crime Survey 2004–5 (unweighted).

statistics and also to calculate how accurate these estimates are likely to be. This is often known as the 'Law of Large Numbers'.

However, not all surveys have such large sample sizes and if, for example, we read a report stating that women were more concerned about walking alone after dark than men, based on twenty-five interviews with men and twenty-five interviews with women, in which four women and one man stated that they felt very unsafe walking alone after dark, we might be rather less convinced.

These are extreme examples with very different sample sizes, but clearly a great deal of research is carried out on moderate sized samples. Therefore, we need some way of deciding, for any specific size of sample, how big a difference is needed between two (or more) groups for the finding to be robust. That is, for the difference observed within the sample to indicate that a similar difference exists in the wider population. This issue brings us to the important topic of 'inferential statistics' i.e. the question of how we can use analysis of data from samples of individuals to infer information about the population as a whole.

When we are dealing with categorical variables, which can be analysed by cross-tabulating them and displaying them in contingency tables such as that shown in figure 7.1 and figure 7.4, a statistic known as 'chi-square' can be calculated which provides useful information about how far the results from the sample can be generalized to the population as a whole. In the next section we will examine in some detail how this statistic is calculated, and indeed for simple tables with only a few cells it is relatively straightforward to calculate by hand. However, the vast majority of researchers rely on statistics packages such as SPSS to provide them with the chi-square statistic and therefore when reading the next section it is more important to follow the logic of what is happening than to worry unduly about the arithmetic.

7.6 Calculating the chi-square statistic – innocent until proven guilty?

In order to understand how the chi-square statistic is calculated and how its value should be interpreted, it is helpful to refer to a concrete example, but one in which the numbers are very straightforward. Therefore let's start with an imaginary piece of research in which 100 men and 100 women are asked about their fear of walking alone after dark. Until we conduct the survey we have no information

Figure 7.5 Feeling safe walking alone after dark by gender (hypothetical survey of 200 individuals).

	Very safe, fairly safe or a bit unsafe		Very unsafe		Total	
	p	N	p	N	p	N
Male	?	?	?	?	1	100
Female	?	?	?	?	1	100
Total	?	?	?	?	1	200

other than the number of men and women in our sample and therefore we have figure 7.5.

Once we carry out the survey let us imagine that we find that in total 20 individuals i.e. 0.1 of the sample state that they feel very unsafe when walking alone after dark. We therefore now have some more information that we can add to our table and this is entered as the column marginals in figure 7.6 below.

Figure 7.6 Feeling safe walking alone after dark by gender (hypothetical survey of 200 individuals).

	Very safe, fairly safe or a bit unsafe		Very unsafe		Total	
	p	N	p	N	p	N
Male	?	?	?	?	1	100
Female	?	?	?	?	1	100
Total	0.9	180	0.1	20		200

If, in the population as a whole, the proportion of men who feel very unsafe walking alone after dark is the same as the proportion of women who feel very unsafe walking alone after dark, we would expect this to be reflected in our sample survey. The **expected** proportions and frequencies would then be as shown in figure 7.7.

Figure 7.7 Feeling safe walking alone after dark by gender – expected values if men and women in the population are equally likely to feel unsafe (hypothetical survey of 200 individuals).

	Very safe, fairly safe or a bit unsafe		Very unsafe		Total	
	p	N	p	N	p	N
Male	0.9	90	0.1	10	1	100
Female	0.9	90	0.1	10	1	100
Total	0.9	180	0.1	20		200

Once we have carried out our survey and cross-tabulated fear of walking alone after dark by gender we will have 'observed' values that we are able to put in our table as shown in figure 7.8.

Figure 7.8   Feeling safe walking alone after dark by gender – **observed** values following the survey (hypothetical survey of 200 individuals).

	Very safe, fairly safe or a bit unsafe		Very unsafe		Total	
	p	N	p	N	p	N
Male	0.95	95	0.05	5	1	100
Female	0.85	85	0.15	15	1	100
Total	0.9	180	0.1	20		200

In order to be able to judge whether there is a relationship between gender and fear of walking alone after dark we need to compare the values we actually observed, following our survey, with the values that we would expect **if there were no differences between men and women.** The chi-square statistic provides a formalized way of making this comparison. The equation for chi-square is given below. In practical terms we need to find the difference between the observed and expected frequencies for each cell of the table. We then square this value before dividing it by the expected frequency for that cell. Finally we sum these values over all the cells of the table.

$$\chi^2 = \sum \frac{(O-E)^2}{E}$$

chi-squared equals

the sum of...

the squared difference between the expected and observed value, divided by the expected value

For the previous example, the computational details are provided in figure 7.9. The total chi-square value is calculated as 5.56. Although this provides a measure of the difference between all the observed and expected values in the table, as a figure on its own it still has little intrinsic meaning. How are we to use this to determine whether there is a relationship between gender and fear of walking alone after dark?

In order to answer this question we need to be aware that the sample of 200 individuals that we took in our particular survey is just one possible sample from the population and that there are many other samples that we might have taken. Each sample would have resulted in a slightly different observed result, but as long as the sample was randomly drawn we would expect the results in the sample to be shaped by the underlying relationships in the population.

Figure 7.9 Computation of chi-square from figures 7.7 and 7.8.

Observed	Expected	O-E	$(O-E)^2$	$(O-E)^2/E$
95	90	5	25	0.28
5	10	−5	25	2.5
85	90	−5	25	0.28
15	10	5	25	2.5
200	200			Total sum: 5.56

Just as in chapter 3 we discussed the normal distribution and areas under the normal curve, the chi-square statistic also has a distribution. If there was no relationship between gender and feeling unsafe walking alone after dark in the population, then taking repeated samples and constructing tables such as that in figure 7.8 would result in many chi-square statistics with low values, but occasionally, just by chance, we would obtain a rather higher value of chi-square. In the same way that for the normal distribution it is possible to use a set of statistical tables (or rely on a computer package) to find out the probability of obtaining a result as big as a particular value, we can find out the probability of obtaining a value of chi-square at least as big as that observed for a particular survey or table. For the current example, the probability of obtaining a chi-square of 5.56 or larger if there was no relationship between gender and fear of walking alone after dark (obtained by looking up the value in a set of statistical tables) is between 0.025 and 0.01. This is often expressed as $p < 0.025$ where 'p' indicates the probability of obtaining a chi-square of a given magnitude. In other words, if there was no relationship between gender and feeling unsafe walking alone after dark in the population as a whole, we would obtain a chi-square this large by chance fewer than twenty-five in every thousand random surveys (or once in every 40 random surveys). This is clearly very unlikely and therefore the balance of probabilities suggests that the result obtained in our sample survey reflects a difference in the population as a whole. Given the low value of this probability we reject the 'null hypothesis' that there is no relationship between gender and feeling unsafe walking alone after dark and conclude that the table shows a **'statistically significant'** relationship between the variables.

This of course still begs the question 'how low does the probability have to be before we consider it to be low enough?' One in forty sounds very low but would one in thirty, one in twenty, or even one in ten be a low enough probability for us to reject the null hypothesis? The answer to this question is not straightforward in that there is no mathematical way of deciding what the cut-off-point should be, below which the null hypothesis is rejected. Rather, the decision is made based on the custom and practice of communities of researchers. For example, in the social sciences the cut-off of $p < 0.05$ is commonly used. In other words we reject the null hypothesis if the probability of obtaining the test statistic (in this case the chi-square) is less than one in twenty. However, in the medical sciences, a cut-off of $p < 0.01$ is more common (i.e. one in a hundred). It is also good practice for researchers to state the probability or 'p value' they have obtained rather than simply writing that a result is statistically significant.

The null hypothesis

Whenever researchers use a statistical test two hypotheses are involved: the null hypothesis and the alternative hypothesis. A hypothesis is simply a factual statement that may or may not be true. We calculate a test statistic (such as a chi-square) to help us decide whether the null hypothesis is true. The null hypothesis is that the two variables we are analysing are not associated in the population as a whole and that any relationship we observe between variables in the sample is small enough to have occurred due to random error. In other words the null hypothesis suggests that in the population of interest, changes in the explanatory variable have no impact on the outcome of the response variable. This is sometimes also described as the two variables being 'independent'. This section has the subheading 'innocent until proven guilty' because in most research situations we start out from the assumption that the null hypothesis is true and that there is no relationship between the variables and then we calculate a test statistic such as chi-square to see if we can disprove the null hypothesis. The null hypothesis is sometimes expressed symbolically as H_0 and you may see it written like this in other books on data analysis.

Let us now turn to an empirical example where chi-square can be used to discover whether there is a statistically significant relationship between gender and feeling unsafe walking alone after dark. Whereas figure 7.4 was based on comparing men and women for the sample as a whole, i.e. some 44,836 individuals, figure 7.10 restricts attention to the 398 men and women in the sample who are of Black Caribbean ethnic origin. Once again we observe a difference in the proportion of men and women stating that they feel very unsafe when they walk alone after dark (0.07 for men vs 0.19 for women), but how confident can we be that these results hold for the population of Black Caribbean individuals given that the sample size is not that large?

Using the SPSS package to calculate chi-square and the associated probability, we see from figure 7.11 that the probability of obtaining a chi-square value of 10.032 or higher is 0.002, i.e. just 2 in 1000, and we therefore reject the null hypothesis and conclude that the fear of walking alone after dark is higher for Black Caribbean women than for Black Caribbean men. Even though our sample

Figure 7.10 Feeling safe walking alone after dark by gender (sample restricted to those of Black Caribbean ethnic origin).

	Very safe, fairly safe or a bit unsafe		Very unsafe		Total	
	P	N	p	N	p	N
Male	0.93	150	0.07	12	1	162
Female	0.81	192	0.19	44	1	236
Total		342		56		398

Source: Analysis of British Crime Survey 2004–5 (unweighted).

Figure 7.11   Chi-square for figure 7.10 calculated using SPSS.

Chi-Square Tests

	Value	df	Asymp. Sig. (2-sided)	Exact Sig. (2-sided)	Exact Sig. (1-sided)
Pearson Chi-Square	10.032[b]	1	.002		
Continuity Correction[a]	9.124	1	.003		
Likelihood Ratio	10.771	1	.001		
Fisher's Exact Test				.002	.001
Linear-by-Linear Association	10.006	1	.002		
N of Valid Cases	398				

a. Computed only for a 2x2 table.

b. 0 cells (.0%) have expected count less than 5. The minimum expected count is 22. 79.

size is moderate, the difference between men and women has been found to be too large to be attributed to chance.

Type 1 and Type 2 errors

Clearly, using the method described above for deciding whether a result is statistically significant or not can never give us a definitive answer as to whether the relationship we observe in our sample reflects what we would observe if we could collect data on the population as a whole. However, the level of probability associated with a particular chi-square gives us a measure of how likely we are to be mistaken. This probability is sometimes thought of as the likelihood that we will make what is called a 'Type 1' error. That is, the probability that we will state a result is applicable to the population, when in fact we have simply been unlucky in selecting a random sample with an unusual profile.

In the example in figures 7.10 and 7.11, the probability of making a Type 1 error is 0.002 or 2 in a thousand and it is this very low value that makes us confident that we should reject the null hypothesis. However, if we obtain a rather higher probability associated with a chi-square, such as 0.02, there is a two in a hundred chance of making a Type 1 error and we may therefore decide not to reject the null hypothesis. As was explained above, custom and practice has led most social scientists to reject the null hypothesis if the probability is less than 0.05 (or 1 in 20) and to accept the null hypothesis if the probability is greater than or equal to 0.05.

In some surveys, particularly where the sample size is small, we may obtain what looks like an interesting difference between two groups, but find that the probability associated with the chi-square is above the conventional cut-off of 0.05. It is in this situation that we run the risk of making a 'Type 2' error. For example, if we use the British Crime Survey to look at the fear of walking alone after dark for individuals of Black Caribbean ethnic origin who are aged between 16 and 39 (see figure 7.12), we still find that women are slightly more likely than men to report that they

Figure 7.12   Feeling safe walking alone after dark by gender (sample restricted to those aged 16–39 of Black Caribbean ethnic origin).

	Very safe, fairly safe or a bit unsafe		Very unsafe		Total	
	p	N	p	N	p	N
Male	0.93	53	0.07	4	1	57
Female	0.91	98	0.09	10	1	108
Total		151		14		165

Source: Analysis of British Crime Survey 2004–5 (unweighted).

Figure 7.13   Chi-square associated with figure 7.12, calculated using the SPSS package.

Chi-Square Tests

	Value	df	Asymp. Sig. (2-sided)	Exact Sig. (2-sided)	Exact Sig. (1-sided)
Pearson Chi-Square	.241[b]	1	.623		
Continuity Correction[a]	.039	1	.843		
Likelihood Ratio	.248	1	.618		
Fisher's Exact Test				.773	.432
Linear-by-Linear Association	.240	1	.624		
N of Valid Cases	165				

[a]. Computed only for a 2x2 table.

[b]. 1 cells (25.0%) have expected count less than 5. The minimum expected count is 4.84.

feel very unsafe see figure 7.12. However, with a sample size of just 165 individuals chi-square is calculated (by SPSS as shown in figure 7.13) to be 0.241 with an associated probability of 0.623 and we do not reject the null hypothesis see figure 7.13.

In this example there is a danger of making a Type 2 error namely that we fail to reject the null-hypothesis even though there is a difference between the groups in the population. As was hinted at above, Type 2 errors are particularly common when we have a small sample size or when we are looking at a small subgroup within a larger survey.

Degrees of freedom

In figure 7.8 and figure 7.10, chi-square was calculated for the smallest table possible, that is with two rows and two columns. As we saw in figure 7.9, this resulted in a chi-square of 5.56 with an associated probability between 0.01 and 0.025. Although we do not need to concern ourselves with the technical details here, the probability associated with a particular value of chi-square does not only depend on the size of the chi-square, but also the size of the table from which chi-square was calculated. A table with two rows and two columns is said to have one degree of freedom because once one cell is known (e.g. once we know how many women are afraid to walk alone after dark) the values in the other cells can be calculated based on the row and column marginals. Similarly, a table with two columns and three rows is said to have two degrees of freedom. In formal terms the number of degrees of freedom for a table with r rows and c columns is given by the equation below:

$$\text{Degrees of freedom (Df)} = (r-1) \times (c-1)$$

So for a table with 4 rows and 5 columns the degrees of freedom would be 12 (and chi-square would be a great deal more cumbersome to calculate). As was shown in figure 7.11, when we use SPSS to produce a cross-tabulation and calculate chi-square it also indicates the degrees of freedom of the table alongside the probability associated with the chi-square value.

One problem which also arises for tables with more than one degree of freedom, and particularly with large tables, is that chi-square only gives an overall measure of whether the two variables are likely to be associated, but it does not tell us where the differences lie within the table. It may therefore be necessary to recode the variables or to select specific groups for more detailed analysis.

Sample size and limitations on using the chi-square statistic

One practical question which is often asked by those planning research is: what is the minimum sample size that yields reliable results? As we have seen from the discussion above, a major problem with small sample sizes is the likelihood of making Type 2 errors. In addition, though, one limitation on using chi-square is that the probability associated with a specific value of chi-square can only be calculated reliably if all the expected frequencies in the table are at least 5. This means that the size of sample required partly depends on the distribution of the variables of interest. In figure 7.13 we can see that the SPSS package provides a note (note b) of how many cells have an expected value less than 5. In this case, one cell has an expected value of 4.84 which is just below the minimum of 5.

A further limitation of using chi-square is that it only enables us to focus on the relationship between two categorical variables. If we are interested in examining the relationship between a number of different categorical variables simultaneously (e.g. if we wanted to understand how gender, ethnic group, and age group all shape feeling unsafe walking alone after dark) we would need to use a procedure such as logistic regression. This is introduced in chapter 12. Alternatively, if we wish to examine the possible association between a categorical variable and a continuous variable we would need to use the analysis of variance procedure. This will be covered in the next chapter.

Interpreting contingency tables and chi-square – the essentials

Many people find the logic of inferential statistics somewhat bewildering at first. This is partly because there are a number of different stages to understanding how to interpret a statistic such as chi-square with its associated probability. For practical purposes it is not necessary to understand exactly how chi-square is calculated or what the distribution of the chi-square statistic might look like. Indeed, the following checklist provides a practical guide to the essentials of interpreting contingency tables:

1. Which way have proportions (or percentages) been calculated, do they sum to one (or one hundred for percentages) within the categories of the explanatory variable? It is important to ensure that the proportions sum to 1 for each category of the explanatory variable (sometimes also referred to as the independent variable).
2. When comparing proportions or percentages ensure that you are comparing numbers which do not add up to 1 (or 100 in the case of percentages).
3. If there are more than two categories of the explanatory variable decide which should be the base category and compare the other categories with this one.
4. Note the size of the table. Are there too many categories to be able to interpret the table easily? If so it may be worth collapsing some of the categories and simplifying the table (review chapter 6 for further discussion of this). Remember that the 'degrees of freedom' can be calculated as (rows-1) multiplied by (columns-1). The smallest possible table is a two-by-two table and this has one degree of freedom.
5. Inspect the value of chi-square associated with the table. The larger it is, the more likely the table is to show a statistically significant association i.e. to have an associated probability less than 0.05 (written $p < 0.05$). For a two by two table (1 degree of freedom) a value of chi-square larger than 3.84 will be significant. For a table with two degrees of freedom a value of chi-square of 5.99 is needed and for a table with three degrees of freedom chi-square needs to be 7.81 to be significant.
6. Check the probability associated with chi-square (or p value). This literally gives the probability that the values observed in the table have occurred by chance under the assumption that in the population as a whole there is **no** association between the variables in the table (this assumption of no relationship is known as the null hypothesis). The smaller the value of p the more comfortable we are in saying that we should reject the null hypothesis and that there is a statistically significant relationship between the variables. As a rule of thumb, social scientists say that if p is less than 0.05 the results are significant.

7.7 Calculating chi-square using SPSS

The previous chapter included instructions about how to create contingency tables using SPSS. Once you have specified the variables that you want displayed in your contingency table it is easy to obtain a value for chi-square by clicking on the 'Statistics . . .' button.

Once you have clicked on the 'Statistics . . .' button you can then specify that you want SPSS to calculate the chi-square statistic as shown in figures 7.14 and 7.15. Then click on the 'Continue' button and click 'OK'.

The output produced by SPSS gives several different statistics. However, you can just focus on the first line labelled 'Pearson Chi-Square' (see figure 7.13). Karl

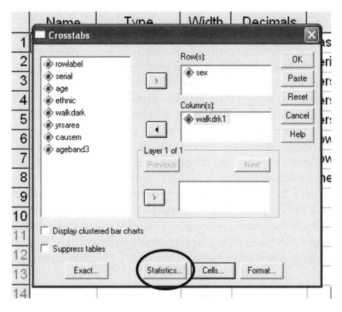

Figure 7.14 Obtaining a value for chi-square using the 'Statistics . . .' button.

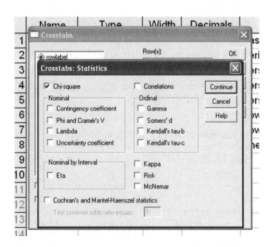

Figure 7.15 Specifying the type of statistics required in SPSS.

Pearson (1857–1936) was a British scientist whose thinking underpins a great many of the statistical procedures we still use today.

7.8 Conclusion

This chapter has provided an introduction to the interpretation of contingency tables and the use of *d* as a measure of association. Given that so much of the data in the social sciences is measured at the nominal or ordinal level these techniques are an extremely valuable part of a researcher's toolkit. It has been shown that using *d* as a measure of association is helpful when we wish to construct a causal path diagram and aim to quantify the magnitude of the effect of an explanatory variable on a response variable. The chapter has also introduced the chi-square statistic, which can be used to decide whether there is a statistically significant relationship between two categorical variables displayed in a table. This is an example of an **inferential statistic** because we use it to decide whether we can infer that the relationships between variables that we observe in our sample would also be observed in the population as a whole. The next chapter will introduce other uses of inferential statistics in the context of looking at relationships between variables measured at the nominal and interval level.

The substantive focus of this chapter has been on measuring perceptions of safety and fear of crime. As was discussed above, a prerequisite for good data analysis is that our variables are good measures of the constructs that interest us. We therefore need to be cautious in interpreting individuals' responses to questions about feeling safe walking alone after dark as indicating their fear of crime.

Exercises

7.1 Examine the data in figure 7.16. Which group of women is most likely to have high levels of worry about violent crime? And which group is least likely to have high levels of worry about violent crime? Using the data in the table create a simpler table with just three age groups: 16–34; 35–54; and 55+. Decide which should be the reference or base category and use the table to construct a causal path diagram similar to that shown in figure 7.3.

Figure 7.16 Women's levels of worry about violent crime by age 2005–6.

Women age group	High levels of worry		Not worried		Total	
	P	N	P	N	P	N
16–24	0.32	686	0.68	1447	1	2133
25–34	0.27	1040	0.73	2815	1	3855
35–44	0.25	1224	0.75	3725	1	4949
45–54	0.24	952	0.76	3008	1	3960
55–64	0.22	943	0.78	3430	1	4373
65–74	0.22	781	0.78	2735	1	3516
75 or older	0.14	511	0.86	3044	1	3555
Total		6,137		20,204		26,341

Source: Table 3.02 Worry about crime by demographic and socio-economic characteristics. 2005–6 report on crime based on BCS.

7.2 Figure 7.17 show the output from SPSS after conducting an analysis of the association between age group and feelings of safety focusing just on the men in the British Crime Survey.

Figure 7.17   SPSS output of the association between age group and fear of crime focusing just on the men in the British Crime Survey.

ageband3 Age groups * walkdrk1 How safe do you feel walking alone after dark Crosstabulation

			walkdrk1 How safe do you feel walking alone after dark		
			1.00 Not very worried	2.00 Very worried	Total
ageband3 Age groups	1.00 16–39	Count	6317	117	6434
		% within ageband3 Age groups	98.2%	1.8%	100.0%
	2.00 40–59	Count	6808	157	6965
		% within ageband3 Age groups	97.7%	2.3%	100.0%
	3.00 60–99	Count	6251	422	6673
		% within ageband3 Age groups	93.7%	6.3%	100.0%
Total		Count	19376	696	20072
		% within ageband3 Age groups	96.5%	3.5%	100.0%

Source: Analysis of data from the 2004–5 British Crime Survey (unweighted)
[Sample restricted to men only].

Chi-Square Tests

	Value	df	Asymp. Sig. (2-sided)
Pearson Chi-Square	245.570[a]	2	.000
Likelihood Ratio	229.460	2	.000
Linear-by-Linear Association	200.701	1	.000
N of Valid Cases	20072		

a. 0 cells (.0%) have expected count less than 5. The minimum expected count is 223.10.

Source: Analysis of data from the 2004–5 British Crime Survey (unweighted)
[Sample restricted to men only].

(a) Have row percentages or column percentages been provided in this table and why?
(b) Which age group appears to show the highest levels of fear of walking alone after dark?
(c) How many degrees of freedom are there in this table?
(d) What is the value of chi-square and is this significant?
(e) Is this sample large enough to enable us to calculate chi-square reliably?

7.3 (a) Using the 'GHS_ind_teach' dataset in SPSS, construct a table to show the cross-tabulation of the variable Sex by DRINKAMT 'Amount of alcohol respondent drinks' by placing Sex in the rows and DRINKAMT in the columns. Indicate your views about the likely causal relationship between these two variables by selecting the appropriate percentages.

(b) How many degrees of freedom does this table have?

(c) Is the value of chi-square significant and what does this mean about the association between the two variables in the table?

8

Handling Several Batches

In this chapter we will first examine the distribution of local unemployment rates within each region of Great Britain. A new graphical method, the boxplot, will be presented which facilitates comparisons between distributions, and the idea of an unusual data value will be given more systematic treatment than previously. This chapter therefore builds directly on the subject matter of the first two chapters. In the second part of the chapter a statistical technique called 'Analysis of Variance' will be introduced and applied to the analysis of the link between children's performance in maths tests at age 11 and their mother's interest in their education. Although the subject matter of the two halves of the chapter may at first sight appear radically different, the unifying link is that in both cases we wish to explore the association between a variable measured at the interval level (i.e. unemployment rate for a particular area; maths test score for an individual) and a variable measured at a nominal level (region; mother's interest in education measured in four categories).

8.1 Unemployment – an issue of concern

The problem of unemployment lies, in a very special sense, at the root of most other social problems. Society is built up on labour; it lays on its members responsibilities which in the vast majority of cases can be met only from the reward of labour . . . Everywhere reasonable security of employment is the basis of all private duties and all social action. (Beveridge, 1909, p. 1)

As this extract from the beginning of Beveridge's book *Unemployment: A Problem of Industry* demonstrates, unemployment has been understood as an issue of concern for both the individuals concerned and the society they are part of, for at least 100 years. Unemployment is viewed as a personal catastrophe by most of its victims, even those who are relatively quickly back in work. Being deprived of work, the unemployed lack not only access to an adequate income, but also access to a routine to organize their lives around, and to one of the most important sources of personal and social esteem. There is now a substantial body of research which documents the negative consequences of unemployment for the individual (for example, see Wadsworth et al., 1999).

Historically, unemployment has also been viewed as a major national problem by the overwhelming majority of adults in Britain, whether employed or unemployed. During the late 1970s and early 1980s every upward spiral of the unemployment figures brought a corresponding increase in the number of people who said, in response to being asked what they think are the most urgent problems facing the country today, that unemployment was top or second from the top (Marsh, 1988). This awareness of the importance of unemployment has made national unemployment statistics a matter of great political sensitivity. Therefore it is important to understand how unemployment statistics are compiled and to look at techniques for comparing levels of unemployment in different areas. In this chapter, some of the problems of using the official unemployment statistics will be discussed.

8.2 Counting the unemployed

Unemployment statistics serve several functions. They are used, along with employment, vacancies, output and earnings statistics, as indicators of the level of economic activity. They are interpreted as an indicator of the size of the potential labour reserve. They suggest levels of social distress in a community. They also have operational uses in guiding the management of employment services, and administrative uses in helping determine, for example, which areas should be granted assisted area status to qualify for various forms of government relief. No single statistical series could hope to serve all these functions at once. Therefore, there is no unique answer to the question of how unemployment should be defined.

The employed and the unemployed between them comprise the **labour force**. The unemployed should ideally be distinguished from the **economically inactive** who would not accept a job in the formal economy if it were offered to them. However, the line between the unemployed and the inactive is, in practice, a hard one to draw: how is one to know what would happen in hypothetical situations? Even the unemployed themselves may not be very good informants about their likely behaviour under different labour market conditions.

The Office for National Statistics (ONS) publishes two different measures of people who want to work but do not have a job – unemployment based on results from the Labour Force Survey, and the Claimant Count. Further information about both of these measures is provided in the appendix to this chapter which can be found on the accompanying website. The Labour Force Survey (LFS) provides estimates of both the unemployment level (i.e. numbers unemployed) and the unemployment rate. It is the rate that is the best indicator, because it measures the proportion of the economically active population who are unemployed and so takes account of changes in the size of the population over time, as well as changes in the level of unemployment. It is a legal requirement for every country in the European Union to conduct a Labour Force Survey. This, together with an agreement to use the ILO definition of unemployment, makes it possible to begin to compare levels of unemployment in different countries. We can see from

Figure 8.1 Unemployment rates across Europe (October 2006).

Unemployment rates across Europe in October 2006	
Denmark	3.5
Netherlands	3.9
Estonia	4.2
Ireland	4.2
Austria	4.7
Luxembourg	4.9
Cyprus	5.1
Slovenia	5.4
United Kingdom	5.6
Lithuania	5.7
Italy	6.8
Latvia	6.8
Czech Republic	6.9
Portugal	7.2
Malta	7.3
Hungary	7.9
Finland	7.9
Germany	8.2
Belgium	8.3
Spain	8.4
France	8.8
Greece	9
Slovakia	12.7
Poland	14

Source: Eurostat: Euro-indicators news release 156/2006.

figure 8.1 that in 2006 the United Kingdom had relatively low levels of unemployment compared with Germany, France and Spain, but rates were even lower in Denmark and the Netherlands. The unemployment rates in Poland can be seen to have been particularly high and this partly explains the high number of Polish people migrating to Britain to look for work.

8.3 Regional variation in unemployment rates

In the 1920s, the unemployed were required to show that they were 'genuinely seeking work' before they could claim benefit. People from Liverpool travelling to Manchester to look for work would pass Mancunians travelling to Liverpool for the same reason, when there was little prospect of work in either place. The futility of this exercise was deeply resented by the unemployed, and campaigning against this rule was one of the principal activities of the National Unemployed Workers' Movement at the time.

Although nothing like this is now enforced, there are still plenty of people who believe that the problem of unemployment would be lessened if the unemployed moved around more. The exhortation of the Secretary of State for Employment in 1981 (Norman Tebbit) that the current unemployed should 'get on their bikes',

Figure 8.2   Sample of unemployment rates by local
area in 2005.

Unitary and Local Authorities	Unemployment rate %
Cambridge	5.3
Colchester	3.8
Harlow	6.9
North Hertfordshire	4.5
Peterborough	4.6
Three Rivers	3.4
Mansfield	8.8
Nottingham	9.9
Ealing	7.9
Sutton	3.8
Chester-le-Street	5.0
South Tyneside	8.4
Allerdale	4.1
Barrow-in-Furness	5.7
Ellesmere Port and Neston	2.0
Ribble Valley	1.8
Rossendale	4.0
Salford	5.7
St Helens	5.6
Trafford	4.7
North Lanarkshire	6.9
Crawley	6.3
Portsmouth	6.6
Tunbridge Wells	3.2
Weymouth and Portland	3.5

Source: 2005 Annual Population Survey.

like those in the Depression, to look for work, has become an emotionally charged
slogan. In this chapter, by looking at regional and local unemployment rates, we
investigate what the unemployed in 2005 would have found if they had pedalled
around the country looking for work.

One of the main geographical units that can be used to divide Great Britain is
Government Office Regions. There are eleven regions in all and this includes Scotland
and Wales, which of course are not regions at all but devolved administrations.
Within each Government Office Region are a number of districts or unitary authorities. The unemployment rate within each district/unitary authority is calculated by
dividing the numbers unemployed by the most recent estimate of the size of the labour
force in the area. For example, the workforce in each area in 2005 was estimated by
taking the 2001 Census of Employment figures as the baseline, and adjusting them
on the basis of their industrial composition and of changes in the industrial composition in that region since 2001 known from other more up-to-date sources.

To get a feeling for how variable the experience of unemployment is in different parts of the country, we will start by examining a sample of towns. Figure 8.2
shows the unemployment rate for a random sample of twenty-five local authorities. Ignore for now the fact that we know which region each district is in, and
treat the data as a single batch.

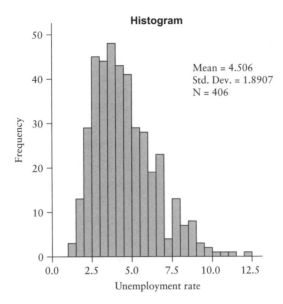

Histogram

Mean = 4.506
Std. Dev. = 1.8907
N = 406

Statistics

unemployment Unemployment rate

N	Valid	406
	Missing	2
Median		4.2
Minimum		1.1
Maximum		12.4
Percentiles	25	3.1
	50	4.2
	75	5.6

Source: 2005 Annual Population Survey.

Figure 8.3 Local area unemployment rate in 2005 across all regions in Great Britain: histogram and descriptive statistics.

The histogram and the five number summary of median, quartiles and extremes are shown in figure 8.3.

As usual, we focus in turn on four different aspects of the distribution: the level, spread, shape and outliers. Typical local unemployment rates in 2005 were around 4.2 per cent, and the middle 50 per cent of areas varied between 3.1 and 5.6 per cent, giving a midspread of 2.5 (i.e. 5.6 − 3.1, and see chapter 2 for an explanation of midspread). The main body of the data is roughly symmetrical, and there are no points that stand out as being a distance from the main bulk of the data.

In order to investigate whether and to what extent unemployment rates are associated with region, we must turn to the distribution of unemployment within regions, rather than over regions. Figure 8.4 shows the detail of the rates in 2005 for all the local areas in the East Midlands.

Figure 8.4   Unemployment rates in the East Midlands in 2005: percentages, histogram and basic descriptive statistics.

	unemployed		unemployed
Amber Valley	2.8	Kettering	3.2
Ashfield	5.6	Leicester City	8.8
Bassetlaw	3.8	Lincoln	5.8
Blaby	2.8	Mansfield	8.8
Bolsover	8.1	Melton	2.6
Boston	5.1	Newark and Sherwood	2.8
Broxtowe	2.6	North East Derbyshire	4.3
Charnwood	3.7	North Kesteven	3.0
Chesterfield	5.6	North West Leicestershire	3.4
Corby	4.7	Northampton	4.3
Daventry	4.5	Nottingham	9.9
Derby City	5.2	Oadby and Wigston	4.0
Derbyshire Dales	3.8	Rushcliffe	3.1
East Lindsey	2.9	Rutland	4.5
East Northamptonshire	2.6	South Derbyshire	4.2
Erewash	4.6	South Holland	4.4
Gedling	3.7	South Kesteven	2.8
Harborough	3.2	South Northamptonshire	2.6
High Peak	3.9	Wellingborough	3.9
Hinckley and Bosworth	3.2	West Lindsey	4.4

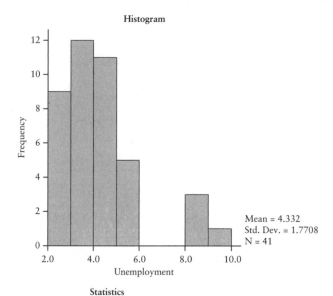

Histogram

Mean = 4.332
Std. Dev. = 1.7708
N = 41

Statistics

Unemployment

N	Valid	41
	Missing	0
Median		3.900
Minimum		2.6
Maximum		9.9
Percentiles	25	3.050
	50	3.900
	75	4.650

Source: 2005 Annual Population Survey.

By comparing figures 8.3 and 8.4, two indications may be gained that unemployment is associated with region. The regional median is not the same as the national average. It is slightly lower (3.9 per cent compared with 4.2 per cent). There is also somewhat less variation in the unemployment rates experienced by towns in the same region than there was in the sample of areas drawn from all over the country. Two areas that appeared relatively normal in the context of the national spread of unemployment rates, Mansfield and Nottingham, are seen from figure 8.4 to be unusually high for the East Midlands.

The exercise can now be repeated for all regions in the country. However, since it is too cumbersome to construct histograms for eleven batches of data at once and to compare their essential features, we will first introduce a new graphical device, and then a more formal way of identifying unusual data points or 'outliers'.

8.4 Boxplots

Most people agree that it is important to display data well when communicating it to others. Pictures are better at conveying the story line than numbers. However, visual display also has a role that is less well appreciated in helping researchers themselves understand their data and in forcing them to notice features that they did not suspect. We have already looked at one pictorial representation of data, the histogram. Its advantage was that it preserved a great deal of the numerical information. For some purposes, however, it preserves too much.

The **boxplot** is a device for conveying the information in the five number summaries economically and effectively. The important aspects of the distribution are represented schematically as shown in figure 8.5.

The middle 50 per cent of the distribution is represented by a box. The median is shown as a line dividing that box. Whiskers are drawn connecting the box to the end of the main body of the data. They are not drawn right up to the inner fences because there may not be any data points that far out. They extend to the **adjacent values**, the data points which come nearest to the inner fence while still being inside or on them. The outliers are drawn in separately. They can be coded with symbols (such as those in figure 8.5) to denote whether they are ordinary or far outliers, and are often identified by name. Outliers are points that are unusually distant from the rest of the data. They are discussed in more detail in the next section. To identify the outliers in a particular dataset, a value 1.5 times the dQ, or a **step**, is calculated; as usual, fractions other than one-half are ignored. Then the points beyond which the outliers fall (the **inner fences**) and the points beyond which the far outliers fall (the **outer fences**) are identified; inner fences lie one step beyond the quartiles and outer fences lie two steps beyond the quartiles.

The boxplot of unemployment in the East Midlands is shown in figure 8.6. It contains the same data as figure 8.4, but in a schematic form, highlighting the summary features, and drawing the eye's attention to the three outliers of Leicester City, Mansfield and Bolsover and the extreme case of Nottingham. It is striking how high

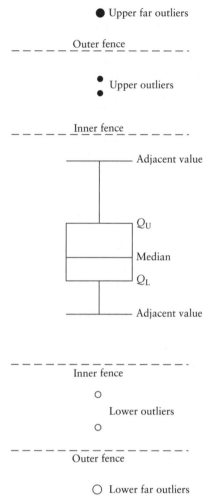

Figure 8.5 Anatomy of a boxplot.

unemployment rates are in these four areas compared with the rest of the region. There are perhaps two separate factors at work here: while Nottingham and Leicester are major cities which have seen a decline in their textile industries, Mansfield and Bolsover are smaller towns that were historically dominated by mining.

8.5 Outliers

Some, but not all, datasets contain points which are a lot higher or lower than the main body of the data. These are called **outliers**. They are always points that require the data analyst's special attention. They are important as diagnostics, and they can arise for one of four reasons:

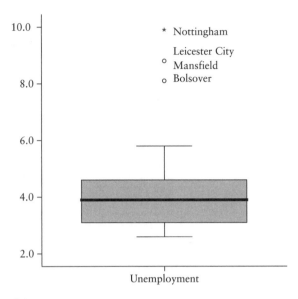

Source: Data in figure 8.4.

Figure 8.6 Unemployment in the East Midlands in 2005: boxplot.

1. They may just result from a fluke of the particular sample that was drawn. The probability of this kind of fluke can be assessed by traditional statistical tests, if sensible assumptions can be made about the shape of the distribution.
2. They may arise through measurement or transcription errors, which can occur in official statistics as well as anywhere else. We always want to be alerted to such errors, so that they can be corrected, or so that the points can be omitted from the analysis.
3. They may occur because the whole distribution is strongly skewed. In this case they point to the need to transform the data. As we will see in chapter 10, transformations such as logging or squaring the values may remove these outliers.
4. Most interesting of all, they may suggest that these particular data points do not really belong substantively to the same data batch.

Up to now the idea of a data point being unusually large or small has been judgemental. It is useful to formalize the idea and define just how far away any case needs to fall from the main body of the data before we will decide that it may be particularly unusual.

We could declare the extremes, or the outside 5 per cent of the distribution, to be outliers. However, this would be totally unsatisfactory as it would result in all distributions containing some, indeed the same proportion of, outliers. A rule is needed which highlights real differences between empirical distributions in the proportion of unusual data points they contain.

It makes sense to use the information about the spread in the main body of the data to define a point that is a long way away. The following has proved a useful rule

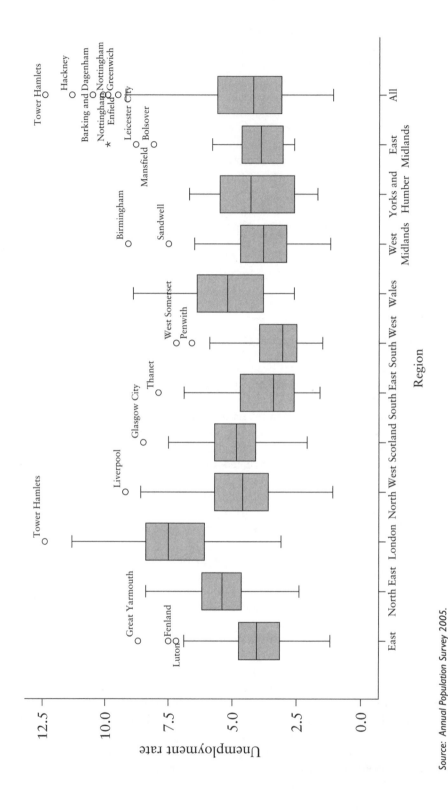

Source: Annual Population Survey 2005.

Figure 8.7   Local unemployment within regions in 2005: multiple boxplots.

of thumb: we define the main body of the data as spreading from one and a half times the dQ higher than the upper quartile to one and a half times the dQ lower than the lower quartile. Values further out than this are outliers. Moreover, it is also useful to define a cut-off for even more unusual points: we treat as a **far outlier** any point which is more than three times the dQ higher than the Q_U or lower than the Q_L.

There is nothing hard and fast about this definition. It is not intended to replace human judgement. If an extreme data point only just qualified as an outlier and there were many other points close to it which did not, we might choose not to so label it. On the other hand, if a point technically just failed to qualify but resembled other outliers more than the rest of the data, or was separated from the rest of the data by a big gap, we might choose to call it an outlier.

8.6 Multiple boxplots

Inspection of the unemployment rates for different districts in figure 8.4 suggested the hypothesis that the unemployment rate in a local labour market might be a function of which region it is in. We can now proceed to display unemployment in each region separately, to investigate this. Note that guidance about how to use SPSS to draw multiple boxplots is provided in section 8.10.

Boxplots, laid out side by side, as shown in figure 8.7, permit comparisons to be made with ease. The figure has been drawn according to the rule of thumb, not using any local knowledge or judgement to decide whether a point should be treated as an outlier. The order in which the regions are drawn is not fixed, since region is measured on a nominal scale. In the absence of any other rationale, it is helpful to order batches by their medians. The boxplot for all the areas is also included, for comparison.

The principal features of unemployment in each region now stand out clearly. The standard four features of each region's distribution can now be compared:

The level As can be seen from figure 8.7, the median unemployment rate varies from approximately 3 per cent in the South West to around 7.5 per cent in London. The original hypothesis was therefore correct: one source of the variation in local area unemployment rates is a regional effect. If there was no such effect, the medians would all be roughly the same. An unemployed worker who travelled from region to region in search of work would certainly find different average levels of unemployment prevailing.

The spread There is some regional variation in spread. The South West and East Midlands have a smaller midspread than other areas, and Yorkshire and Humberside has a larger midspread. However, the differences are not very marked (it is not unusual to find batches of data where the midspread of one batch is ten times the midspread of another). Importantly, there is no systematic evidence that the spread increases as the median increases, although this could be checked by plotting midspreads against medians. We should always watch out for such a pattern, as it usually suggests that looking at the data on a transformed scale might be better, as we will see in chapter 10.

The shape The datasets seem about as symmetrical as batches of data ever are. Some of the batches have longer upper tails than lower tails; this is because unemployment overall was relatively low in 2005 (i.e. when compared with the mid 1980s). The floor of zero unemployment prevents the possibility of a long lower tail at a time when median unemployment is relatively low.

Outliers Our attention is then drawn to several districts which do not fit the pattern of unemployment exhibited in the rest of the data. There seem to be slightly different forces operating depending on whether we focus on regions in the North or South of Great Britain. Whereas in the North the outliers tend to be large cities such as Liverpool, Glasgow, Nottingham and Birmingham, in the South the outliers include remote areas such as Penwith and Fenland which might be thought of as relatively remote.

   The regional outliers are generally not the same as the outliers in the whole batch. For example, Greenwich and Enfield appear to be outliers when viewed in the context of the country as a whole, but are seen to be almost normal in the context of London's unemployment rate.

8.7 Decomposing the variation in unemployment rates

The boxplot of unemployment rates in all local areas in Britain (figure 8.7) is longer than the plots for any of the individual regions. This indicates that the variation in unemployment rates in the country as a whole could be broken down into two components: between region variation and within region variation. This corresponds to the idea of a **conditional fit,** where the value to be fitted is not fixed, but itself depends upon which category the case falls in.

   The implicit model suggested by figure 8.7 is that variation in unemployment rates can be accounted for partly by region. This can be formalized as follows:

$$\text{Unemployment rate} = \text{Regional fit} + \text{Residual}$$

This model says that part of the reason for variation in all the local areas in the country stems from the fact that they are in different regions, and in part stems from other factors unconnected with region. The unemployment rate in Ealing, for example (7.9 per cent), can be decomposed into a typical rate for London (7.5 per cent) and a residual of +0.4 per cent.

   The regional medians could themselves be decomposed into two parts: a grand median and a regional effect, which indicates how far the median rate in a particular region deviates from the grand median:

$$\text{Unemployment rate} = \text{Grand median} + \text{Regional effect} + \text{Residual}$$

   The median unemployment rate in the whole of Great Britain was 4.2 per cent, so the London regional median of 7.5 per cent was 3.3 per cent higher. The unemployment rate in Ealing can therefore also be decomposed as 4.2 + 3.3 + 0.4 or 7.9 per cent as before.

An **effect** is here calculated as the difference between a conditional fit and the grand median. It is the value that is entered on the arrows in causal path models. If we ask 'What is the effect of region on local unemployment rates?', ten answers would have to be given, one for each region.

To quantify how much of the variation in unemployment rates is accounted for by region, the regional median is fitted to each value, residuals from the fit are calculated, and the variation in the residuals is compared with the original variation. Figure 8.8 shows a worksheet where this is done for the sample of local areas. The residuals from the regional fit show the variation in unemployment rates not accounted for by region; Ribble Valley, for example, has a very low unemployment rate for the North West.

The residuals can be displayed using a histogram and summary descriptive statistics (figure 8.9). Whereas the midspread in the original sample batch was 2.5, the residual midspread is now reduced to only 2.0. This corresponds with the feature observable in figure 8.7 that the variation in all areas taken together is larger than that in the regions taken separately. This reduction in midspread is an indicator of the strength of the effect of the explanatory variable on the response variable; in this case the reduction is modest and we therefore consider the impact of region on unemployment to be only modest.

Figure 8.8 Worksheet for fitting conditional regional medians.

District	Region	Unemployment rate	Fit (regional median)	Residual
Cambridge	East	5.3	4.05	1.3
Colchester	East	3.8	4.05	−0.3
Harlow	East	6.9	4.05	2.9
North Hertfordshire	East	4.5	4.05	0.5
Peterborough	East	4.6	4.05	0.6
Three Rivers	East	3.4	4.05	−0.7
Mansfield	East Midlands	8.8	3.90	4.9
Nottingham	East Midlands	9.9	3.90	6.0
Ealing	London	7.9	7.50	0.4
Sutton	London	3.8	7.50	−3.7
Chester-le-Street	North East	5.0	5.40	−0.4
South Tyneside	North East	8.4	5.40	3.0
Allerdale	North West	4.1	4.60	−0.5
Barrow-in-Furness	North West	5.7	4.60	1.1
Ellesmere Port and Neston	North West	2.0	4.60	−2.6
Ribble Valley	North West	1.8	4.60	−2.8
Rossendale	North West	4.0	4.60	−0.6
Salford	North West	5.7	4.60	1.1
St Helens	North West	5.6	4.60	1.0
Trafford	North West	4.7	4.60	0.1
North Lanarkshire	Scotland	6.9	4.85	2.1
Crawley	South East	6.3	3.40	2.9
Portsmouth	South East	6.6	3.40	3.2
Tunbridge Wells	South East	3.2	3.40	−0.2
Weymouth and Portland	South West	3.5	3.05	0.5

Source: Sample as figure 8.2.

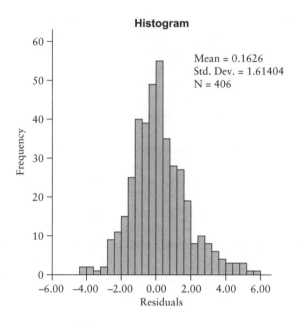

Statistics

Residuals

N	Valid	406
	Missing	2
Median		.0000
Minimum		-4.40
Maximum		6.00
Percentiles	25	-.9000
	50	.0000
	75	1.1000

Source: Data in final column of figure 8.8.

Figure 8.9   Displaying residuals from conditional regional fit: histogram and descriptive statistics.

8.8 Moving to the individual as a unit of analysis and using a statistical test

In the example of unemployment rates above, the unit of analysis was the local authority. Data were available for every local authority in Great Britain and there was no need to take a sample. It was therefore possible to use boxplots to carry out an exploratory analysis of how unemployment rates vary between and within region. In this type of example there is no need to focus on the question of statistical significance, introduced in the previous chapter.

Comparing the mathematics scores of boys and girls

Let us now turn to a rather different topic, but use the same approach to examine whether there are any differences between the mathematics scores of boys and girls. Figure 8.10 displays two boxplots, one for girls' mathematics score and one for boys' mathematics score at age eleven. The data originate from the National Child Development Study (introduced in chapter 3), and so these are historical data collected in 1969.

We can see that the scores of boys and girls on the maths tests at age 11 have a very similar distribution. The two boxplots look almost identical, but the girls' scores appear to have a very slightly lower median and a slightly lower upper quartile. As was described in chapter 3, the National Child Development Study is a longitudinal cohort study that has followed every individual born in one week of 1958. The sample size is considerable with 7,253 boys and 6,874 girls taking the mathematics test at age 11. Because the sample is so large, even if there are only small differences between boys and girls in the sample these differences may be statistically significant. That is to say, the differences we observe in the sample may also exist in the population and may not be a result of sampling error. In the previous chapter we introduced the chi-square statistic as a method for testing whether the results observed in a sample were also likely to exist in the population as a whole. However, the chi-square statistic can only be used when we are focusing on variables that are measured at the ordinal or nominal level. In the example above, mathematics score is an interval level variable and we therefore need a different statistical test to check whether the results are significant. In this specific example we have two groups (boys and girls) defined by a dichotomous variable and we are comparing them on an interval level variable (mathematics score). In these circumstances the statistical test that we need to use is called the T-test.

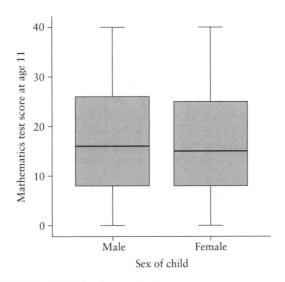

Source: Analysis of the National Child Development Study.

Figure 8.10　Boxplots comparing girls' and boys' mathematics scores at age 11.

8.9 The T-test

In simple terms the T-statistic provides a measure of the difference between the means of two groups. However, as well as taking account of the magnitude of the difference between the two groups it also takes account of the amount of variation within each group. The formula for T is given below for completeness, but it is rarely, if ever, necessary to calculate it by hand as statistical packages such as SPSS will calculate it automatically. If the sample sizes in the two groups you are comparing are small then the data must come from populations that have normal distributions. However, once the size of the whole sample is greater than 40 this assumption of normality can be relaxed.

Figure 8.11   Extract from SPSS output showing T-test results.

Group Statistics

	sex 0-3D Sex of child	N	Mean	Std Deviation	Std Error Mean
n926 2T Mathematics test score at age 11	1 Male	7253	16.81	10.598	.124
	2 Female	6874	16.44	10.083	.122

Independent Samples Test

		Levene's Test for Equality of Variances		t-test for Equality of Means						95% Confidence Interval of the Difference	
		F	Sig.	t	df	Sig. (2-tailed)	Mean Difference	Std Error Difference	Lower	Upper
n926 2T Mathematics test score at age 11	Equal variances assumed	30.577	.000	2.163	14125	.031	.377	.174	.035	.718
	Equal variances not assumed			2.166	14124.785	.030	.377	.174	.036	.718

Source: Analysis of data from the National Child Development Study.

T-test formula
The formula for a two-sample t-test where the samples are independent (as in the example of boys' and girls' mathematics test scores) is

$$t = \frac{\overline{X}_1 - \overline{X}_2}{S_{X_1 X_2} \cdot \sqrt{\frac{1}{n_1} + \frac{1}{n_2}}}$$

Where X_1 and X_2 are the means of the two samples and S_{X1X2} is known as the pooled standard deviation and is calculated as follows:

$$S_{X_1 X_2} = \sqrt{\frac{(n_1 - 1)S_{X_1}^2 + (n_2 - 1)S_{X_2}^2}{n_1 + n_2 - 2}}$$

here S_{X1} is the standard deviation of one sample and S_{X2} is the standard deviation of the other sample. In these formulae n_1 is the sample size of the first sample and n_2 is the sample size of the second sample. In simple terms therefore the size of the t-statistic depends on the size of the difference between the two means adjusted for the amount of spread and the sample sizes of the two samples.

Returning to our example, in order to test whether boys' and girls' mathematics scores are significantly different (that is whether the differences in the sample represent differences in the population) we first need to be clear about our null hypothesis. In this example it would be that boys' and girls' mathematics scores are the same, or in other words that there is no association between the variables gender and mathematics score. The T-statistic is then calculated in order to help us decide whether to reject the null hypothesis. If we find that we can reject the null hypothesis this would lead us to believe that there is an association between gender and mathematics score in the population of interest.

If SPSS is used to carry out a T-test, two short tables of statistics are produced (see figure 8.11). The first provides a simple descriptive summary of the distribution of the variables of interest (in this case mathematics score) for the two groups. In this example we can see that the results confirm what we observed in the boxplot. Boys' mathematics scores are very slightly higher than girls' mathematics scores and in addition the variability of scores (here measured using the standard deviation) is also slightly higher for boys than for girls. The second table produced by SPSS provides the T-statistic which in this case is 2.163. As explained above, this provides a type of standardized measure of the differences between the means that takes account of the variation within each group. The larger the T-statistic the more likely we are to reject the null hypothesis that there is no difference between the groups. Once again this raises the question of how big T needs to be before we can reject the null hypothesis. You may remember that in chapter 7 the chi-square statistic had a probability associated with it which allowed us to decide whether to reject the null hypothesis. We follow the same process with the T-statistic. In figure 8.11 we can see that the probability associated with the T-statistic (labelled 'sig. 2-tailed') is 0.031. Using the cut-off points, discussed in chapter 7, we note that this is less than 0.05. This means that there is less than a one in twenty chance that we would have obtained a T-statistic of this magnitude, based on our sample data, if there was no difference between boys and girls in the population as a whole. We therefore reject the null hypothesis and state that there is a significant difference between the mathematics test scores of boys and girls at age 11. Or alternatively that mathematics score is significantly associated with gender. Given that the data are from the National Child Development Study we should also be clear in our reported results that this result is historical and that boys were scoring significantly higher than girls on a mathematics test in 1969.

Using SPSS to carry out a T-test

The National Child Development Study also asked members of the cohort to complete a mathematics test at age 16. In order to use SPSS to carry out a T-test to determine whether there is still a statistically significant difference between the mathematics scores of boys and girls at age 16 the first step is to select 'Compare Means' from the 'Analyze' menu and then select 'Independent-Samples T Test' (see figure 8.12).

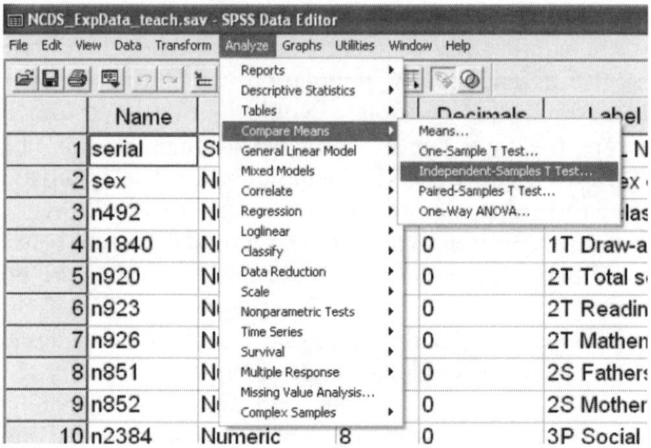

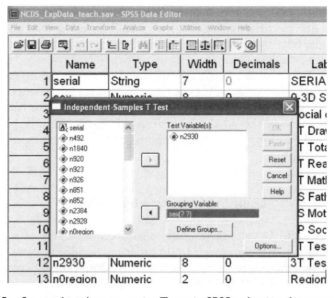

Figure 8.12 Screenshot demonstrating T-test in SPSS.

The next stage is to specify the 'Test variable' and the 'grouping variable'. In this example the test variable is mathematics test score at age 16 while the grouping variable is sex. In general terms it is the interval level variable that is the test variable and the dichotomous variable that defines the two groups is therefore the grouping variable.

The final stage is to click on the 'Define Groups . . .' button and define the values of the groups you are interested in comparing. In this example the grouping variable is sex and the values are 1 (for boys) and 2 (for girls). Having defined these groups you can then click on the Continue button and then on the OK button in the next dialogue box and SPSS will calculate the T-statistic.

Figure 8.13 Screenshot demonstrating T-test in SPSS: selecting the test variable(s) and grouping variable.

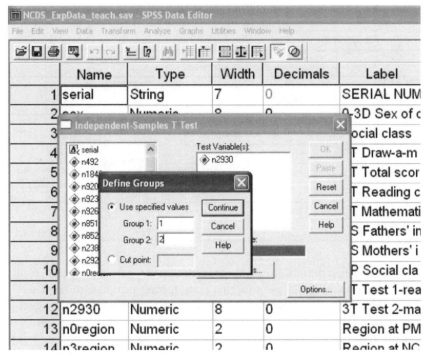

Figure 8.14 Screenshot T-test in SPSS: define groups.

Following these steps but then clicking the 'Paste' button will write the following syntax to a syntax file.

```
T-TEST
    GROUPS = sex(1 2)
    /MISSING = ANALYSIS
    /VARIABLES = n2930
    /CRITERIA = CI(.95).
```

The results of the T-test comparing boys' and girls' mathematics scores at age 16 are shown in figure 8.15. First it can be seen that there is still a difference in the mean scores of boys and girls, with boys scoring higher on average than girls (13.39 vs 12.09). Examination of the second table shows that the T-statistic has been calculated to be 10.15 and the associated probability is printed as 0.000 indicating that there is less than a 1 in a 1,000 chance that the null hypothesis is true and that such a big difference between the boys' scores and girls' scores could have arisen due to sampling error. For this reason we reject the null hypothesis and state that there is a significant difference between boys' and girls' mathematics test scores at age 16.

Figure 8.15   T-test output from SPSS comparing boys' and girls' mathematics scores at age 16.

Group Statistics

	sex 0-3D Sex of child	N	Mean	Std Deviation	Std Error Mean
n2930 3T Test 2-mathematics comprehension at age 16	1 Male	6104	13.39	7.267	.093
	2 Female	5816	12.09	6.639	.087

Independent Samples Test

		Levene's Test for Equality of Variances		t-test for Equality of Means						
							Mean Difference	Std Error Difference	95% Confidence Interval of the Difference	
		F	Sig.	t	df	Sig. (2-tailed)			Lower	Upper
n2930 3T Test 2-mathematics comprehension at age 16	Equal variances assumed	85.365	.000	10.150	11918	.000	1.296	.128	1.046	1.546
	Equal variances not assumed			10.172	11897.173	.000	1.296	.127	1.046	1.546

It is helpful at this point to make some brief comparisons between the results at 16 and the results at age 11 because this gives further insight into the T-test. For example it should be noted that the T-statistic at age 16 is considerably higher than it was at age 11 (10.15 compared with 2.16). This makes intuitive sense because we can see that the difference between the mean scores of boys and girls is considerably greater at age 16 and also that the standard deviation of the scores appears somewhat lower. We can also see that the sample size has declined somewhat between age 11 and age 16 from a total of 14,127 to a total of 11,920. This is reflected in the degrees of freedom associated with the T-test (labelled df on the output) which reduces from 14,125 to 11,918. You may remember from the previous chapter that for a contingency table, the degrees of freedom are equivalent to (rows – 1) multiplied by (columns – 1). When calculating a T-statistic the degrees of freedom are equivalent to the size of the sample minus the number of groups (sample size – 2).

Assuming equal variances?

So far we have been keeping things simple by just focusing on the first row of results in the output from SPSS, labelled 'Equal variances assumed'. However, you will have noticed that there is a second row of results, which looks almost identical, but is labelled 'Equal variances not assumed'. This is because there is a slightly different formula for calculating the T-statistic depending on whether the two groups have similar levels of variability within them. In figure 8.15 we can see that the standard deviation for boys is 7.267, whereas the standard deviation for girls is 6.639. In other words, the boys' mathematics scores are more spread out or heterogeneous than the girls' scores. As part of the T-test procedure, SPSS tests whether these variances are equal using 'Levene's test for the equality of variances'. From figure 8.15 we can see that the significance value for Levene's test is printed as 0.000. So in other words, there is less than a one in a thousand chance that the variance of boys'

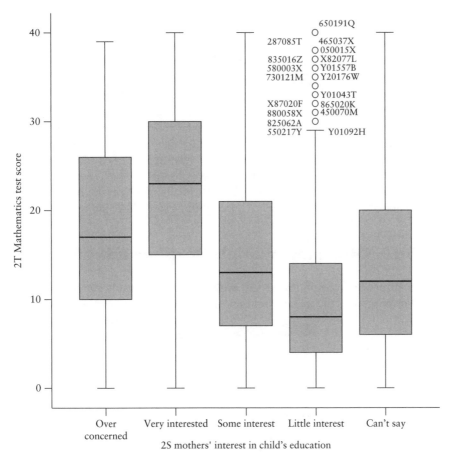

Source: Data from the National Child Development Study.

Figure 8.16 Mathematics test scores at age 11 by mother's interest in education: multiple boxplots.

and girls' scores is equal in the population as a whole. This implies that, strictly speaking, the second row of results corresponding to 'Equal variances not assumed' should be used. In this example we can note that the results are almost completely identical regardless of whether equal variances are assumed. This is always the case when the sample size in the two groups is almost the same.

Comparing more than two groups: parental interest and children's mathematics scores

In the example above we focused on just two groups i.e. boys and girls. However, we also need a technique and a statistical test that is appropriate for comparing more than two groups. For example, if we wish to examine the impact of mothers' interest in education on their children's performance on the maths test we can once again use the technique of multiple boxplots to explore the data. Figure 8.16 displays the multiple boxplot and we can clearly see that children's mathematics score and their mothers' interest in their education appear to be closely associated. If we start by focusing on the medians (denoted by the thick black horizontal lines in the middle of the boxplots) we can see that children whose mothers are 'very interested' in their education have the highest mathematics scores followed by children whose mothers are 'over concerned' about their education. Unsurprisingly, perhaps, children whose mothers are reported to have 'little interest' in their education have the lowest scores of all. These multiple boxplots are useful because they reveal more than simply the level or average mathematics score for each of these groups of children. If we focus for a moment on just the second and fourth boxplots in figure 8.16 we can see that the lower quartile for those children with mothers who are 'very interested' is *higher* than the upper quartile for children whose mothers show little interest.

8.10   Obtaining multiple boxplots using SPSS

In order to obtain a graph displaying multiple boxplots using the SPSS package, select 'Graphs' from the menus and then 'Boxplot', as shown in figure 8.17.

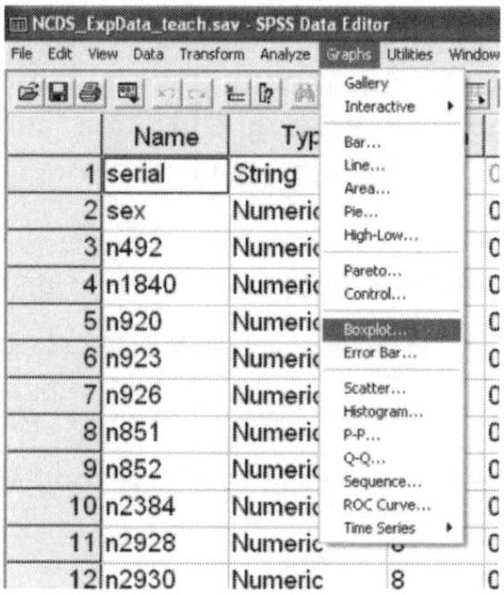

Figure 8.17   Screenshot from SPSS showing the boxplot command.

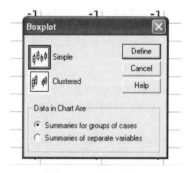

Figure 8.18   Screenshot from SPSS showing boxplot options.

Next a dialogue box will appear; choose 'Summaries for groups of cases' and then click on the 'Define' button.

The next step is to specify the 'Variable' you want to be displayed. In this case it is maths score at age 11. The category axis is the variable that defines the separate boxplots, in this case, mothers' interest in education.

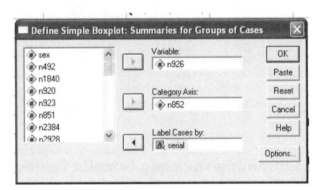

Figure 8.19   Screenshot from SPSS showing how to define a simple boxplot.

In this example we are examining a sample of children, namely those included in the National Child Development Study. If we wish to ascertain whether the relationship between mother's interest in education and mathematics test score observed within this sample is also present in the wider population we need to use inferential statistics.

8.11 One-way analysis of variance

When we have a continuous dependent variable (such as maths test score) and a categorical independent variable with more than two categories (such as mother's interest in education), the appropriate statistical procedure to use is 'One-way analysis of variance'. Once we shift from exploratory data analysis, in the form of comparing boxplots, to inferential statistics we also need to shift our description of the level and spread of the data from the median and the interquartile range to the mean and the standard deviation. One-way analysis of variance is used to test the null hypothesis that a number of independent population means are equal. In the current example we are going to test whether the mean mathematics scores for different groups of children, defined by their mothers' interest in education, are equal.

Before carrying out a one-way analysis of variance it is important to examine the data. We have already produced boxplots and noticed that there appear to be large differences between the groups of children. A further way to examine the data is to produce descriptive statistics for each of the groups. We can see from figure 8.20 that the average (mean) mathematics score for children with 'Very interested' mothers is 22.27, compared with 18.07 for the 'Over concerned' mothers and just 9.83 for the mothers who have 'little interest'.

Figure 8.20   Extract from SPSS output showing mathematics scores by mother's reported interest in child's education.

Descriptives

n926 2T Mathematics test score

	N	Mean	Std. Deviation	Std. Error	95% Confidence Interval for Mean		Minimum	Maximum
					Lower Bound	Upper Bound		
1 Over concerned	521	18.07	9.867	.432	17.22	18.92	0	39
2 Very interested	4875	22.27	9.808	.140	22.00	22.55	0	40
3 Some interest	4841	14.55	9.307	.134	14.28	14.81	0	40
4 Little interest	1903	9.83	7.901	.181	9.47	10.18	0	40
5 Can't say	1584	13.73	9.116	.229	13.28	14.18	0	40
Total	13724	16.68	10.342	.088	16.50	16.85	0	40

The one-way analysis of variance procedure is based on the fact that there is a known statistical relationship between the variability of means and the variability of individual observations from the same population. If the independent sample means vary more than would be expected, if the null hypothesis is true, the null hypothesis should be rejected in favour of the alternative hypothesis that the means of the separate groups within the population are not all equal. The information needed to test the null-hypothesis that all population means are equal is provided in figure 8.21.

The between-groups mean square indicates how much individual observations should vary if the null hypothesis is true. This is computed based on the variability of the sample means. In this case it is based on the variability between the five mean mathematics test scores for the groups defined by mothers' interest in education. The within groups mean square indicates how much the observations within the groups really do vary. The F statistic is then calculated based on the **ratio** of these two estimates of the variance. The between-groups mean square is divided by the within groups mean square. The larger the value of the F statistic the more likely you are to reject the null hypothesis. The distribution of the F statistic depends both on the number of groups that are being compared (5 in this example) and the number of cases in the groups (13,724 in total). The between-groups degree of freedom is one fewer than the number of groups (i.e. 5–1 = 4 in this example), and the within groups degree of freedom is the number of case minus the number of groups (i.e. 13,724 − 5 = 13,719, in this example).

Figure 8.21   Extract from SPSS output showing one-way Anova results.

ANOVA

n926 2T Mathematics test score

	Sum of Squares	df	Mean Square	F	Sig.
Between Groups	278803.0	4	69700.757	804.164	.000
Within Groups	1189091	13719	86.675		
Total	1467895	13723			

The most important pieces of information that you need to focus on in order to be able to interpret the results of this one-way analysis of variance are in the last two columns of figure 8.21: the F statistic and its associated probability or 'significance'. If the observed probability is small then the null hypothesis that all group means are equal within the population can be rejected. In this example the probability is so small (less than 0.001) that the computer prints the value as .000. Therefore we can reject the null hypothesis that mothers' interest in education is *not* associated with children's score on the maths test.

However, having rejected the null hypothesis that all the group means are equal, it is still not clear which pairs of mean maths scores are statistically different from each other. Children whose mothers are 'very interested' in their education have a very high mean score of 22.27 and we would expect this to be significantly different from the very low score for children whose mothers have 'little interest' in their education (9.83). But are there any real differences between children whose mothers show 'some interest' (14.55) and children whose mothers are 'over concerned' (18.07)? Within SPSS the multiple comparison procedures associated with one-way analysis of variance allow you to pinpoint exactly which groups are significantly different from each other. Indeed, SPSS offers a slightly overwhelming choice of 18 different types of multiple comparison procedures. Tukey's 'honestly significant difference' (HSD) test is one of the oldest and is still routinely used. For the sake of simplicity, we will focus on just this test here. Figure 8.22 lists all the different comparisons between the five groups (defined by mother's interest in education).

Figure 8.22 Comparisons between the five groups (defined by mother's interest in education).

Multiple Comparisons

Dependent Variable: n926 2T Mathematics test score
Tukey HSD

(I) n852 2S Mothers' interest in child's education	(J) n852 2S Mothers' interest in child's education	Mean Difference (I-J)	Std. Error	Sig.	95% Confidence Interval	
					Lower Bound	Upper Bound
1 Over concerned	2 Very interested	-4.202*	.429	.000	-5.37	-3.03
	3 Some interest	3.528*	.429	.000	2.36	4.70
	4 Little interest	8.247*	.460	.000	6.99	9.50
	5 Can't say	4.339*	.470	.000	3.06	5.62
2 Very interested	1 Over concerned	4.202*	.429	.000	3.03	5.37
	3 Some interest	7.729*	.189	.000	7.21	8.24
	4 Little interest	12.449*	.252	.000	11.76	13.14
	5 Can't say	8.540*	.269	.000	7.81	9.27
3 Some interest	1 Over concerned	-3.528*	.429	.000	-4.70	-2.36
	2 Very interested	-7.729*	.189	.000	-8.24	-7.21
	4 Little interest	4.720*	.252	.000	4.03	5.41
	5 Can't say	.811*	.269	.022	.08	1.55
4 Little interest	1 Over concerned	-8.247*	.460	.000	-9.50	-6.99
	2 Very interested	-12.449*	.252	.000	-13.14	-11.76
	3 Some interest	-4.720*	.252	.000	-5.41	-4.03
	5 Can't say	-3.909*	.317	.000	-4.77	-3.04
5 Can't say	1 Over concerned	-4.339*	.470	.000	-5.62	-3.06
	2 Very interested	-8.540*	.269	.000	-9.27	-7.81
	3 Some interest	-.811*	.269	.022	-1.55	-.08
	4 Little interest	3.909*	.317	.000	3.04	4.77

*. The mean difference is significant at the .05 level.

Source: Analysis of NCDS data.

The differences between pairs of means are provided in the column labelled Mean Difference (I-J). For example, looking at the first row we can see that the difference between children whose mothers were 'over concerned' and those whose mothers were 'interested' is −4.202, this is 18.07 − 22.27. The column labelled 'Sig.' is the Tukey significance value. This has been 'corrected' to allow for the fact that we are making multiple comparisons between all the different combinations of pairs of means (in this case 20 in all). If you run your eye down the significance column you will see that all the groups are significantly different from each other (i.e. all the values are less than 0.05) even though in some cases the mean difference is relatively small. When interpreting this you should bear in mind that the sample size is relatively large so that even relatively small differences between groups reflect a real (though possibly small) difference within the population.

8.12 Using SPSS to carry out a one-way analysis of variance

In order to carry out a one-way analysis of variance in SPSS, for example to test whether mathematics score (a variable measured on a continuous scale) is associated with mothers' interest in their child's education (a variable measured on a nominal or categorical scale), the first step is to select 'Compare Means' from the 'Analyze' menu and then select 'One-Way Anova . . .'

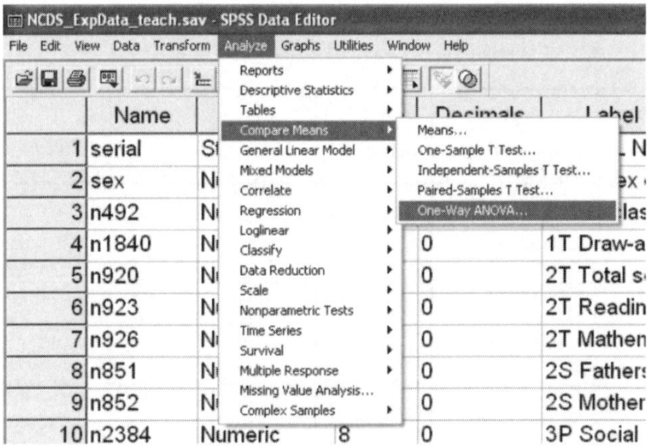

Figure 8.23   Screenshot demonstrating one-way Anova in SPSS.

The next step is to specify the 'dependent' variable, and you should note that this will be the variable measured on a continuous or 'interval' scale. In this case mathematics test score at age 11. It is this variable that will be summarized using mean values. The 'Factor' or categorical variable in the analysis must also be specified. This is the variable that will define the separate groups for which means will

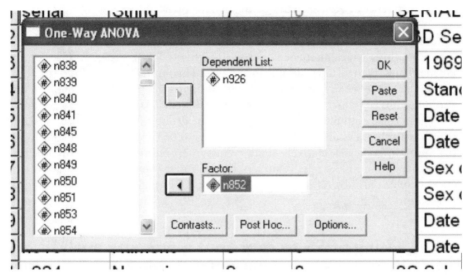

Figure 8.24 Screenshot demonstrating specification of one-way Anova in SPSS.

be calculated. In this example it is the nominal variable that records a mother's interest in her child's education at age 11.

The One-Way Analysis of Variance procedure in SPSS only allows the researcher to specify a single factor for the analysis. For more complicated analysis where you may, for example, want to examine the association between mothers' interest in education and mathematics test scores at age 11, *separately for boys and girls*, the General Linear Modelling procedure should be used. For more details about this, see Norusis (2005).

The next stage is to click on the 'Post Hoc . . .' button and to specify the multiple comparison procedure you wish SPSS to use. As was discussed above, this will enable you to identify which specific groups are significantly different from each other. In this case we have selected 'Tukey' see figure 8.25.

Click on 'Continue' and then click on the 'Options . . .' button in order to specify that you would like descriptive statistics displayed.

The 'Continue' button will return you to the main One-Way Anova dialogue box, where clicking the 'OK' button will simply run the analysis, or clicking the 'Paste' button will paste the syntax into a syntax window. The syntax associated with this example is as follows:

```
ONEWAY
    n926 BY n852
    /STATISTICS DESCRIPTIVES
    /MISSING ANALYSIS
    /POSTHOC = TUKEY ALPHA(.05).
```

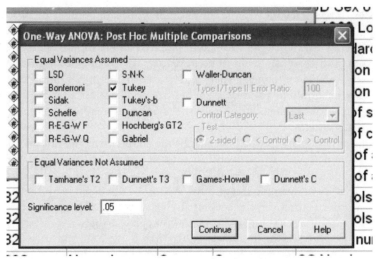

Figure 8.25   Screenshot demonstrating specification of post-hoc comparisons for one-way Anova in SPSS.

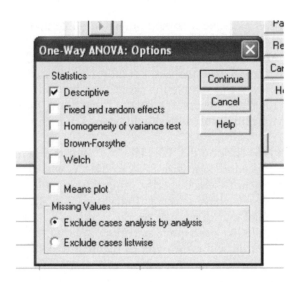

Figure 8.26   Screenshot demonstrating specification of display options for one-way Anova in SPSS.

8.13 Conclusion

This chapter had three methodological aims. First, a useful graphical device known as the boxplot was introduced, which facilitated focused comparison. Secondly, a rigorous definition of an unusual data point was given; a rule of thumb for identifying unusual values relative to the midspread in the main body of the data was advanced. The third goal was to introduce statistical techniques for testing associations between categorical (nominal level) variables and continuous (interval level) variables or in other words for comparing two or more groups.

Despite being used since the 1930s, boxplots are rarely shown in newspapers or on television and currently seem to be in regular use by only a minority of statisticians (Reese, 2005). However, their wider use for the presentation of different batches of data should be promoted as they are excellent for allowing researchers simultaneously to take account of both the level and spread when comparing different batches of data.

The substantive theme of the first part of the chapter was the rate of unemployment in Britain. Despite the relatively low rates of unemployment in Britain in 2005, particularly compared with the mid-1980s, we saw that there is still considerable regional variation in unemployment rates. As will be discussed in more detail in the appendix to this chapter (on the accompanying website), although unemployment statistics are useful in enabling us to make comparisons between different regions and different countries, we should be aware that, as with all statistics, unemployment rates come with a certain amount of conceptual and political baggage.

Exercises

8.1 The midspread (i.e. the distance between the upper and lower quartile) of the sample of unemployment rates drawn from all regions was 2.5 per cent (figure 8.3). If region had no effect on unemployment, what would you expect the residual midspread to be once the regional median was fitted? At the other extreme, what would the residual variation be if an area's unemployment level could be predicted perfectly from its region?

8.2 Figure 8.27 displays the boxplots for economic inactivity rates in London and the South East. What does this tell us about levels and variation in economic activity rates in these two regions? Southampton and Oxford are both identified as outliers, having high rates of economic inactivity compared with the rest of the South East. Would they be classified as outliers if they were districts within London? Why / Why not?

8.3 The output below in figure 8.28 results from a one-way analysis of variance examining the impact of father's interest in education on child's mathematics test score at age 11. How do the results compare with those shown in figure 8.20 for mother's interest in child's education?

8.4 Using the teaching dataset NCDS_ExpData_Teach, use boxplots and the One Way analysis of variance procedure to explore the mathematics test score at age 11 of children with fathers in different social classes at the child's birth.

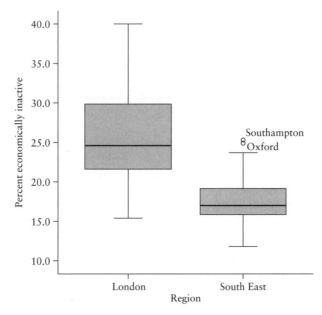

Figure 8.27 Boxplots for economic inactivity rates in London and the South East.

Figure 8.28 Results from a one-way analysis of variance examining the impact of father's interest in education on child's mathematics test score at age 11.

Descriptives

n926 2T Mathematics test score

	N	Mean	Std. Deviation	Std. Error	95% Confidence Interval for Mean		Minimum	Maximum
					Lower Bound	Upper Bound		
1 Over concerned	344	18.35	9.748	.526	17.32	19.39	0	39
2 Very interested	3679	23.64	9.561	.158	23.33	23.95	0	40
3 Some interest	3494	16.04	9.394	.159	15.73	16.35	0	40
4 Little interest	2332	10.37	8.043	.167	10.05	10.70	0	39
5 Can't say	3293	14.19	9.346	.163	13.87	14.51	0	40
Total	13142	16.76	10.356	.090	16.58	16.94	0	40

ANOVA

n926 2T Mathematics test score

	Sum of Squares	df	Mean Square	F	Sig.
Between Groups	293847.6	4	73461.911	865.237	.000
Within Groups	1115381	13137	84.904		
Total	1409229	13141			

9

Scatterplots and Resistant Lines

9.1 Introduction: lone parents and deprivation

Over recent decades the proportion of households headed by lone parents has increased dramatically. This increase has been observed across Western Europe but is particularly marked in Britain. Whereas in Britain in 1971, 8 per cent of households with dependent children were headed by a lone parent (i.e. less than one in ten), by 1991 this figure had increased to 20 per cent and by 2001 it had increased still further so that nearly a quarter (22.9 per cent) of children were living in a household headed by a lone parent, and over 90 per cent of these children were living with a lone mother. Research regularly shows that households headed by a lone mother are strikingly worse off than other households in Britain. This is largely because the many lone mothers are not in paid work and are therefore reliant on state benefits. Due to the association between material deprivation and lone parenthood, many commentators have focused on the growth in lone parent families as a social problem. The New Deal for Lone Parents, launched across Britain by the Labour government in 1998, is one response to this problem and represents an attempt to help more lone mothers into paid employment. However, others have portrayed the dramatic increase in lone parents, and particularly single, never-married mothers, as a social threat. In particular, during the 1990s, Charles Murray, an American academic, wrote a number of polemic articles highlighting the concentration of large percentages of lone parents in particular areas of Britain and warning that in neighbourhoods with concentrations of un-married mothers, children would lack positive male role models and that this would lead to high levels of crime and unemployment.

In this chapter we will start by using data from the 2001 Census to look at the relationship between the proportion of lone parents in an area and other measures of deprivation, such as the percentage of households with no access to a car or van, levels of overcrowding, the percentage unemployed and percentage long-term unemployed. In these analyses the *unit of analysis* can be understood as a region, neighbourhood or local authority area. Data from the Census are readily available at the level of the local authority. For example, statistics from the Census website tell us that Liverpool has 2.4 per cent long-term unemployed compared with only

0.3 per cent in South Oxfordshire (in the 2001 Census an individual was classified as long-term unemployed if they had not worked since 1999 or earlier). In
addition, while in Liverpool 11.5 per cent of households consist of a lone parent
with dependent children, in South Oxfordshire the figure is 4.1 per cent.

The methodological focus of this chapter is to learn techniques for dealing
with the relationship between two interval level variables. Such data are often
called paired, *X–Y* data, since for each case we have a pair of values which we
want to display together. We will learn how to construct a suitable display and
how to interpret it and summarize it effectively. Chapters 1 and 2 are essential
reading for understanding this chapter, and chapter 3 also provides useful
background.

The techniques described in this chapter can also be used to analyse data at the
level of the individual, rather than using local authorities as the unit of analysis.
Towards the end of the chapter this will be illustrated by looking at the relationship between mathematics scores at age 16 and general ability scores at age 11,
using data from the National Child Development Study.

9.2 Scatterplots

To depict the information about the value of two interval level variables at once,
each case is plotted on a graph known as a **scatterplot**, such as figure 9.1. Visual
inspection of well-drawn scatterplots of paired data can be one of the most effective ways of spotting important features of a relationship.

A scatterplot has two **axes** – a vertical axis, conventionally labelled *Y* and a horizontal axis, labelled *X*. The variable that is thought of as a cause (the explanatory variable) is placed on the *X*-axis and the variable that is thought of as an effect
(the response variable) is placed on the *Y*-axis. Each case is entered on the plot at
the point representing its *X* and *Y* values.

Scatterplots depict bivariate relationships. To show a third variable would
require a three-dimensional space, and to show four would be impossible.

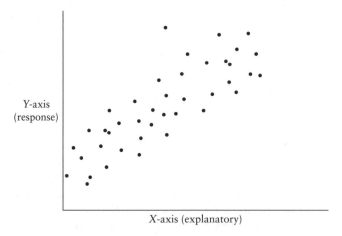

Figure 9.1   A scatterplot showing a moderately strong relationship.

However, the value of a third nominal variable can often usefully be shown by using a different symbol for each value of a third variable.

Scatterplots are inspected to see if there is any sort of pattern visible, to see if the value of Y could be predicted from the value of X, or if the relationship is patternless. If there does appear to be something interesting going on, there are several further useful questions that we can ask:

1. Is the relationship **monotonic**? In other words, does Y rise or fall consistently as X rises? The relationship in figure 9.1 is monotonic. A U-shaped relationship would not be.
2. Are the variables positively or negatively related? Do the points slope from bottom left to top right (positive) or from top left to bottom right (negative)?
3. Can the relationship be summarized as a straight line or will it need a curve?
4. How much effect does X have on Y? In other words, how much does Y increase (or decrease) for every unit increase of X?
5. How highly do the variables **correlate**? In other words, how tightly do the points cluster around a fitted line or curve?
6. Are there any gaps in the plot? Do we have examples smoothly ranged across the whole scale of X and Y, or are there gaps and discontinuities? Caution may need to be exercised when one is making statements about the relationship in the gap.
7. Are there any obvious outliers? One of the major goals of plotting is to draw attention to any unusual data points.

In this chapter we will investigate the answers to some of these questions by using Census data to explore how the concentration of lone parents in an area is associated with other measures of deprivation.

9.3 Lone parents

The data in figure 9.2 relate to the percentage of households that are headed by a lone parent and contain dependent children, and the percentage of households

Figure 9.2   Lone parent households and households with no car or van, % by region.

Government Office Region (2001)	% Lone parent households	% Households with no car or van
North East	7.35	35.94
North West	7.67	30.21
Yorkshire/Humber	6.58	30.31
East Midlands	6.08	24.25
West Midlands	6.73	26.77
Eastern	5.29	19.80
London	7.60	37.49
South East	5.22	19.43
South West	5.42	20.21
Wales	7.28	25.95

Source: 2001 Census.

that have no car or van for each of the ten Government Office Regions of England and Wales.

9.4 Linear relationships

The scatterplot of the percentage of lone parent households by the percentage of households with no car or van is shown in figure 9.3. The pattern is not terribly tight, but inspection of the plot suggests a monotonic, positive relationship. In other words, as the percentage of lone parent households in a region increases, the percentage of households with no car or van also increases.

In order to summarize the relationship between two interval-level variables, we will try to fit a line if we possibly can. When describing the apparent relationship, instead of making the somewhat vague generalization 'the higher the X, the higher the Y', the linear summary permits a more precise generalization 'every time X goes up a certain amount, Y seems to go up a specified multiple of that amount'.

Straight lines are easy to visualize and to draw on a graph, but they can also be expressed algebraically. Equations of the form:

$$Y = a + bX$$

always describe lines. In this equation, Y and X are the variables, and a and b are coefficients that quantify any particular line; figure 9.4 shows this diagrammatically.

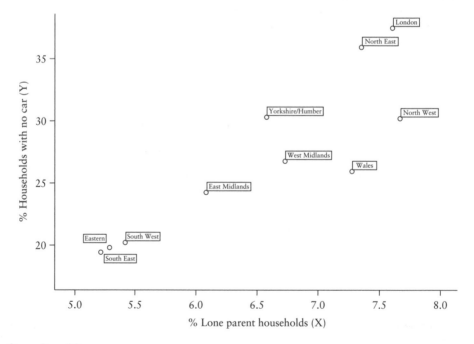

Source: Figure 9.2.

Figure 9.3   Lone parent households by households with no car or van: scatterplot.

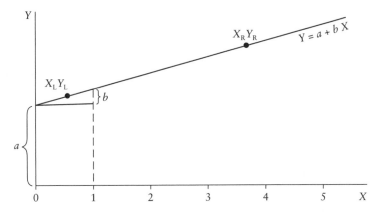

Figure 9.4 Anatomy of a straight line.

The degree of **slope** or gradient of the line is given by the coefficient b; the steeper the slope, the bigger the value of b. As we can see from figure 9.4, the coefficient b gives a measure of how much Y increases for a unit increase in the value of X. The slope is usually the item of scientific interest, showing how much change in Y is associated with a given change in X. The **intercept** a is the value of Y when X is zero, or where the line starts. Frequently, the intercept makes little substantive sense – for example, a mortality rate of zero is an impossibility. This value is also sometimes described as the **constant**.

The slope of a line can be derived from any two points on it. If we choose two points **on the line**, one on the left-hand side with a low X value (called X_L, Y_L), and one on the right with a high X value (called X_R, Y_R), then the slope is

$$\frac{Y_R - Y_L}{X_R - X_L}$$

If the line slopes from top left to bottom right, $Y_R - Y_L$ will be negative and thus the slope will be negative.

We only want to try to run a straight line through a cloud of data points if the relationship looks linear. *Never* try to fit a line before you have plotted the data to see if it is a sensible thing to do.

9.5 Where to draw the line?

Let us turn now to the relationship between the percentage of lone parent households and the percentage of households with no car in each region. Inspection of the scatterplot suggested that it would be worth trying to fit a line. The task is to find one which will come as near as possible to the data points. A technique such as smoothing, discussed in chapter 5, will not do because it does not ordinarily produce a linear outcome. One possibility would be to try and draw a straight line through the points by eye. However, drawing a line so roughly has its limitations: the eye can deceive and the heart may secretly desire a particular outcome. It would be better to fit a line which met some predetermined criterion. There are many different rules one could try to follow:

1. Make half the points lie above the line and half below along the full length of the line.
2. Make each point as near to the line as possible (minimizing distances perpendicular to the line).
3. Make each point as near to the line in the Y direction as possible (minimizing vertical distances).
4. Make the squared distance between each point and the line in the Y direction as small as possible (minimizing squared vertical distances).

The choice of criterion is a matter of judgement. When drawing a line by eye, many people seem to try to follow rule 1 or rule 2. The technique explained in the first half of this chapter, resistant line fitting, produces a line which makes the absolute value of the deviations in the Y direction as small as possible (rule 3). Another very popular criterion for line fitting is minimizing squared deviations from the line in the Y direction (rule 4). This technique is known as **linear regression** and will be covered in the second half of the chapter.

9.6 Fitting a resistant line

One simple method of line fitting involves joining two typical points: the X-axis is roughly divided into three parts, conditional summary points for X and Y are found in each of the end thirds, and then a line is drawn connecting the right-hand and left-hand summary points. We choose to use the outer thirds because we want the line to be drawn between two points as far away from each other as possible without being so far out that they risk being unreliable.

Ordering and grouping

In dividing the X-axis, the aim is to get one-third of the cases into each of the three parts. To do this, the cases are reordered so that the X values are in order, as shown in the first two columns of figure 9.5. Notice that the corresponding Y value has been kept with each X, and the Y values are therefore not in order. (Ignore the third and fourth columns for now.)

Dividing the X-axis into three is in principle straightforward, but in practice there are snags, especially where there are not many data points. Here are guidelines which are usually helpful:

1. The X-axis should be divided into three approximately equal lengths.
2. There should be an equal number of data points in each third.
3. The left and the right batch should be balanced, with an equal number of data points in each.

Figure 9.5   Worksheet for calculating a resistant line.

	1 X	2 Y	3 Fit Y *	4 Residual Y
South East	5.22	19.43	18.39	1.04
Eastern	5.29	19.8	18.88	0.92
South West	5.42	20.21	19.79	0.42
East Midlands	6.08	24.25	24.40	−0.15
Yorkshire/Humber	6.58	30.31	27.89	2.42
West Midlands	6.73	26.77	28.94	−2.17
Wales	7.28	25.95	32.79	−6.84
North East	7.35	35.94	33.28	2.66
London	7.6	37.49	35.02	2.47
North West	7.67	30.21	35.51	−5.30

Source: X and Y data from figure 9.2.

* Y has been fitted by the equation Y = −18.1 + 6.99X: this is explained in section 9.6.

4. Any points which have the same X value must go into the same third.
5. No subdivision of the X-axis should account for more than half the range of the X-values found in the data.

Since these rules are not always compatible, compromises will be needed. In this example, the number of data points is not an exact multiple of three, so the second guideline could not be met; balance in the two outer batches has been preserved by putting three points into each of them and four into the middle.

Obtaining the summary value

A summary X and Y value must now be found within each third. The summary X value is the median X in each third; in the first third of the data, the summary X value is 5.29, the value for the Eastern region. Similarly, the median Y in each third becomes the summary Y value, here 19.8. **This does not have to be the value paired with the summary value for X,** although in this instance it happens also to be the value for the Eastern region.

The summary X and Y values for each of our batches can be read off figure 9.5:

$$X_L = 5.29 \quad Y_L = 19.8$$

$$X_M = 6.66 \quad Y_M = 26.36$$

$$X_R = 7.6 \quad Y_R = 35.94$$

It is left to the reader to plot these points on figure 9.3, and to connect the first and third.

The middle summary point is not used to draw a straight line, but it should not lie too far from the line if the underlying relationship really is linear. It can be used to provide a more systematic evaluation of linearity.

The method involves calculating two **half-slopes**: the left-hand half-slope is calculated between the first and the middle summary point, and the right-hand half-slope between the middle and the third point. If the half-slopes are nearly equal, the relationship is fairly linear. If one is more than double the other, we should not fit a straight line.

Deriving the coefficients of the line

The slope and the intercept could be read off a graph. It is, however, quicker and more accurate to calculate them arithmetically from the summary points. The slope is given by

$$\frac{Y_R - Y_L}{X_R - X_L} = \frac{35.94 - 19.8}{7.6 - 5.29} = 6.99$$

This is not very different from the slope of the eyeballed line.

The intercept is the value of Y when X is zero, often a pretty meaningless value and in this case suggesting the percentage of households with no car or van if there were no lone parent households in a region. We can just treat this as a scaling factor, needed to predict a given Y value from a given X value. It is obtained by inverting the equation for a line. If $Y = a + bX$, then $a = Y - bX$. Either the upper or lower summary X values could be used to find the intercept: $a = Y_R - bX_R$, for example. But we will get a more accurate estimate of the intercept if the mean of all three summary values is used:

$$a_R = Y_R - bX_R = 35.94 - (6.99 \times 7.6) = -17.1$$

$$a_M = Y_M - bX_M = 26.36 - (6.99 \times 6.66) = -20.2$$

$$a_L = Y_L - bX_L = 19.8 - (6.99 \times 5.29) = -17.1$$

Because we used the upper and lower summary points in finding the slope, the a_L and a_R estimates will always be the same. The intercept is given by the average of -17.1, -20.2 and -17.1, i.e. -18.1. As noted above, this figure is meaningless if we try to apply it to the real world, as it is not possible to have a negative percentage of households without a car or van (percentages must vary between 0 and 100 in this case). However the intercept has a role to play within the equation of a straight line.

The full prediction equation for each region is therefore:

$$\% \text{ no car} = -18.1 + (6.99 \times \% \text{ lone parent})$$

We would predict, for instance, that the South East, with only 5.22 per cent of households headed by a lone parent, would have a percentage of households with no car of:

$$18.1 + (6.99 \times 0.0522) \text{ or } 18.39$$

We can find such a predicted, or fitted, value for each case. The full set of predicted values is shown in column 3 of figure 9.5; the column is headed $\hat{Y}$ (pronounced 'Y-hat'), a common notation for fitted values.

In fact, in the South East the percentage of households with no car is 1.04 higher than the predicted 18.39, namely 19.43. Residuals from the fitted values can also be calculated for each region, and these are shown in column 4 of figure 9.5. Now all the data values can be recast in the traditional DFR form:

$$\text{Data } (19.43) = \text{Fit } (18.39) + \text{Residual } (1.04)$$

As was mentioned above, this simple technique for fitting the 'best' straight line through the scatterplot minimizes the total sum of these residual values. Inspection of the column of residuals in figure 9.5 shows that most of the residuals are relatively small compared with the observed values (Y) of the percentage of households without a car. The two residuals which stand out as being rather larger in magnitude than the rest are for Wales and the North West. Both these regions would appear to have a lower percentage of households without a car than would be predicted based on the percentage of households headed by a lone parent in the region. With such a small dataset it is difficult to draw any firm conclusions from the residuals but methods for examining the residuals to assess the fit of the line will be returned to below.

This 'pencil and paper' example, with a relatively small number of cases (ten Government Office Regions) has been used to demonstrate how a straight line can be used to describe the relationship between two interval level variables and to show how a straight line can simply be defined in terms of a slope and a constant. However, the wide availability of personal computers and statistical packages such as SPSS or spreadsheets such as Excel make it rare for researchers to use this 'pencil and paper' technique for fitting a straight line. Before discussing the residuals in more detail, let us therefore move on to consider a slightly more 'real' example. In the following example we will also focus on the association between the percentage of lone parent households and the percentage of households without a car. However, rather than looking at data aggregated to regional level we will examine data from each of the 376 local authorities in England and Wales.

9.7 Using SPSS to fit a resistant line

In order to create a scatterplot using SPSS, go to the *Graphs* menu and select *Scatter* (see figure 9.6).
Once you select Scatter, a dialogue box will appear as in figure 9.7.
Choose *Simple* and then *Define*. A new dialogue box will appear so that you can select the two variables you wish to plot see figure 9.8.
As in the simple example given in figure 9.3, we wish to plot the percentage of lone parent households on the X axis and the percentage of households without a car or van on the Y axis. We therefore select these variables and transfer them to the appropriate boxes. Click OK and the output in figure 9.9 will be generated.

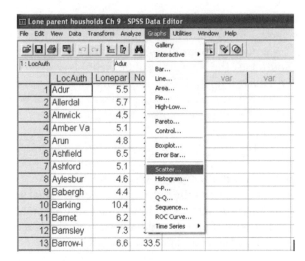

Figure 9.6 Using SPSS to create a scatterplot.

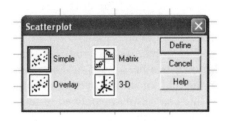

Figure 9.7 Choosing the type of scatterplot in SPSS.

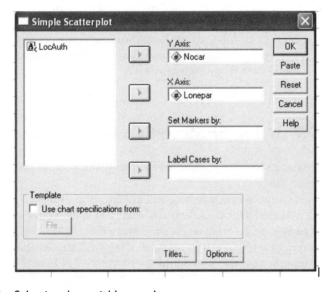

Figure 9.8 Selecting the variables to plot.

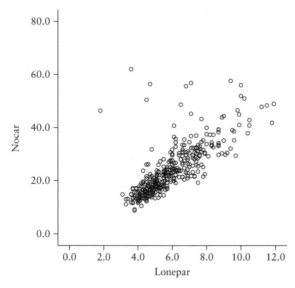

Figure 9.9 Percentage of lone parents and car ownership.

There are many more points plotted on this graph than in figure 9.3, but the basic principle is the same. In this example each circle represents a single Local Authority with a specific percentage of lone parent households and an associated percentage of households with no car or van. Where lots of cases are clustered together the plot looks rather messy but the scatterplot in figure 9.9 suggests a moderately strong relationship between the two variables. Local Authorities with a large percentage of lone parent households also tend to have a large percentage of households with no car or van.

Using SPSS, the plot can be modified slightly to display a fitted line to summarize this relationship. Double click on the chart to open the Chart editor, then select all the plotted points and then click on the icon to add a 'fit line'.

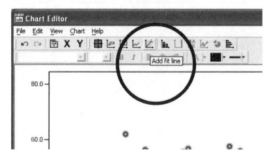

Figure 9.10 Using SPSS to add a fit line.

This will produce a plot, like the one shown in figure 9.11, that includes a regression line. This example has also been annotated to indicate two outliers, both with relatively low percentages of lone parent households, but high percentages of households with no car or van. How would you explain the reasons behind these

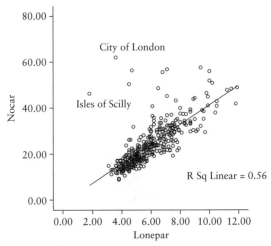

Figure 9.11   Percentage of lone parents and car ownership including a resistant line.

two outliers? In other words why do you think these two places have such a high percentage of households with no cars even though the percentage of lone parent households is relatively low?

We can also use SPSS to provide the equation of this straight line by using Regression analysis. To do this select Analyze, Regression and then Linear as in figure 9.12.

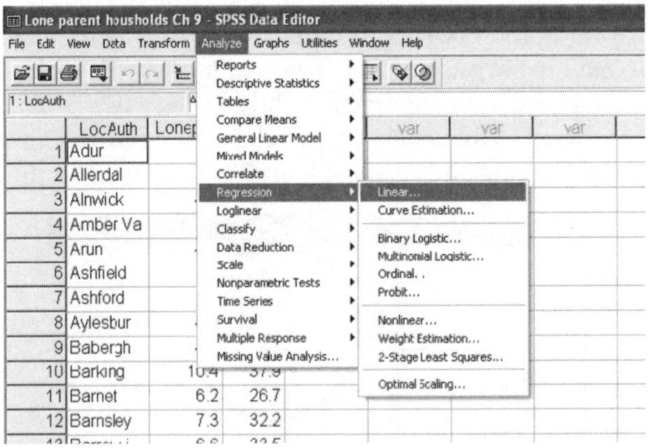

Figure 9.12   Using regression analysis in SPSS to provide an equation for a straight line.

This will produce the dialogue box shown in figure 9.13, which you can use to specify the dependent variable 'Nocar' and the independent variable 'Lonepar'.

Next click on OK to get the output shown in figure 9.14.

The 'Model Summary' provides an indication of how well the line fits the data. The value R square is used to indicate what proportion of variance in the dependent variable (% households without car) is 'explained' by the variance in the

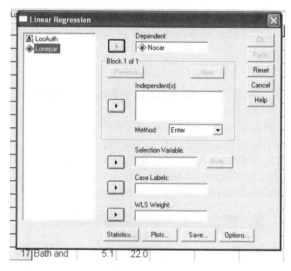

Figure 9.13 Specifying the dependent and independent variables in SPSS.

independent variable (% lone parent households). You will see that by default this figure of 0.56 is also provided in figure 9.11.

The table of coefficients provides the figures we need to define the straight line plotted in figure 9.11. We can see that the constant is −1.34 and the slope is 4.26. In other words

$$\% \text{ households without a car} = 4.26(\% \text{ lonepar}) - 1.34$$

Therefore if a local authority has 8 per cent of lone parent households we would predict it to have 32.74 per cent households without a car. Inspection of figure 9.11

Figure 9.14 A model summary produced by SPSS.

Model Summary

Model	R	R Square	Adjusted R Square	Std. Error of the Estimate
1	.749(a)	.560	.559	6.3718

a Predictors: (Constant), Lonepar

Coefficients(a)

Model		Unstandardized Coefficients		Standardized Coefficients	t	Sig.
		B	Std. Error	Beta		
1	(Constant)	-1.341	1.203		-1.115	.266
	Lonepar	4.263	.195	.749	21.832	.000

a Dependent Variable: Nocar

suggests that this is indeed a plausible figure. For example, inspection of data from the 2001 Census shows that Hastings has 8 per cent households headed by a lone parent and has 33.8 per cent of households with no access to a car or van.

9.8 Inspection of residuals

In the same way that it is possible to calculate fitted or 'predicted' values and residuals when fitting a line by hand (as shown in section 9.6 and figure 9.5), it is also possible to use SPSS to calculate predicted values and residuals as part of the regression analysis discussed above. Once you have specified the dependent and independent variables click on the Save button see figure 9.15A. Then check

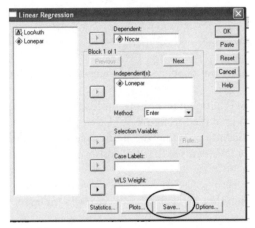

Figure 9.15A Using SPSS to save predicted values and residuals as part of the regression analysis.

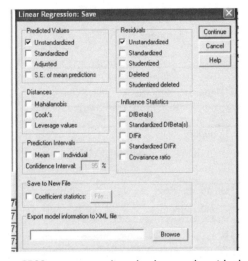

Figure 9.15B Using SPSS to save predicted values and residuals as part of the regression analysis.

the boxes to indicate that you want the predicted values and residuals saved, and the SPSS program will automatically create two new variables 'PRE_1' and 'RES_1' for the predicted values and residuals see figure 9.15B. In addition the output will include a listing of any residual values that are particularly high (i.e. with a standardized value of more than 3).

In this example figure 9.16 shows the unusually large residuals.

Figure 9.16   The SPSS output identifying unusually large residuals.

Casewise Diagnostics(a)

Case Number	Std. Residual	Nocar
1	6.273	46.3
7	7.533	62.0
76	5.110	50.4
107	5.918	56.4
255	3.489	48.6
270	4.387	55.6
292	4.375	56.8

a Dependent Variable: Nocar

By examining the original data from the 2001 Census it is possible to identify that these residuals are for the following local authorities: Isles of Scilly; City of London; Kensington; Westminster; Hammersmith; Camden; and Tower Hamlets.

In each case the residual is positive which means that there is a *higher* percentage of households with no car than would be expected given the percentage of households headed by a lone parent. A little knowledge of the local authorities in question suggests that with the exception of the Isles of Scilly, all the other local authorities are in London, where traffic congestion is a real problem and public transport is relatively good, so that some households may be choosing not to run a car. This means that in these localities access to a car is a less reliable measure of deprivation than in other areas. The Isles of Scilly are accessible only by boat and helicopter and it is perhaps unsurprising that the levels of car ownership are relatively low.

Having automatically calculated the residuals using SPSS they can also be displayed as a histogram. We would always like residuals from a fit to be small and patternless. This means that a histogram of the residuals should be approximately normally distributed and centred around zero. In figure 9.17 we can see that the histogram of the residuals in the current example is centred around zero but that it is slightly positively skewed (with a tail of positive residuals straggling upwards).

The residuals can also be used to indicate whether we have fitted the correct functional form or not. For this purpose, they are best plotted against predicted Y values. If the relationship is mildly curvy, or if the spread of the Y values is not constant for all X values, this may stand out more clearly in the plot of residual Y versus fitted Y than in the original scatterplot. What to do if the relationship is curved is discussed fully in the next chapter.

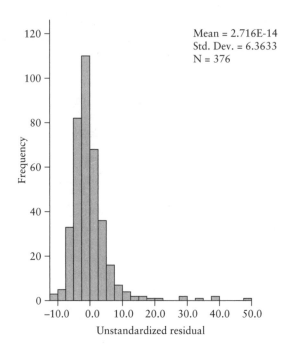

Figure 9.17 Residuals from regression of nocar on lonepar.

9.9 Further examples

So far we have concentrated on using scatterplots and resistant lines to examine the relationship between the percentage of households headed by a lone parent and the percentage of households with no access to a car or van. However, the same techniques can be used to explore the relationship between any two variables measured on a continuous or 'interval' scale. For example figure 9.18 shows a scatterplot illustrating the relationship between the percentage of people aged 16–74 who are unemployed and the percentage of households living in owner occupied accommodation, in each local authority. The pattern is rather different from that shown in figure 9.11 in two respects. First it can be seen that there is a negative relationship between the two variables, so that as the percentage unemployed in each local authority *increases* the percentage of households that are owner occupied *decreases*. Second the points are not clustered so tightly around the line of best fit and this is also reflected in the slightly lower value of R square which is 0.49 compared with a value of 0.56 in figure 9.11.

In all the examples discussed so far, the unit of analysis has been a geographical area. In section 9.4 the focus was on government regions, while from section 9.7 onwards the focus has been on local authorities. However, the technique of drawing scatterplots and constructing resistant lines is just as effective when the unit of analysis is the individual, as long as the variables of interest are still measured on an interval scale. For example, figure 9.19 displays a scatterplot showing the relationship between children's ability scores at age 11 and their mathematics scores at age 16, using data from the National Child Development Study. As

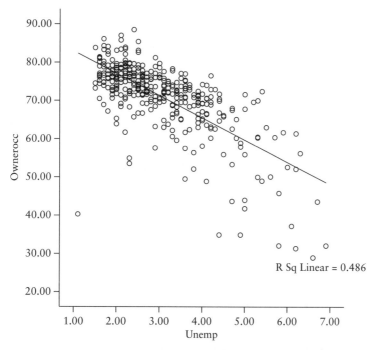

Figure 9.18 Unemployment rate and proportion of households that are owner occupied.

would be expected there is a positive relationship between these two variables such that the higher a child's general ability score at age 11, the higher their mathematics score at age 16 is likely to be. By using regression analysis in SPSS to calculate the equation of this straight line we obtain the output in figure 9.19. As discussed previously, the value of R square, in the model summary, indicates what proportion of the variance in children's mathematics scores at age 16 is accounted for by the variance in ability scores at age 11 – this figure is 0.47. It is the table of coefficients that provides us with the equation of the straight line plotted in figure 9.19. In this case the constant is: −.310 and the slope, or gradient, of the line is 0.301. In other words, for every additional mark scored at age 11 we would predict the child to score an additional 0.301 marks in the mathematics test at age 16. This means that we would predict a child who scored 50 in the ability test at age 11 to score 14.74 in the mathematics test at age 16.

The unstandardized residuals from the regression analysis are displayed in figure 9.20. The fact that they are normally distributed and centred around 0 is further confirmation that there is a linear relationship between ability at 11 and mathematics score at age 16. However, the existence of these residuals highlights the fact that the ability scores at age 11 do not perfectly predict the maths scores at age 16. This is partly because the scores at each age do not provide a perfect measure of the child's ability and partly because there will be other factors that are likely to have an impact on a child's maths score at age 16. Although this chapter has only introduced scatterplots and regression as

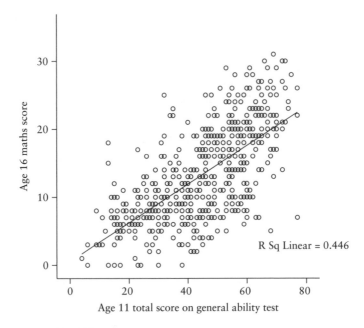

Model Summary

Model	R	R Square	Adjusted R Square	Std. Error of the Estimate
1	.683(a)	.466	.466	5.112

a Predictors: (Constant), n2totsc Age 11 total score on general ability test

Coefficients(a)

Model		Unstandardized Coefficients		Standardized Coefficients	t	Sig.
		B	Std. Error	Beta		
1	(Constant)	-.310	.148		-2.096	.036
	n2totsc Age 11 total score on general ability test	.301	.003	.683	94.848	.000

a Dependent Variable: n3maths Age 16 maths score

Figure 9.19 Scatterplot of mathematics score at age 16 by general ability test score at age 11.

techniques for looking at the relationships between two variables, the next chapter will extend this discussion to demonstrate how we can quantify the relationship between a number of different independent variables and a single dependent variable.

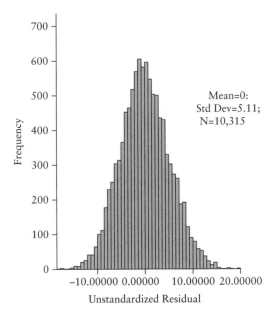

Figure 9.20   Residuals from regression of mathematics score at age 16 on general ability at age 11.

9.10 Conclusion

In this chapter we have used Census data to look at the association between the percentage of lone parents and measures of deprivation such as the percentage of households without access to a car. The relationship was first examined by means of a useful pictorial device: the scatterplot. This relationship was next summarized by fitting a straight line. The strength of the association was given by the slope of this line, indicating how the percentage of households without access to a car goes up for each point increase in the percentage of lone parent households.

In the second half of the chapter the technique was extended to a much larger number of cases by using the Multiple Regression procedure in the SPSS package. In regression, the criterion for line fitting is to minimize the sum of the squared residuals, the 'least-squares' rule 4 of section 9.5. It is the variance, not the midspread, which is broken down into a fitted ('explained') and residual ('unexplained') component. The correlation is given by the Pearson's correlation coefficient r. Regression techniques have their advantages: the lines can be derived in one fell swoop from a formula, and do not require iterating. Moreover, if the residuals are well behaved (Gaussian, without freak values) then the calculation of the likely error associated with the coefficients is fairly straightforward.

However, error terms are often highly non-Gaussian, and outliers from the line are the rule rather than the exception. Regression techniques, because they set out to make the *squared* distances of the residuals from the line as small as possible, can be unduly influenced by a few exceptional data points. They are therefore much less resistant than the pencil and paper techniques introduced in the first half of this chapter.

The slope, b, is mathematically very close to the proportion difference, d. It is an asymmetric measure, just like d: the slope depends on which variable is treated as the response variable, just as d depends on which way the percentages have been run. Exercise 9.2 has been set to illustrate this.

Exercises

9.1   A key assumption in economics is that money can be used to buy things that satisfy people's wants and make them happy ('utilities'). Surveys *within* different countries seem to confirm this. The wealthier people in those countries are actually happier than the poorer. The data in figure 9.21, assembled by Easterlin (1974, p. 105), however, examined the relationship *across* various countries from surveys conducted around 1960; the personal happiness rating was the average reply to a scale where 0 indicated that respondents were very unhappy and 10 that they were very happy.

   If money can buy happiness, what would you expect the relationship between the two variables to look like? Plot the data points and discuss the apparent relationship. Then calculate a resistant line and find the slope and intercept. How well does the line summarize the scatterplot? Polish the fit and adjust your estimate of the slope.

9.2   Plot the two variables in figure 9.2 the other way round from the plot in figure 9.3, as if one wanted to predict the percentage of households headed by a lone parent in each region from the percentage of households with no access to a car or van. Draw in a line by eye, read off the slope and intercept, and confirm that the line is different from the line fitted in the chapter.

9.3   It is hard to assess the IQ of young children. Rather than set formal tests, some researchers prefer to base their inferences on the child's performance on less formal tasks; the Goodenough draw-a-man test, for example, scores

Figure 9.21   Rating of personal happiness by real GNP per head.

	Rating of personal happiness	Real GNP per head ($US)
United States	6.6	2790
Cuba	6.4	516
Egypt	5.5	225
Israel	5.3	1027
West Germany	5.3	1860
Japan	5.2	613
Yugoslavia	5.0	489
Philippines	4.9	282
Panama	4.8	371
Nigeria	4.8	134
Brazil	4.6	375
Poland	4.4	702
India	3.7	140
Dominican Republic	1.6	313

Source: Easterlin, 1974.

how sophisticated children's pictures are. Other researchers have criticized this test for being insufficiently rigorous. The dataset NCDS_ExpData_Teach contains the results of the Goodenough test at age 7 and standard tests of verbal and non-verbal ability at age 11. Using SPSS, plot the score on general ability test at age 11 against the Goodenough test scores, and fit a resistant line. How well do you think the Goodenough test at 7 predicts general ability at 11?

10

Transformations

We will now take up an issue that has been touched on several times before: power transformation of the scale of a variable in order to make its analysis easier. This chapter has been placed after chapter 9 since one of the most appealing uses of such transformations is to unbend curvy lines. However, it follows on very naturally from the introduction to techniques of scaling and standardizing provided in chapter 3, and some may want to read it directly after that. Some of the illustrations require an understanding of boxplots, introduced in chapter 8, and line fitting, introduced in the previous chapter. The substantive focus of this chapter is the list of eight Millennium Development Goals and all the data used in the examples and exercises in this chapter are extracted from the *World Bank, World Development Indicators* (2000).

10.1 The Millennium Development Goals

The stated goal both of leaders of poor nations and of agencies and banks in the richer countries is the 'development' of the poorer countries. The nature of that development, however, has been a matter of some dispute. National income, or its rate of growth, has most often been used in the West to indicate 'success'. For many poorer countries, however, the idea of turning into a replica of one of the industrialized countries, pursuing high money incomes and high growth rates as goals in their own right, appears neither feasible nor desirable.

At the United Nations Millennium Summit in September 2000, world leaders agreed to a set of targets for combating poverty, hunger, disease, illiteracy, environmental degradation and discrimination against women. One of the key features of these targets is that they are time bound and measurable, so that it is possible to track progress towards achieving them. In the year 2000 the aim was to achieve each of the goals by the year 2015. The eight 'Millennium Development Goals' (MDGs) are at the heart of the current global agenda and are intended to provide a framework for the entire UN system to work together towards a common end. Each of the eight goals has a number of associated targets. For example, the first goal, to eradicate extreme poverty and hunger, is operationalized through two main targets: first to halve between 1990 and 2015 the proportion of people whose income is less than one dollar a day, and second to halve between 1990 and 2015 the proportion of people who suffer from hunger. Clearly, indicators are needed in order to monitor progress towards these targets and these are provided by data that are routinely collected by organizations such as the World Bank, the World Health Organization, UNICEF and the International Labour Organization. A list of the Millennium Development Goals, targets, and associated indicators for monitoring progress is available via the UN website at http://unstats.un.org/unsd/mdg/default.aspx under 'Indicators'.

The eight Millennium Development Goals

- Eradicate extreme poverty and hunger
- Achieve universal primary education
- Promote gender equality and empower women
- Reduce child mortality
- Improve maternal health
- Combat HIV/AIDS, malaria and other diseases
- Ensure environmental sustainability
- Develop a global partnership for development

In this chapter we will first take a look at how the most commonly used measure of national wealth – gross national income (GNI) – is constructed, and consider the distribution of GNI across several countries. We will return to the question of whether GNI is in fact a good indicator of well-being later, and consider a newer approach which examines the extent to which the basic human needs of citizens are being met.

Most countries in the world attempt to monitor the total value of their output, or **gross national income**. This can be defined abstractly as the sum of values of both final goods and services and investment goods in a country. Final goods are things that are consumed directly and not used to produce something else. If all goods were included in the estimate of GNI, then the cost of flour would be double-counted when the final cost of bread was included. However, a final good is not easy to operationalize. Logically, even consumption activities such as eating could be viewed as an investment required to sustain the producer; this is perhaps clearer in the case of the agricultural labourer's meal which is essential to production, than the executive's expense-account lunch which may actually impede it. However, rules have been developed to standardize what is to be included in the definition of final product; meals, for example, are always included as final goods.

Goods and services which in some countries are circulated by being exchanged on the market are circulated by the state in others – health care and medicines are a good example. It is clearly desirable that the amount that a nation spends on health be included in the estimate of GNI, so the total expenditures of the state as well as private individuals are included. Moreover, part of a nation's wealth is spent on investment goods, and not on consumption goods. Therefore these are also included in the calculation.

Two methods can be used to estimate GNI. One can either directly estimate the value of all the final goods and services (a variant would be to estimate what every branch of production adds to the value of the goods it uses as raw materials). Or one can assess the earnings which are received by those involved in production, both wages and profits, interest and the like. The job of the statisticians employed by governments to produce national accounts is to piece together the picture as best they can, using both methods, and as much of the available data as possible. Further details of the methods used to calculate GNI in the UK can be found in the 'UK ESA95 Gross National Income Inventory of Methods', which is available on the National Statistics website at www.statistics. gov.uk. Follow the links to: Economy > National accounts > Gross national income.

A distinction is made between domestic product and national income. If one focuses on all the production that takes place within national boundaries, the measure is termed the **gross domestic product** (GDP). If, on the other hand, one focuses on the production that is undertaken by the residents of that country, the income earned by nationals from abroad has to be added to the gross domestic product, to arrive at the gross national income.

In a country where most of the goods and services are exchanged for money, GNI can be defined and estimated fairly reliably, given sufficient care. In countries where large proportions of goods and services are produced by those who consume them, or are exchanged on a very small scale without coming to the market, estimates have to be made, and these are of varying accuracy. 'We should ask national income estimators conceptual questions such as: which of the activities a farm family does for itself without payment, such as haircutting for example, have you included in the national income?', says a leading development economist (Seers, 1979, p. 15).

GNI is commonly used as a measure of well-being of individuals in a country. For this purpose, it is often expressed per head of population, which also brings problems of estimation. Most countries organize censuses of their population on something like ten-yearly intervals, but not all do, and they certainly do not do them at the same point in time. The quality of many of these censuses is low, and error rates of 20 per cent are not unusual. Moreover, population size changes and thus the errors are not constant.

In order to compare the GNI of different nations, the income has to be expressed in a common currency unit. US dollars are conventionally used, but the method of conversion to that scale is problematic. The World Bank method, used in the data in this chapter, follows the Atlas method of conversion. This uses a three-year average of exchange rates to smooth the effects of short-term fluctuations in the exchange rate. Therefore there are several problems in measuring GNI. The value of the statistics from poor countries which have neither a large statistical staff nor routine data collection activities is often especially questionable. The World Bank does its best to adjust the estimates made by the individual countries for comparability, but the process is inevitably inexact.

10.2 The distribution of GNI per capita

Let us now consider the distribution of GNI in a sample of countries in the world, as shown in figure 10.1. The boxplot of the distribution of GNI per capita is shown in figure 10.2.

The distribution of incomes across countries looks similar to the distribution of incomes one finds within a country: it straggles upwards, the midspread is above the median, the midextreme is above the midspread, the lower whisker is very short and there are upper outliers, namely Germany and the United States. There are relatively few countries at the top of the spectrum: uncomfortably, many have per capita incomes that are very low indeed.

If we consider the boxplots of GNI per capita for all the countries in the world, broken down into different country groups (figure 10.3), they also straggle upwards, in data batches at different levels, with different midspreads and shapes. One reason for the upward straggle is the existence of a floor of zero dollars below which no country can fall (in theory), whereas there is no ceiling. Moreover, the batches form a characteristic wedge shape: batches with lower medians have lower midspreads, and those with higher medians have higher midspreads; this is always a tell-tale sign that a transformation might be in order.

The upward straggle of income distributions is, in one sense, a truth about the world that we must not obscure. However, it does pose difficulties for the data

Figure 10.1   GNI per capita in 2000 in 20 sampled countries.

Country	GNI per capita in 2000 ($US)
Australia	20,060
Benin	340
Burundi	120
China	930
Czech Republic	5,690
Estonia	4,070
Germany	25,510
Haiti	490
Israel	17,090
Korea, Rep.	9,790
Lithuania	3,180
Malta	9,590
Mozambique	210
Nigeria	280
Philippines	1,040
Sudan	310
United States	34,400
Togo	270
Zimbabwe	460
Tanzania	260

Source: Sample of 20 countries from the World Bank World Development Indicators Teaching Dataset (WorldBank_2000_Teach.sav).

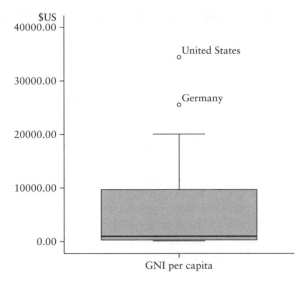

Source: Data in figure 10.1.

Figure 10.2   The distribution of GNI per capita in 2000: boxplot.

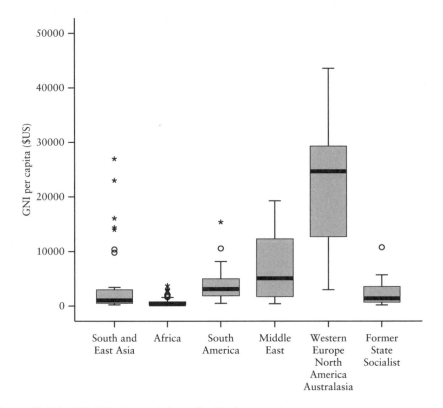

Source: World Bank World Development Indicators Teaching Dataset.

Figure 10.3   Distribution of GNI per capita in 2000 within country groups.

analyst. Differences at the lower end of the scale are obscured by the massive differences at the top end. In particular in figure 10.3 any variations between countries in Africa are masked by the fact that African countries have a much lower GNI than countries in the Middle East or in Western Europe. Multiple boxplots such as those in figure 10.3 are hard to summarize succinctly: not only do typical income levels in each group vary, but the spread and shape also vary. Finally, if income were plotted against another interval level variable, the relationship would almost certainly be curved rather than straight. In this chapter, we will consider a family of transformations of the scale of measurement which help make the variables easier to handle in data analysis.

10.3 The log transformation

One method for transforming data or re-expressing the scale of measurement is to take the logarithm of each data point. This keeps all the data points in the same order but stretches or shrinks the scale by varying amounts at different points. A quick revision for those who have forgotten about logarithms is provided in the appendix to this chapter, which can be found on the website accompanying this book. Don't worry if you don't understand exactly what logarithms are, it is more important to notice carefully what they do to a set of numbers. In particular it is worth noting that while the log of 10 is 1, the log of 100 is 2, the log of 1000 is 3, and the log of 10,000 is 4. Taking logs of a dataset therefore has the effect of

Figure 10.4   Logging the numbers in figure 10.1.

	GNI per capita in 2000 ($US)	Log GNI per capita
Australia	20060	4.3
Benin	340	2.53
Burundi	120	2.08
China	930	2.97
Czech Republic	5690	3.76
Estonia	4070	3.61
Germany	25510	4.41
Haiti	490	2.69
Israel	17090	4.23
Korea, Rep.	9790	3.99
Lithuania	3180	3.5
Malta	9590	3.98
Mozambique	210	2.32
Nigeria	280	2.45
Philippines	1040	3.02
Sudan	310	2.49
United States	34400	4.54
Togo	270	2.43
Zimbabwe	460	2.66
Tanzania	260	2.41

Source: Sample of 20 countries from the World Bank World Development Indicators Teaching Dataset.

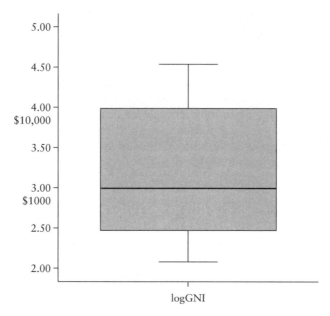

Source: Column 2 of figure 10.4.

Figure 10.5 Logging GNI per capita in 2000 in 20 selected countries.

counteracting upward straggle. Figure 10.4 shows what happens if we take a logarithm of every number in figure 10.1; the resulting shape is shown in figure 10.5.

You will notice that all the GNI per capita figures between 100 and 1000 have been transformed, by taking logs, to lie between 2 and 3 (e.g. Benin with a GNI per capita of 340 has a log GNI per capita of 2.53). While all the data lying between 10,000 and 100,000 have been transformed to lie between 4 and 5 (e.g. Australia with a GNI per capita of 20,060 has a log GNI per capita of 4.3). The higher values have therefore been pulled down towards the centre of the batch, bringing the United States and Germany into the main body of the data, and the bottom of the scale has been stretched out correspondingly. The shape is now more symmetrical.

It would not be necessary to transform every single data value in order to draw the boxplot in figure 10.5; it is sufficient to transform the median, the quartiles and the extremes, and to recalculate the midspread and adjacent values. Only order-based summaries such as medians can be transformed in this way; it is *not* the case that mean (log X) is the same as log (mean X), for example. However, given the widespread use of packages such as Excel and SPSS it is likely that most researchers would simply create a variable LOGGNI using the original GNI variable, by taking the log to base 10 of each value. In Excel the function is as follows:

$=$Log10(number)

Further information about how to transform data using SPSS is given in the appendix to this chapter, which can be found on the website accompanying this book.

The principles of logarithms were discovered in the seventeenth century. They gave a tremendous technical spur to navigation, astronomy and to the growing commercial sector, facilitating tedious calculations, like nineteen months' interest at an annual rate of 2.79 per cent. In the days of calculators and computers, we no longer use log tables to speed up hand calculations. But logs have a vital role to play in data analysis, providing one of the most useful ways of re-expressing data that straggle upwards. As is shown in the appendix to this chapter, logs convert multiplicative processes into additive ones, since $\log (ab) = \log (a) + \log (b)$. Whenever we work with data values that have been generated by a growth process, we will have a better chance of revealing regularities in their behaviour if we convert them first to logs.

10.4 The ladder of powers

However, not all variables straggle upwards. Consider life expectancy, a measure indicating the number of years a newborn infant could typically be expected to live if patterns of mortality prevailing for all people in the year of its birth were to stay the same throughout its life. The distribution of life expectancy across countries is not symmetrical: the lower half of the distribution is more spread out than the upper half (figure 10.6); many countries are pushing up against what looks like some kind of a ceiling of around eighty years, while some poorer countries trail down in the forties and two countries (Zambia and Zimbabwe) even register under forty years. A log transformation of the life expectancy distribution would make the downward straggle even more pronounced, since logs have the effect of stretching the bottom end of any scale.

There is a general family of power transformations that can help promote symmetry and sometimes Gaussian shape in many different data batches. Look what

Mean = 65.9114
Std. Dev. = 11.7439
N = 193

Source: World Bank World Development Indicators Teaching Dataset.

Figure 10.6 Life expectancy in the world in 2000: histogram of raw data.

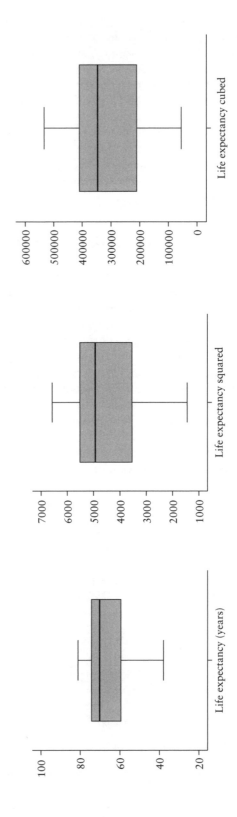

Source: As figure 10.6.

Figure 10.7 Life expectancy in the world in 2000: boxplots of raw and transformed data.

Power	Expression	Name
•		
•		
3	X^3	cube
2	X^2	square
1	X^1	raw data
0.5	$\sqrt{X}$	square root
0	X^0	? (log)
–0.5	$1/\sqrt{X}$	reciprocal root
–1	$1/X$	reciprocal
–2	$1/X^2$	reciprocal square
•		
•		

Figure 10.8   The ladder of powers.

happens, for example, when the life expectancy in each country is raised to powers greater than 1 (figure 10.7). Squaring the values makes the batch slightly more symmetrical, and cubing them even more; the effects are not dramatic, but the improvement is visible.

The effect is the opposite to taking logs: squaring stretches out the upper values and compresses the lower ones, and cubing does so even more powerfully. Both transformations keep the data points in the same order, just as logging did.

There are an infinite number of possible powers to which data can be raised. The commonest values are shown in figure 10.8, placed, as Tukey (1977) suggests, on a 'ladder' in terms of their effect on distributions. There are many other points besides the ones on this **ladder of powers**, both in between the values shown and above and beneath them, but we shall rarely have any need to go beyond those shown.

Since these transformations must preserve the order of the data points, all the transformations which are powers of less than zero are multiplied by −1. The transformation is then strictly the negative reciprocal and not the reciprocal; otherwise, the order of 2 and 3 would be reversed, as the reciprocal of 2 (0.5) is larger than the reciprocal of 3 (0.33).

If we start from the raw data values X^1 we can either proceed up the ladder of powers by squaring or cubing each number, or down the ladder by taking square roots or reciprocals. **Going up the ladder of powers corrects downward straggle, whereas going down corrects upward straggle.** We went up the ladder of powers when we squared the data. It was not far enough, as there was still downward straggle, so we moved further up the ladder to cubes.

What about the mystery exponent, X^0? Any number raised to the power of exactly zero is unity. Clearly, it would be no help to make all the numbers identical.

But we can treat the zero exponent on the ladder of powers as the log, since its effect on the shape of data batches fits exactly at this point; it corrects upward straggle more powerfully than taking roots, but it is not as strong a transformation as the reciprocal root, or reciprocals.

There are two refinements to notice about power transformations. In general, exact zeros cannot be transformed in this way (the log of zero is undefined), so it is conventional to add a very small amount (usually one-sixth or one-half) to all the values in a batch containing zeros before transforming. The second problem comes with negative numbers. If all the numbers are negative, the simplest thing is to multiply them all by −1. If some are negative and some positive, it may be possible to add a constant to make them all positive, or it may be necessary to consider treating the positive and negative numbers separately.

10.5 The goals of transformation

The number systems we use as yardsticks should be thought of as being made not of wood but of elastic which can be stretched or shrunk to our convenience. Transforming the original numbers by taking logs (or by one of the other transformations considered below) is an essentially trivial operation: the order of the numbers is preserved, and they can easily be recast in their original form by taking antilogs. There is nothing God-given about any particular system of measurement. Indeed, when pay increases are negotiated in percentage terms, trade unions and employers implicitly acknowledge that money is most naturally dealt with in multiplicative rather than in additive units. Ideally, we should feel as comfortable working with logged GNI per capita or life expectancy cubed as we feel about working with the raw numbers.

However, it is reasonable to demand a more positive rationale for transforming data, especially as the resulting numbers seem so unfamiliar. There are five principal advantages to be gained, listed below in rising order of importance.

1. Data batches can be made more symmetrical.
2. The shape of data batches can be made more Gaussian.
3. Outliers that arise simply from the skewness of the distribution can be removed, and previously hidden outliers may be forced into view.
4. Multiple batches can be made to have more similar spreads.
5. Linear, additive models may be fitted to the data.

Symmetry on its own is not very important, but the advantages of the Gaussian shape were discussed in chapter 3. The third goal attempts to focus the data analyst's attention on data points that are unusual for a substantive reason, not just because of the shape of the distribution. Equality of spread in multiple batches promotes comparability between them. It is hard to summarize differences in level when spreads also vary. Linear, additive models are easier to work with than more complex mathematical models. The last two goals are the most important, and we will consider them further in the following sections. But it is often the case that, by finding a transformation that will promote equality of spread or linearity, it is possible to achieve the first three at the same time.

If these goals can be achieved, a loss of the intuitive appeal of the simple number scale will have been worthwhile. For those who find it hard to work with or explain coherently to others a set of numbers which have been raised to a power or logged, Mosteller and Tukey (1977, p. 194) suggest a technique which they call 'matched re-expression' to rescale the transformed values to fall within the main range of the original number scale.

10.6 Promoting equality of spread

It is important for the spread to be independent of level in data analysis, whether fitting lines, smoothing, or dealing with multiple boxplots. No simple statement can be made summarizing typical differences in GNI between the country groups in figure 10.3, for example, because they differ systematically in spread as well as in level. A tell-tale wedge-shaped pattern appears in the multiple boxplots: batches with higher medians tend also to have higher midspreads, a sign that usually indicates the need for transformation.

Figure 10.9 shows the effect of taking logs on the distribution of GNI in the different country groups. Logging GNI per capita goes a long way towards holding the midspreads constant by making them similar in size. This means that

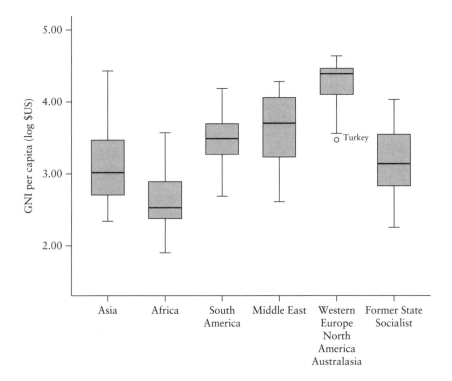

Source: *World Bank World Development Indicators Teaching Dataset.*

Figure 10.9 Logged GNI per capita in 2000 by country group.

statements can be made describing typical differences in wealth between the country groups without needing to mention the differences in spread in the same breath. But, by transforming, progress has also been made towards the first three goals: the batches are more symmetrical and bell-shaped, and some of the outliers in the original batch were not really unusual values, but merely a product of the upward straggle of the raw numbers.

There are no far outliers in the logged distribution, and the outlier that remains does seem to differ substantively from the body of the data. It was always debatable whether Turkey should have been included as a European country; its GNI suggests that it fits more comfortably with other Asian countries.

It is not always easy to spot the fact that the spread increases as the level increases. The fact may stand out in higher relief if the residuals are plotted against the fitted values. We should be concerned whenever there appears to be a positive association between the level and spread (or between residuals and fitted values), whatever data analytic technique is being used.

10.7 Alternatives to GNI as a measure of welfare

Before we look at the last goal of transformation, unbending curved relationships, it will be helpful to return briefly to the debate about the goals of development. There are formidable problems in estimating GNI reliably in many countries of the world. Even if these were surmounted, two fundamental questions would remain about using the average wealth of a country as an index of the well-being of its citizens. First, while the wealthier members of any society claim to be more happy than poorer members of that society, the cross-cultural association between the average amount of wealth in a country and the proportion who claim to be happy is extremely weak. In particular, for countries with over $20,000 US per head additional income is not associated with extra happiness (Layard, 2005, pp. 31–2). Moreover, the measure of GNI per capita says nothing about how the wealth is distributed; a country could raise its GNI by expanding capital-intensive industries which leave the poorest sectors of that society completely untouched.

Alternative indicators of well-being have therefore been sought. Summary measures of inequality, such as quantile shares or Gini coefficients, are not available in enough countries. Moreover, measures such as the Gini coefficient treat inequalities at different points in the income distribution as equivalent, whereas many development economists have argued that the goal of economic aid should be to meet the basic needs of all the citizens in any country. This usually involves focusing on how well a society is doing by its poorest members.

While the logic of this 'basic needs' approach is appealing, there is still room for argument about precisely which needs are basic. Many writers on welfare have viewed life expectancy rates as the most fundamental indicator of well-being in a society. They have the advantage that they can be calculated for most countries in the world. However, a country could have a moderately high average level, while some sections of society still had very short life expectancy. Long life expectancy also indicates the success of development rather than the potential for it.

A case has also been made for using educational variables as an alternative. Suggestions have included the proportion of adults who can read, or the proportion of females attending primary school. One can be sure that the higher either of these indicators go, the more the basic educational needs of *all* members of a given society are being met. Moreover, an educated workforce is argued to be one of the important prerequisites for economic expansion and advance. You can explore the relationships between some of the basic indicators published by the World Bank in the teaching dataset based on the World Bank World Development indicators that accompanies this book.

10.8 Unbending curvy lines

In this section, we will consider the relationship between life expectancy and national wealth in 2000 (it is arguable that life expectancy in 2000 would respond to the prevailing GNI sometime in the past, but we will ignore that refinement here). The scatterplot in figure 10.10 reveals a clear relationship between the two variables. However, the relationship is curved; fitting a straight line will not provide a sensible summary. Either a curve must be fitted, a job which is difficult to do well, or the data must be manipulated so that a straight line becomes a good summary.

Logging GNI per capita and cubing life expectancy did the best job of promoting symmetry and Gaussian shape in these two variables taken individually. The same transformations also help clarify the bivariate relationship (figure 10.11): the

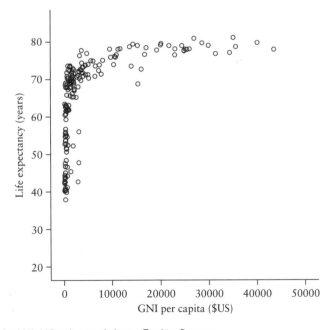

Source: World Bank World Development Indicators Teaching Dataset.

Figure 10.10 Life expectancy by GNI per capita in 2000.

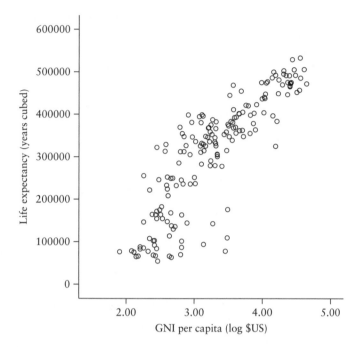

Source: World Bank World Development Indicators Teaching Dataset.

Figure 10.11   Cubed life expectancy by logged GNI per capita in 2000.

scatterplot is more nearly linear, the relationship is capable of easy summary, and previously hidden unusual values are revealed.

We fit lines whenever possible because they are simple, not only for our computers but also for our own brains. However, if you prefer, you can think of fitting a line to transformed data as equivalent to fitting a curve to the raw data; in effect one is saying that the relationship between the two variables takes the form of a particular curve.

The curvy pattern in figure 10.10 was very clear, but sometimes, when the relationship is not so strong, it is hard for the eye to tell if a transformation is required. A useful diagnostic guide is given by the half-slope ratio, introduced in section 9.6. As a rule of thumb, we should explore the possible improvement of fit that a transformation would bring whenever the half-slope ratio is greater than 2.

The overall picture in figure 10.11 suggests that life expectancy can be predicted pretty accurately from a country's GNI: wealthy countries have healthier populations. GNI could be vindicated as a measure of welfare by this finding.

However, life expectancy is still an average measure and might conceal problems for some groups within wealthy countries. As we will discuss in the next chapter, there is a lot more work to be done before the causal process underlying this relationship is laid bare: we do not know whether it is through buying a better diet or better medical care, for example, that richer countries improve their life expectancy. (Exercise 10.5 casts some light on this.)

10.9 Determining the best power for transformation

There are many clues in the course of data analysis that suggest that it might be better to work on a transformed scale. We have concentrated on the three most important diagnostic signs: upward or downward straggle in individual batches (figure 10.2), wedge-shaped data where batches with higher medians have greater spread (figure 10.3), and curvy lines in a scatterplot (figure 10.10).

Identifying the need for a transformation, however, does not tell us which one will do the best job of achieving the five goals mentioned above: so far we have guides to diagnosis but not to cure. There are three different ways we can get such guidance: from our substantive knowledge of the world, by experimenting with the ladder of powers, and by constructing special diagnostic plots.

We may have a theoretical reason for believing that the variable we are studying will require a particular transformation. We have already noted that a log transformation often helps when the data are the result of some process of growth. The square root transformation will often work well in cases where the data are rare occurrences, like suicide or infant mortality. There are situations where the reciprocal of a rate would make more sense than the original rate: ergonomists, for example, might find it more natural to look at the time it takes a person to produce a fixed number of items rather than at the output a person produces from a machine in a fixed period of time.

In the absence of a rationale for a particular transformation (or in the face of competing rationales) the ladder of powers provides a useful guide. When investigating a transformation to promote symmetry in a single batch, we first examine the midpoint summaries – the median, the midquartile, and the midextreme – to see if they tend to increase or decrease. If they systematically increase in value, a transformation lower down the ladder should be tried. If the midpoint summaries the trend downwards, the transformation was too powerful, and we must move back up the ladder somewhat. We continue experimenting with different transformations from the summary values until we have done the best we can to promote symmetry and Gaussian shape.

In trying to unbend curvy lines, there is another way of deciding how to proceed on the ladder of powers. Curves which are monotonic and contain only one bend can be thought of as one of the four quadrants of a circle. To straighten out any such curves, first draw a tangent to see what you are trying to achieve. Then imagine pulling the curve towards the tangent (as shown in figure 10.12). Notice the direction in which you are having to pull the curve on each axis, and move on the ladder of powers accordingly: down in the Y-direction? go down on the ladder of powers with Y, and so on.

To straighten the data in figure 10.12, for example, the curve has to be pulled down in the Y-direction and up in the X-direction; linearity will therefore probably be improved by raising the Y variable to a power lower down on the ladder and/or by raising the X variable to a power higher up on the ladder.

If the curve is not a single bend, monotonic curve, power transformations will probably not straighten it out, though they may help. A logistic transformation can also help straighten out a flat S-shaped curve. Transformations for more complex curves are rarely needed.

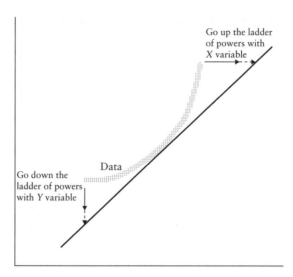

Figure 10.12   Guide to linearizing transformations for curves.

When there is a systematic relationship between the level of the batch and the spread of that batch, plotting the log of the dQ against the log of the median for each batch produces a useful diagnostic picture. Tukey (1977) suggests that, if a line is sketched to fit the points, (1 – slope) will yield the power which should help promote equality of spread. Thus, for instance, if the line had a slope of 1, a log transformation would be indicated; if the line had a negative slope, it would be necessary to raise the data values by a power of more than 1; if there is no relationship and the line has zero slope, power transformations are not likely to help.

10.10 Conclusion

We have looked at the distribution of two variables in this chapter: an indicator of the monetary wealth of a nation, GNI per capita, and an indicator of the material standard of living of a nation, the average age to which people can expect to live. Neither variable was symmetrical in its raw form. Altering the scale of measurement of each of these variables altered the shape of the distribution of each. A general family of transformations – involving raising the data values to different powers – was introduced as a guide to correcting straggle: if the straggle is downward, go up on the ladder of powers, and vice versa. The log transformation was found to fit nicely at the zero position on the ladder of powers.

However, the main goal of transformation is not aesthetic. The aim is to express numbers on a scale of measurement which makes data analysis easier, often by allowing simple models to be fitted, and thus enhancing our ability to understand the data. In particular, we saw how such transformations can help make the dQ of different batches more similar, and help unbend curvy lines. The result in both cases is to enable the data analyst to re-express the data simply in the conventional form: data = fit + residual.

Power transformations are a very important part of the researcher's armoury; the exponents of exploratory data analysis stress them (Tukey, 1977; Mosteller and Tukey, 1977), and their use is applauded by many statisticians (e.g. Kruskal, 1978). Although it may take some practice to get used to the idea of changing the seemingly natural number scale, you will soon find that you automatically consider whether a transformation would aid analysis when you first look at a batch of data.

The most difficult problem comes with conveying the effect of transformation to lay audiences, who may be suspicious of statisticians 'fiddling with the numbers'. Someone might fear, for example, that by taking logs in figure 10.9 the real upward straggle in national wealth has been hidden. Data analysts must not be put off using the best techniques available in case they are misunderstood, but they have an important responsibility to explain what they have done to try to ensure that misunderstandings do not arise. For presentation purposes, this usually involves converting key elements of the analysis back to the original scale. It may be possible to explain line fitting with transformed data in terms of fitting curves. However we achieve it, great care must be taken to make the exposition clear to a non-technical audience.

Exercises

10.1 Using logs to the base 10 (see the appendix to this chapter on the accompanying website), what is:
(a) $\log(1)$
(b) $\log(0)$
(c) $\log(pqr)$
(d) $\log(p/q)$
(e) $\log(p^n)$?
Write down the value of:
(f) $\log_{10}(2)$
(g) $\log_e(2)$

10.2 The boxplot in figure 10.13 shows the CO_2 emissions per capita for all the countries in the *World Bank World Development Indicators Teaching Dataset*. What type of transformation would be needed to aid the analysis of these data? Using the ladder of powers, suggest two possible transformations that might be appropriate.

10.3 The *World Bank World Development Indicators Teaching Dataset* has been used to produce a scatterplot of GNI per capita and CO_2 emissions per capita, shown in figure 10.14. What would you expect this graph to show and why is it difficult to interpret?

10.4 Using SPSS or a similar package, open the *World Bank World Development Indicators Teaching Dataset* (WorldBank_2000_Teach.sav) into the worksheet.

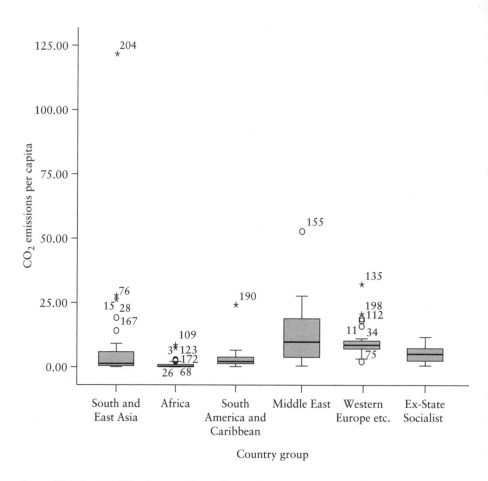

Source: *World Bank World Development Indicators Teaching Dataset.*

Figure 10.13 Boxplot of CO2 emissions per capita.

(a) Find a transformation suitable for the ratio of females to males in secondary education.

(b) Plot the log of GNI per capita versus ratio of females to males in secondary education as transformed in (a). Can you predict gender disparity in secondary education using GNI?

10.5 Goal 4 of the Millennium Development Goals is represented by Target 5 'Reduce by two-thirds, between 1990 and 2015, the under-five mortality rate'.

(a) Find a transformation suitable for the under-five mortality rate in the *World Bank World Development Indicators Teaching Dataset* (WorldBank_2000_Teach.sav)

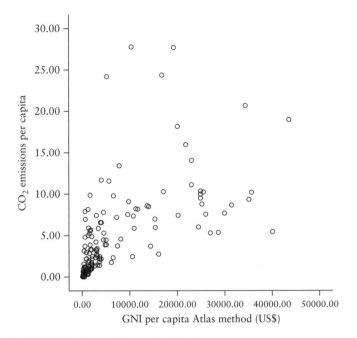

Source: *World Bank World Development Indicators Teaching Dataset.*

Figure 10.14 Scatterplot of GNI per capita by CO_2 emissions per capita.

(b) Examine the under-five mortality rate in the different country groups (using your transformed variable). Which countries in Africa have the lowest under-five mortality rates? Is this what you would expect?

(c) Plot the log of GNI per capita versus under-five mortality rate as transformed in (a). Can you predict under-five mortality rate using GNI?

Part III

Introducing a Third Variable

In the third part of this book, we consider ways of holding a third variable constant while assessing the relationship between two others. In chapter 12 we discuss how this is done with contingency tables and using logistic regression. However, before proceeding to the techniques of controlling extraneous variables, we must devote a chapter to discussing the logic of the procedure. Chapter 11 is devoted entirely to thinking about the causal issues at stake. The final chapter of the book, chapter 13, provides an introduction to the advantages of longitudinal research and the analysis of longitudinal data.

11

Causal Explanations

You will by now have developed some experience of handling batches of data, summarizing features of their distributions, and investigating relationships between variables. We must now change gear somewhat and ask what it would take for such relationships to be treated as satisfactory *explanations*. One of the challenges of introducing the concept of causal explanations in the context of a book about exploring data is that philosophers of science have been struggling with the problem of defining causality since at least the time of David Hume in the mid eighteenth century. Hume suggested that 'We may define a cause to be *an object followed by another, and where all the objects, similar to the first, are followed by objects similar to the second. Or, in other words, where, if the first object had not been, the second never had existed*' (1748, Section VII). This statement, rather confusingly, starts by suggesting that causality can be defined in terms of regularity but then moves on to link the notion of causality to the concept of counterfactual dependence (i.e. if the cause had not occurred the effect would not have occurred). It is these kinds of tensions around the best way of understanding the concept of causality that the philosophy literature has been struggling with for many years.

Writing just before the First World War, Bertrand Russell claimed that the word 'cause' should be banished from philosophy altogether, and argued that in advanced sciences, such as gravitational astronomy, the word 'cause' never occurs. Russell therefore suggested that the concept of causality was only of use in everyday life and in sciences that are still in their infancy (Russell, 1913). However, as Gillies (2005) has argued, the notion of cause is regularly used and has practical utility in sciences such as medicine (which many people would acknowledge to be an advanced science). When a doctor performs a medical diagnosis he, or she, is aiming to identify the cause of the symptoms that the patient is exhibiting. It is also the case that in medical research the aim is often to understand the underlying causes of diseases and then to use any discoveries to help with prevention or cure. Gillies therefore suggests that Russell's attempt to prevent the use of the term causality is unhelpful and he argues instead that causal laws are useful and appropriate in situations where there is a close link between the law and action based on the law (Gillies, 2005, p. 827). The acknowledgement of the utility of the concept of cause within the field of medicine is helpful here. It could be argued that the focus on symptoms and the causes of diseases in the medical sciences, is mirrored in the social sciences by a concern with the causes of social ills. Just as within medicine an understanding of the cause of disease is seen as useful if it can form the basis of action to cure or prevent disease, in the social sciences the aspiration to understand causal processes is often motivated by the desire to intervene or act in some way that will have a positive impact on the outcomes for individuals or society. This chapter will therefore deliberately leave on one side the philosophical difficulties of providing an adequate definition of the concept of causality. It will instead focus on some of the practical ways that researchers can explore datasets in order to develop a better understanding of how variables are linked, and to what extent these links can be interpreted as evidence of underlying causal processes.

11.1 Why did the chicken cross the road?

An **explanation** is a human construction. It is an answer to the question 'why?' In everyday terms, a successful explanation is simply one that satisfies the person who asked the question. Since people who ask questions about the world vary in their interests, curiosity and knowledge, what counts as a successful explanation is also likely to vary greatly.

The question 'why?' is notoriously ambiguous. It can have many different kinds of answers. Some are motivational: 'in order to . . .' some imply a causal relationship: 'because . . . happened first'; some are typological: 'because it is an instance of . . .'; some invoke the existence of a social rule: 'because it is the custom'. The type of answer required will depend on the social context and the perceived motivation behind the question. For this reason it is impossible to come up with universal rules dictating how explanations are to be provided.

This chapter focuses on a particular subset of answers to the question 'why?' When social scientists use data to try and understand a particular set of outcomes they are usually aiming to provide an account that goes beyond the specific and that describes some of the processes and mechanisms that lead to the results that have been observed. If they were to try to give an answer to the question at the head of this section, they would probably try to give a general account of factors which encourage or discourage chickens from crossing roads.

Causality and correlation

It is now widely recognized that establishing a statistically significant correlation or association between two variables using quantitative analysis is not the same as establishing a causal relationship. Whereas, as discussed above, in the 18th century the philosopher David Hume tried to define causality in terms of constant conjunction or statistical association it is clearly not sufficient for one event invariably to precede another for us to be convinced that the first event **causes** the second. Night follows day, but we would not suggest that day 'causes' night. To give another example, the time recorded on two different wrist watches can be perfectly associated: the time on one of them can be correctly predicted from the time on the other, but not because the time on one of them *causes* the time on the other; altering the time on one of them would have absolutely no impact on the other.

However, few people would question the statement that causes exist in the real world. They are not just human constructions to help us understand it. They have been called 'the cement of the universe' (Mackie, 1974). One way that we might define the concept of causality is to say that causes are processes which, once started, end up producing a particular outcome at a later point in time. In other words, to say that X causes Y is to say that, if X changes, it will produce a change in Y. For example, going back to some of the analysis in chapter 8, to say that a mother's interest in her child's education has a causal effect on that child's performance in a maths test is to say that if a mother's level of interest changes this will change the child's performance. In this case we might expect that if a mother became more interested in her child's education, the child's learning would improve and he or she would perform better in tests, and vice versa. It is this practical definition of causality that will be used throughout the rest of this chapter. Although it may not hold up to rigorous scrutiny among those interested in the philosophy of science it has practical utility in the context of the quantitative analysis of data.

Some people get very upset about the idea that there might be any causes operating in the social world; they fear that causal influences on human action rob people of their freedom of choice and dignity of action. This is a mistaken fear: if causes are the cement of both the natural and social universe, refusal to consider their existence will not stop them operating; it will merely mean that such causes are not uncovered, and, ironically, therefore will not be harnessed to give people greater control over and choice in their lives.

In fact, there is nothing to prevent us thinking of choice, intentions and motives in causal terms. One aim within psychology is to understand some of the causal determinants of motivations and to show when conscious intentions really do cause behaviour and when they do not. Many different social sciences – economics, geography and sociology in particular – show how individually intended actions combine to produce social outcomes which may not have been the intentions of the actors.

Some authors have also complained that in the process of manipulating large datasets and examining the ways that variables are associated with each other, researchers have developed a discourse that prioritizes and reifies variables while simultaneously obscuring the actions of individual cases. For example, in his chapter 'What do cases do?' Andrew Abbott provides an interesting analysis of the language used in papers published in the *American Sociological Review* (Abbott, 1992). He demonstrates that the narrative sentences within such articles usually have variables as their subjects. He also argues that 'it is when a variable does something narratively that the authors think themselves to be speaking most directly of causality' (Abbott, 1992, p. 57). This is not to argue against conducting the kind of careful multivariate analysis that is described in the remaining chapters of this book. However, Abbott's work does serve as an important reminder that it is individuals, rather than abstract variables who act in the social world and in our research accounts we should endeavour to reflect this.

Multiple and complex causality

One of the dangers of trying to find a precise definition of causality and of aiming to describe what differentiates a causal relationship from a mere statistical association is that causality can begin to be viewed as a single monolithic concept (Cartwright, 2004). However, recent work in this area has stressed that there is a great variety of causal systems and different ways in which factors may operate together to produce a particular outcome. This in turn means that there will be a number of different methods for testing whether hypotheses about causal relationships are confirmed by patterns in the data we collect and observe. For example, Byrne (2002) has argued that

> To say that causes are real is to say that something generates something else. The something can be a generative mechanism rather than any single factor but something does have generative capacity. When we look for causes we are seeking to identify and to understand the nature of that generative capacity. (Byrne, 2002, p. 2)

It is beyond the scope of this chapter to provide a full discussion of the recent literature on causation or to catalogue the many different types of causal relationships and causal systems which we may be able to observe in the social world. The aim is rather to focus on an introduction to some of the most common ways in which social scientists systematically explore and analyse data to take account of the fact that an observed relationship between two variables may be accounted for, or modified by, a third variable.

Without pushing the notion of complex causality very far at all it is important to recognize that many different component causes can add together to produce a particular outcome, a process sometimes known as **multiple causality**. Given this, we should not expect the relationship between one cause among many and an effect to be perfect. However, much everyday reasoning about causes seems to demand perfect relationships: 'Smoking doesn't cause lung cancer; the man next door to us got lung cancer and he had never smoked a cigarette in his life', implying that the only cast-iron proof would be for all smokers to get lung cancer and for no non-smokers to get it.

11.2 Direct and indirect effects

As has been discussed above, causality should not necessarily be understood as a simple process in which one factor or variable has an impact on another. For example, it is likely in many cases that two or more factors will tend to work together to produce an effect. Moreover, the factors or variables contributing to the effect may themselves be causally related. For this reason, we have to keep a clear idea in our heads of the relationships between the variables in the whole causal process.

In investigating the causes of absenteeism from work, for example, researchers have found different contributory factors. We will consider two possible causal factors: being female and being in a low status job. Let us construct a causal path diagram depicting one possible set of relationships between these variables.

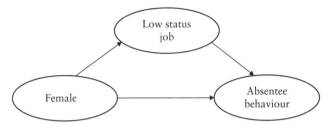

Figure 11.1   Causes of absenteeism.

The diagram in figure 11.1 represents a simple system of multiple causal paths. There is an arrow showing that those in low status jobs are more likely to go absent. Being female has a causal effect in two ways. There is an arrow straight to absentee behaviour; this says that women are more likely to be absent from work than men, regardless of the kind of job they are in. This is termed a **direct effect** of gender on absenteeism. There is also another way in which being female has an effect; women are more likely to be in the kind of low status, perhaps unpleasant, jobs where absenteeism is more likely, irrespective of gender. We can say that being female therefore also has an **indirect effect** on absenteeism, through the type of work performed. Without some empirical evidence we cannot be sure that this 'model' of the relationships between the variables is correct. In the sections which follow we will think through the different ways in which variables like these might be related.

11.3 Controlling the world to learn about causes

It is one thing to declare confidently that causal chains exist in the world out there. However, it is quite another thing to find out what they are. Causal processes are not obvious. They hide in situations of complexity, in which effects may have been produced by several different causes acting together. When investigated, they will reluctantly shed one layer of explanation at a time, but only to reveal another deeper level of complexity beneath.

For this reason, something that is accepted as a satisfactory causal explanation at one point in time can become problematic at another. Researchers investigating the causes of psychological depression spent a long time carefully documenting how severe, traumatizing events that happen to people, such as bereavement or job loss, can induce it. Now that the causal effect of such life events has been established, the research effort is turning to ask how an event such as unemployment has its effect: is it through the loss of social esteem, through the decline of self-evaluation and self-esteem, through lack of cash or through the sheer effect of inactivity (Eales, 1988)?

In order to answer such causal questions, careful observation of what goes on is simply not sufficient. There was a celebrated individual who devoted a large part of his life to carefully recording everything that he observed. Upon his death, this complete set of observations was presented to the Royal Society in the hope that it would be of use to scientists. It was, of course, utterly useless. Deliberate learning situations have to be constructed if we want to pin down causes and further our grasp on the world.

Central to the creation of such learning situations is the idea of **control**. There are two ways in which scientists attempt to impose controls on the wayward world in order to learn. The first involves controlling the setting of the research to prevent certain variables operating. This is the method of the hard sciences like physics. Unlike physicists, however, social scientists cannot easily construct social circuits in a social vacuum so that they are uncontaminated by other factors. The second type of control is therefore also necessary; it involves drawing inferences by comparing like with like. Let us consider both types of control a little more fully.

Sometimes social researchers are not able to achieve any control at all over the research setting, and are forced to observe the world as it occurs naturally. At the other extreme, they may decide they must contrive an artificial research setting in order to exclude the operation of unwanted variables. There is a continuous set of possibilities in between, and the particular design chosen is a matter of judgement. In a study investigating the effect of a particular teaching method on speed of learning, many factors could be held constant if a laboratory experiment were conducted – the identity of the teacher, the way the material was introduced and so on. A trial in real schools would be more realistic, but also more susceptible to the slings and arrows of fortune in the classroom. Researchers who were interested in people's views on what should be done about global warming could either hang around waiting for respondents spontaneously to bring the subject up, or they could ask directed questions about this on a structured questionnaire, taking care to ask everybody exactly the same question.

A balance has to be struck, since too much control of the research setting can lead to situations that lack naturalism and to indicators that lack external validity. For example, the results to structured questions on a topic may not reflect the views respondents would express in any other situation. It is obviously desirable to obtain as much of this type of control as is consistent with naturalism.

Many people believe that it is the careful controlled setting of a laboratory that makes experiments very powerful situations in which to draw causal inferences. They are wrong; highly controlled settings can be achieved without any experimental manipulation. What differentiates true experiments from non-experimental enquiries is the attempt, either in the laboratory or field, to produce an effect among groups which have been randomly formed. In the simplest experiment, the researcher deliberately alters the X values of an experimental group, and sees what effect this has on their Y values by comparing them with a control group.

Unlike the first type of control, which was a spectrum, the second type – the making of controlled comparisons – forms a natural dichotomy: controlled experiments and non-experimental enquiries. In the former, the researcher can draw very strong inferences from comparisons between randomized groups. The importance of their being formed at random cannot be overemphasized; control groups start life the same as experimental groups in all respects simply by virtue of having been formed at random. When such preformed randomized control groups do not exist, inferences have to be drawn *post hoc* from comparisons between unrandomized groups.

The causal inferences that can be drawn from experiments are often thought to be direct and unproblematic, at least in comparison with the inferences that can be drawn from non-experimental enquiries. If randomized control and experimental groups end up substantially different, something that happened to them in the experiment almost certainly caused this. If two uncontrolled groups prove to be different in some respect, we can only treat this as evidence of a causal relationship if we are convinced that they are not also different in some other important respect, as we will see.

11.4 Do opinion polls influence people?

Let us take an example to illustrate the different inferences which can be drawn from experiments and non-experiments.

Some people believe that hearing the results of opinion polls before an election sways individuals towards the winning candidate. Imagine two ways in which empirical evidence could be collected for this proposition. An experiment could be conducted by taking a largish group of electors, splitting them into two at random, telling half that the polls indicated one candidate would win and telling the other half that they showed a rival would win. As long as there were a substantial number of people in each group, the groups would start the experiment having the same political preferences on average, since the groups were formed at random. If they differed substantially in their subsequent support for the candidates, then we could be almost certain that the phony poll information they were fed contributed to which candidate they supported.

Alternatively, the proposition could be researched in a non-experimental way. A survey could be conducted to discover what individuals believed recent opinion polls showed, and to find out which candidates the individuals themselves supported. The preferences of those who believed that one candidate was going to win would be compared with those who believed that the rival was going to win. The hypothesis would be that the former would be more sympathetic to the candidate than the latter.

If the second survey did reveal a strong relationship between individuals' perception of the state of public opinion and their own belief, should this be taken as evidence that opinion polls have a causal effect on people's voting decisions? Should policy-makers consider banning polls in pre-election periods as a result? Anyone who tried this line of argument would be taken to task by the pollsters, who have a commercial interest in resisting such reasoning. They would deny that the effect in any way proves that polls influence opinion; it could, for instance, be that supporters of a right-wing candidate are of a generally conservative predisposition, and purchase newspapers which only report polls sympathetic to their candidate.

In short, comparing individuals in a survey who thought that candidate A would win with those who believed that candidate B would win, would not be comparing two groups similar in all other possible respects, unlike the experiment discussed above.

An experiment would have a better chance of persuading people that the publication of opinion polls affected individual views. However, it is possible that the experimental data would not be thought conclusive either; most of the experiments that have been done of this type have been rather artificial (Marsh, 1985). The famous social scientist, D. T. Campbell, once proposed a more naturalistic experiment, in which scores of towns would be selected and formed into two groups at random, the newspapers in each town would be persuaded to take part in the experiment by publishing phony articles about the state of candidates, and comparisons would be made at the end between the two groups of towns (Campbell, 1951). It will come as no surprise to learn, however, that this experiment has never been conducted.

Experiments are strong on causal logic, which accounts for the enthusiasm some social scientists have had for them. But the situations in which they can be carried out are few. Some have tried to get round this problem by constructing small-scale models of the world that they really want to study, simulating wars, prison situations and so on. But only social psychologists who research aspects of small group behaviour have managed to achieve any kind of realism with such models. For practical and ethical reasons, many interesting and important issues cannot be researched by experiments: the effect of low dosage radiation on human beings, of young maternal age on child abuse, or the effects of authoritarian upbringing on fascist political views, to name but three examples.

By and large, therefore, most social science data are non-experimental, and this leads to some challenging difficulties with the process of drawing causal inferences. We cannot directly infer a causal effect from a statistical effect.

11.5 Assumptions required to infer causes

Does this mean that non-experimental data are useless for addressing causal issues? Not at all. It does mean, however, that the process of drawing inferences is more tentative than in experiments, based on if-then reasoning: if it is the case that the true causal story about the variables is as we imagine, then we would expect to find a statistical effect of X on Y. Any effect discovered is merely consistent with these assumptions; it does not prove that they are true. If it is not discovered, however, it is highly likely that there is something wrong with the assumptions; the data can certainly dampen over-enthusiastic imagination.

Researchers rarely conduct research with a finished model of the causal process they want to test in mind. They usually build up to a more complete description of the causal processes slowly, starting from a simple relationship, imagining how it might be more complex, testing to see if that is in fact the case, and so on. This process is known as **elaboration**, and involves a fruitful interaction between theory and data.

Imagine a common situation. A survey is conducted and an interesting statistical association between X and Y is discovered. There are two basic assumptions that have to be made if we wish to infer from this that X may cause Y. These involve the relationship between X and Y and other variables which might be operating. They are designed to ensure that when we compare groups which differ on X, we are comparing like with like. Before giving an exposition of these assumptions, we need a bit more terminology: other variables can be causally **prior** to both X and Y, **intervene** between X and Y, or **ensue** from X and Y, as shown

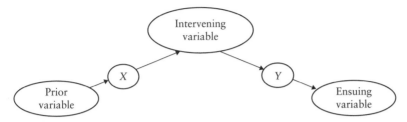

Figure 11.2 Different causal relationships between variables.

in figure 11.2. These terms are only relative to the particular causal model in hand: in a different model we might want to explain what gave rise to the prior variable.

Let us discuss each of the two core assumptions in turn.

Assumption 1

X is causally prior to Y.

There is nothing in the data to tell us whether X causes Y or Y causes X, so we have to make the most plausible assumption we can, based on our knowledge of the subject matter and our theoretical framework.

There are some rules which can guide us. Things which are not open to change, such as a person's age, are often treated as causes. They are certainly best thought of as prior variables. However, while some researchers like to reserve the term 'cause' for such factors, others argue that these are not real causes as a causal connection only exists where we can manipulate the cause to bring about the observed effect. The time ordering can sometimes help out; since causes occur before effects, knowing which variable occurred first can help. However, this is not watertight; human beings can anticipate and respond to future events before they occur. Sometimes a theoretical framework prescribes that particular factors are considered causally prior to others. Marxists, for example, assume that in the last instance economic variables take precedence over cultural, political variables. Sometimes careful measurement can indicate whether the occurrence of a variable is independent of a possible cause.

One particular problem comes from situations in which we suspect that X and Y influence each other in a reciprocating process. There is no way that non-experimental data can be made to yield two independent estimates of the effect of X on Y and of Y on X; we have to plump for one or the other. In such reciprocating systems, the magnitude of causal effect of X on Y or Y on X depends strictly on the exact time at which we conduct the survey. However, such systems tend to settle down after a time. As long as the feedback process is not in full swing, we can often assume that the net effect has balanced out in one direction or the other.

Assumption 2

Related prior variables have been controlled.

All other variables which affect both *X* and *Y* must be held constant. In an experiment, we can be sure that there are no third variables which give rise to both *X* and *Y* because the only way in which the randomized control groups are allowed to vary is in terms of *X*. No such assumption can be made with non-experimental data. If we compare non-experimental groups which vary on *X*, we cannot automatically assume that they are alike in other respects. We have to control for the other ways in which they might vary.

To illustrate this point, imagine a survey of all the fires occurring in a particular neighbourhood. If the number of fire engines which turned up was correlated with the amount of damage done at those fires, a positive relationship would probably be discovered. However, beware of letting simple-minded politicians bent on public expenditure cuts get their hands on such bivariate statistics. Should fewer fire engines therefore be sent to fires? No; control for a prior variable (size of the fire) and the relationship will be shown to be negative.

There are different ways to control for a third factor when investigating a relationship between two variables. Precisely how third variables are brought under control will be discussed in the rest of the book. For the moment, just imagine holding variables constant. For example, to control for the size of the fire one might only consider cases where an isolated car had caught fire.

If we want to infer that the relationship between *X* and *Y* is a direct causal effect, rather than an indirect causal effect, a third assumption must be made.

Assumption 3

All variables intervening between *X* and *Y* have been controlled.

This assumption is not required before you can assume that there is a causal link between *X* and *Y*, but it is required if you aim to understand *how* *X* is causing *Y*. The distinction between controlling for a prior variable and for an intervening variable is drawn more sharply in the next section.

In general, variables that are brought into the picture and controlled are called **test factors**. Controlling for them tests the original relationship between *X* and *Y*, and checks that it holds up. In order to infer that the effect of *X* on *Y* is a direct causal effect, any variable which is related to both *X* and *Y* and causally prior to at least one of them must be controlled.

Never forget that these assumptions are just that. We can never *prove* that a variable is prior rather than intervening or ensuing. To order the variables and decide which should be brought under control, we have to use all the theoretical and rational resources available to us; we cannot appeal to the data for help. (An excellent and eminently readable discussion of the whole logic of control in causal models can be found in Davis, 1985. Balnaves and Caputi, 2001 also provide a useful introduction.)

11.6 Controlling for prior variables

In the next two sections we will pay special attention to situations in which an original effect disappears when a third variable is brought under control. The importance of such an outcome is very different depending on where in the hypothesized causal chain the third variable comes. Obviously, if it ensues from the two variables originally considered, it does not need to be controlled. However, there is a big difference between controlling for a prior variable and finding that the original relationship disappears, and controlling for an intervening variable with a similar result.

Let us first consider a hypothetical example drawn from the earlier discussion of the causes of absenteeism. Suppose previous research had shown a positive bivariate relationship between low social status jobs and absenteeism. The question arises: is there something about such jobs that directly causes the people who do them to go off sick more than others? Before we can draw such a conclusion, two assumptions have to be made.

The first decision is whether the status of the job influences the absentee rate or the absentee rate influences the type of job people get. As we argued earlier, we cannot usually allow a model which depicts reciprocal causation. While absence-prone individuals may have difficulty getting good jobs, the former effect is probably the stronger.

The second assumption is that there are no uncontrolled prior variables influencing both the type of job and the absentee rate. In fact, we already thought that gender might fit into this category: it is likely to be associated with status (women tend to do lower status jobs) and absenteeism (domestic commitments might make women more absence prone than men). It is also the case that people's gender cannot be held to be an *effect* of their job or their work record. Gender must be assumed to be causally prior to both of these variables.

Gender must therefore be held constant while the relationship between job type and absenteeism is 'tested'. While we are at it, we will check whether we were right to believe that being female may have an influence upon both job type and absenteeism.

There are many possible outcomes once the relationship between all three variables is considered at once, four of which are shown in figure 11.3.

We will systematically ask about each outcome: would it change our original interpretation of the bivariate effect?

In the first outcome (I), we discover that being female does affect likelihood of absence, but being female does not increase the chances of being in a low status job. The strength of the effect of type of job on absenteeism would not change by controlling for gender in this case.

In the second outcome (II), we discover that females are more likely to be in low status jobs, and that people in such jobs are more likely to go absent, but that being female, once type of job is controlled, does not affect absentee behaviour directly.

Once again, the strength of the relationship between job and absenteeism would remain the same as in the bivariate case. The first part of the definition of a test factor should now be clear: test factors need to be introduced only when they are related to both the variables under consideration.

However, the third situation (III) is radically different.

Being female dictates the type of job, and being female affects absentee behaviour, but once gender is controlled there is no link at all between the type of job and absenteeism. The direct effect of job on absenteeism is shown to be zero.

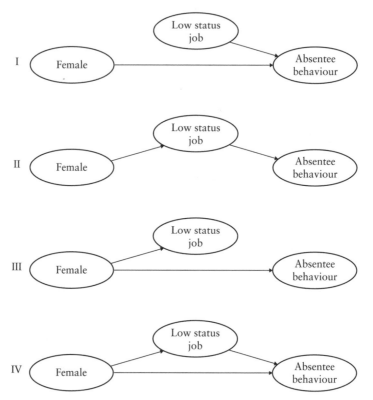

Figure 11.3 The effect of job status on absenteeism: controlling a prior variable.

Figure 11.4 Outcome I from figure 11.3.

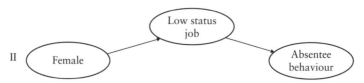

Figure 11.5 Outcome II from figure 11.3.

A causal interpretation of the bivariate effect would have been entirely faulty: it was purely a product of women being both more likely to be in low status jobs and more likely to be absent. Or, to put it another way, changing the status of a job would not have any impact on the behaviour of its incumbents.

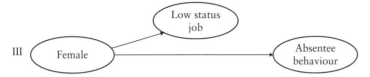

Figure 11.6 Outcome III from figure 11.3.

If the relationship between two variables entirely disappears when a causally prior variable is brought under control, we say that the original relationship was **spurious**. By this we do not mean that the bivariate effect did not really exist, but rather that any causal conclusions drawn from it would be incorrect. We can now introduce another meaning for that verb 'to explain': in this situation, many researchers say that the proportion of females in a job 'explains' the relationship between the status of the job and absenteeism, in the sense that it accounts for it entirely.

But what of the fourth situation which is actually the most likely outcome? It was the situation portrayed in figure 11.1.

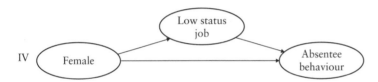

Figure 11.7 Outcome IV from figure 11.3.

We discover that there is a direct effect of both being female and job type on absentee behaviour, and an indirect effect of being female on absenteeism through the type of job women tend to hold. Since the direction of the direct and the indirect effect is the same (which need not always be so), the size of the effect of job type on absenteeism would not be as large once gender was controlled as it had seemed in the bivariate relationship. We now know that the strength of that original relationship contained a **spurious component**.

Simpson's paradox

In some cases the relationship between two variables is not simply reduced when a third, prior, variable is taken into account but indeed the direction of the relationship is completely reversed. This is often known as Simpson's paradox (named after Edward Simpson who wrote a paper describing the phenomenon that was published by the Royal Statistical Society in 1951). However, the insight that a third variable can be vitally important for understanding the relationship between two other variables is also credited to Karl Pearson in the late nineteenth century. Simpson's paradox can be succinctly summarized as follows: every statistical relationship between two variables *may* be reversed by including additional factors in the analysis.

Figure 11.8   Success of application to graduate school by gender and department: an example of Simpson's paradox.

Department	Men				Women			
	Accepted		Rejected		Accepted		Rejected	
	N	%	N	%	N	%	N	%
A	512	62%	313	38%	89	82%	19	18%
B	353	63%	207	37%	17	68%	8	32%
C	121	37%	204	63%	202	34%	391	66%
D	138	33%	279	67%	131	35%	244	65%
E	53	28%	138	72%	94	24%	299	76%
F	16	6%	256	94%	24	7%	317	93%
total	3714	44%	4728	56%	1512	35%	2809	65%

Source: Extract from P.J. Bickel, E.A. Hammel and J.W. O'Connell (1975). 'Sex Bias in Graduate Admissions: Data From Berkeley'. *Science* 187: 398–404.

One of the best known examples of Simpson's paradox is based on data on graduate admissions to departments of University College Berkeley in the early 1970s. An extract from the data is reproduced in figure 11.8. It can be seen that there are three variables represented in this table, namely i) gender ii) outcome of application iii) department. If we start by just focusing on the first two variables, we might be tempted to use the percentage of men who were successful in their application compared to the percentage of women who were successful in their application to suggest that there is a gender bias operating such that men are more likely to be admitted than women. It is certainly clear that when we aggregate the data across all six departments 44 per cent of men compared with only 35 per cent of women made successful applications. However, if we introduce a third variable, namely department, any simplistic interpretation of the apparent link between gender and successful admission is challenged.

It can be seen that in four out of six of the departments (A, B, D and F) women were actually more likely to be successfully admitted for graduate study and in the other two departments the differences between the success rates of men and women were relatively small. Careful examination of these data demonstrates that these apparently contradictory results are a product of the fact that the largest numbers of women applied for admission to departments C and E, which both have relatively low acceptance rates whereas the largest numbers of men applied to departments A and B, which have the highest acceptance rates.

11.7 Controlling for intervening variables

Superficially, the act of controlling for a variable which intervenes between the two original variables of interest is much the same. The third factor is held constant while the original relationship is reassessed. But the logic of the procedure is very different.

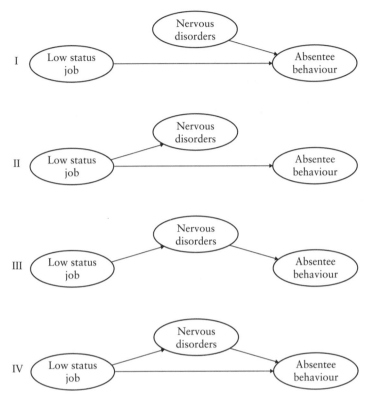

Figure 11.9 The effect of job status on absenteeism: controlling an intervening variable.

Imagine now that we introduce, as a test factor, a variable which represents the extent to which the respondent suffers from chronic nervous disorders, such as sleeplessness, anxiety and so on. Such conditions would be likely to lead to absence from work. It is also quite conceivable that they could be caused in part by stressful, low-status jobs. Let us therefore assume that nervous disorders act as an intervening variable.

What will happen to the original relationship if we control for this test factor? Figure 11.9 shows similar possible outcomes.

As before, in the first two situations controlling for the third variable will not affect the estimate of the causal effect of the type of job on absentee behaviour. In the first, nervous disorders are just an additional cause of absenteeism, but are unrelated to the type of job. In the second, nervous disorders have no effect on absenteeism, despite the fact that they are caused by poor jobs.

But in the third, the relationship between job type and absenteeism disappears when the existence of nervous disorders is brought under control. This test factor is said to **interpret** the relationship between the two variables; it opens up the black box to show how the effect occurs. This is radically different from showing that the original effect was spurious. It is still the case that the type of job affects the absentee behaviour. We now know *how* the causal effect works: poor jobs lead to more stress-related disorders, and these in turn lead to absence from work.

In the fourth situation, nervous disorders partially interpret the relationship between the two variables, but there is still a direct effect remaining after that variable has been brought under control.

The process of drawing inferences from non-experimental data is usually one of slowly elaborating a relationship between two variables, testing that it contains no spurious component due to the operation of a prior variable, and testing to see if one can pin down whether the cause influences the effect directly or through an intervening variable.

Ultimately, of course, whether a cause is held to be direct or indirect is a statement about the state of scientific knowledge at the time. While one variable may provide an illuminating explanation for a puzzle at one point in time, it is likely to provoke further questions about how it operates at a later date. (Further discussion of using quantitative data to understand causal processes can be found in chapter 6 of Elliott, 2005.)

11.8 Positive and negative relationships

There is a further important refinement to the preceding discussion that we must now address. The effect on the original relationship of controlling a test factor is affected by whether the third variable is positively or negatively related to the other variables. Test factors can sometimes suppress and sometimes enhance the size of the original effect, as we will see.

Look back to figure 11.3, at outcome IV (also shown in figure 11.7). We noted that controlling for gender would have reduced the size of the original effect, because there would have been a spurious component stemming purely from the fact that more women are in low status jobs and more women go absent. In this case, the test factor was positively related to both the variables. Now consider two other possible outcomes, as shown in figure 11.10.

In situation V, the test factor, gender, is related negatively to both the other two variables. Being female makes you less likely to be in a low status job, and less likely to go absent. The original bivariate effect would have been larger than the effect once gender is controlled in this case, because once more it will contain a

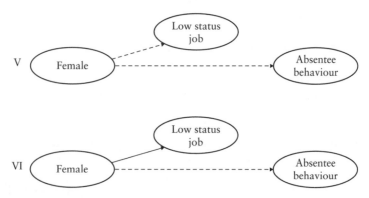

Figure 11.10 Other outcomes for figure 11.3.

spurious component. Test factors which are either positively related to both the other variables or negatively related to both of them are called **enhancer variables**.

However, in case VI, gender is negatively related to one of the variables (absenteeism) and positively to the other (job type). What will happen to the original effect when gender is controlled? The size of the effect will *increase*, because the original effect was being artificially suppressed by failing to control for gender. The fact that women were less likely to go absent, but more likely to be in unfavourable jobs meant that we were misled about the effect of low-status jobs on absence before we controlled for gender. Test factors which are positively associated with one variable and negatively with the other are called **suppressor variables** for this reason.

Sometimes the action of a suppressor variable can be so strong that controlling for it can actually reverse the sign of the effect. If women were much more likely than men to be in low status jobs, and if female employees almost never went absent from work, it might seem that people doing low status jobs were no more likely or even *less* likely than others to be absent. Suppressor variables such as this which are strong enough to reverse the sign of the relationship are called **distorter variables**.

If you have been stimulated by all this consideration of hypothetical possibilities to find out what relationships actually hold between gender, job type and absenteeism, you might like to read Chadwick-Jones *et al.*, 1982.

11.9 Conclusion

Only when we are sure that all possible test factors have been controlled can we feel confident that we begin to understand the possible causal processes at work. Since no survey ever measures all variables, this requirement is never met in full. But in the better, more carefully planned investigations, the variables which are the most important test factors are measured, and brought under control in the analysis.

The same point is made another way when we demand that our residuals should be patternless. If there are important test factors which have been excluded from the model, the residuals from the model will contain an important degree of pattern: they will be systematically related to the omitted variable. We may or may not be aware of this.

Causal inferences are constructions built upon foundations of assumptions. They cannot be more valid than the assumptions. If this induces a feeling of unease in you such that you start routinely checking the concrete around the foundations of inferences drawn from social science data, so much the better. Your job, however, is to mend any plausible cracks you observe – to do a better survey, measuring and controlling important new variables – not to walk away from the edifice declaring it to be a hazard. Be sure to remember how poor lay reasoning about causation is: not to even try to collect the data required to test a hypothesis about the relationship between smoking and lung cancer would be to leave the doors open only to those who jump to conclusions on the basis of a sample of one.

Those of you who are anxious to get back to some real data can now relax: the excursion into philosophy is over, and we return to the nuts and bolts of describing patterns in batches of numbers.

But take with you the lessons of this chapter. A statistical association between one variable and another cannot just be accepted as causal at face value. If we want to show that it is not spurious, we have to demonstrate that there are no plausible prior variables affecting both the variables of interest. If we want to argue that the causal mechanism is fairly direct, we have to control for similar intervening variables.

The act of controlling for a third variable can have many possible results. It can both suggest that an effect previously believed to exist does not exist and that one thought not to exist does exist. It can enhance or suppress its magnitude. As summarized by Simpson's paradox, it can even reverse the sign of the original effect.

The first-order task is to think logically about which variables need to be included in any model, and what types of mechanisms and processes may explain the links between them. While it is important to know that your sample size is big enough for safe conclusions to be drawn (that effects are 'statistically significant'), this is secondary in comparison with the issue of whether a relationship can be given a causal interpretation, or is merely the spurious result of the operation of third factors. The relationship between the number of fire engines and the amount of damage caused could be derived from a sample size of ten thousand and still utterly mislead if taken at face value.

This chapter was therefore important in linking the second and third parts of the book. It should have convinced you of the importance of proceeding beyond bivariate relationships to considering systems in which three or more variables are operating together.

Exercises

11.1 Decide on balance which variable you think would be the cause and which the effect in the following pairs:
  (a) party supported in an election and the type of newspaper read
  (b) wage rises and inflation (both measured over time)
  (c) unemployment and ill health
  (d) attitude towards abortion and religion
  (e) Gross National Income in a country and life expectancy.

11.2 Consider three variables: financial circumstances of family (comfortable vs struggling); marital status of parents (married and cohabiting vs divorced or separated) and educational outcomes for children. Draw a causal path diagram indicating the relationships you would assume to exist between these variables. Suppose the bivariate effect of parents' marital status on educational outcomes for children was strongly positive. What would you expect to happen to the magnitude of the effect once you had controlled for financial circumstances?

11.3 In 2001 there was a special edition of the journal *European Sociological Review* which focused on causality in the social sciences. Read the paper by Ni Bhrolchain entitled: ' "Divorce effects" and causality in the social sciences' (vol. 17, pp. 33–57) and make a list of the main problems that the author identifies with the majority of research which aims to identify the consequences of divorce for children.

12

Three-Variable Contingency
Tables and Beyond

12.1 Trust and reciprocity

In this chapter we will use data from the 2004 Social Attitudes Survey to explore the possible link between an individual's membership of voluntary associations and his or her levels of 'social trust'. In order to understand these possible links we will also need to take account of other factors such as an individual's level of qualifications. This empirical investigation has its theoretical underpinnings in recent influential work on communities and social capital (see for example Putnam (2000) and for a good discussion of social capital see Halpern (2005)). For Putnam, 'social capital refers to connections among individuals – social networks and the norms of reciprocity and trustworthiness that arise from them' (Putnam 2000, p. 19). Putnam argues that trustworthiness 'lubricates' social life and that communities in which there is a high level of trust between members will have a measurable economic advantage. It is perhaps no wonder then that it is not just academics, but also government advisers, civil servants and ministers who have shown an interest in Putnam's work over the past few years.

Putnam makes a distinction between what he calls 'thick trust' and 'thin trust'. Trust and honesty based on personal experience and on knowing people well over a number of years is conceptualized as 'thick trust'. However, this is only possible with a relatively small number of people and is therefore not as useful within a community as 'thin trust'. This can be understood as the decision that an individual might make to give most people – even those one doesn't know personally – the benefit of the doubt. Putnam argues that there is a strong association between 'thin trust' and engagement in community life. Those who trust others are all-round good citizens who are more likely to be members of voluntary associations, contribute to charity, get involved with politics, etc.

The techniques to be presented in this chapter are designed to examine the relationships between three or more categorical variables. They are an extension of the techniques considered in chapters 6 and 7 and they also build on the arguments about the need for controls presented in chapter 11. In addition to introducing how to produce and interpret three-variable tables, this chapter will also provide an introduction to logistic regression analysis. For the sake of simplicity, we will stick to analysing dichotomies, but the principles established in this chapter are easily extended to situations where the explanatory variables have three or more categories. Further information about the 2004 British Social Attitudes Survey can be found in the appendix to this chapter on the accompanying website.

12.2 Controlling for a prior variable

As part of the self-completion section of the survey, respondents to the Social Attitudes Survey in 2004 were asked:

Generally speaking, would you say that people can be trusted or that you can't be too careful in dealing with people?

Overall, just under half (45.2 per cent) said that people can usually or almost always be trusted, with 51.2 per cent stating that 'you can't be too careful'. A further 3.6 per cent didn't answer the question, or said they couldn't choose between the options offered. Given the importance of 'thin trust' for a healthy and functioning society, discussed in the introduction above, it is interesting to explore which factors may lead certain individuals within the population to be less trusting than others.

The self-completion section of the British Social Attitudes Survey in 2004 also asked respondents about their membership of a number of different types of clubs and associations. In response to the question:

People sometimes belong to different kinds of groups or associations. Please indicate whether you: belong and actively participate; belong but don't actively participate; used to belong but do not any more; or have never belonged to . . . A voluntary association

approximately one in six (16.2 per cent) of individuals stated that they were currently members of some kind of voluntary group or association. Of these, 11.6 per cent were active members and a further 4.6 per cent were members, but did not actively take part, while 20.4 per cent used to belong to a voluntary group or association (the total sample size was 853). Recent work on social capital, social participation and social trust would suggest that membership of a voluntary organization may well be associated with higher levels of social trust. Those who are more engaged with community life are likely to be more trusting and more trustworthy (Putnam, 2000, p. 137). As was demonstrated in chapter 6, we can investigate the possible links between trust and membership of voluntary groups by using data from the Social Attitudes Survey to construct a simple contingency table as shown in figure 12.1. (Note that in this table we express the percentages in the different categories as proportions in the same way that we did in chapter 7, because this approach makes it more straightforward to calculate and compare effect sizes.)

Figure 12.1 Membership of voluntary organization by social trust.

	Can't be too careful	People can be trusted	N
Not a member of voluntary group	0.550	0.450	689
Currently a member of a voluntary group	0.436	0.564	133
D		0.114	
missing cases = 31			

Source: Analysis of data from the 2004 British Social Attitude Survey.

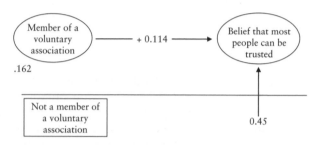

Figure 12.2 Causal path diagram based on contingency table in figure 12.1.

These results could be depicted in a causal path diagram as shown in figure 12.2. The model tells us that 0.450 of those who are not currently members of a voluntary group say that most people can be trusted (the baseline). While for those who are members of a voluntary association this baseline figure can be increased by 0.114.

The result confirms the existing literature on the link between community involvement and social trust, although the difference between the two groups is not enormous, those who are a current member of a voluntary association are more trusting. If we create this table in a package such as SPSS, it is straightforward also to calculate chi-square and this was found to be 5.817 with one degree of freedom and an associated p value of 0.016 indicating a significant relationship between the two variables. (You may wish to look back at chapter 7 to make sure that you understand this before reading on.) However, this is just the beginning of the process of analysis. This association raises questions about what types of people are most likely to be members of voluntary associations and what types of people are most likely to have high levels of social trust. Before we embark on any further analyses, however, we need to be sure that the association between volunteering and social trust is some kind of real causal link and not just the spurious result of joint association with a prior explanatory variable, as explained in chapter 11. We need to think about any additional factors or individual characteristics that are likely to be related to both volunteering behaviour and social trust. We control for these factors and find out whether the relationship between volunteering and social trust remains.

Figure 12.3 Highest level of qualifications by membership of a voluntary association.

	Currently member of voluntary association	Not currently a member	N
Degree or above	0.226	0.774	239
A-level or below	0.137	0.863	614
d	0.089		

Source: Analysis of data from the 2004 British Social Attitudes Survey.

One variable which is a good candidate for such a test factor is level of qualifications. Previous research has shown that those who are highly qualified are most likely to do voluntary work and become members of community groups (Bynner and Parsons, 2003). It is also possible that the level of qualifications an individual has will be associated with whether an individual expresses high levels of trust in others. We might predict that those with high level qualifications are more trusting. Using data from the 2004 British Social Attitudes Survey we can check whether these associations are present within this sample of the British population.

Figure 12.3 shows an association in the direction that we might expect from previous research, namely that those with higher levels of qualifications are more likely to be members of voluntary associations. Once again, using SPSS chi-square can be calculated to check the significance of this association (chi-square=10.079, df=1, p=0.001).

Figure 12.4 also confirms that those with higher levels of qualifications tend to be more trusting.

Figure 12.4 Highest levels of qualifications by social trust.

	People can be trusted	Can't be too careful	N
Degree or above	0.572	0.428	229
A-level or below	0.428	0.572	593
d	0.144		

Source: Analysis of data from the 2004 British Social Attitudes Survey.

Computation of chi-square showed this to be a statistically significant relationship (chi-square = 13.705, df = 1, p<0.001). By comparing the relative size of *d* in figures 12.3 and 12.4 we can also see that level of highest qualifications appears to have a greater impact on trust than it has on being a member of a voluntary group (discussion of effect size '*d*' was introduced in section 7.3 and it may help to go back and read this again if you are unclear what is being measured here). However, in the current example the important thing to note here is that qualifications are associated with both volunteering and social trust and that therefore we need to **control** for qualifications in our analysis of volunteering and social trust. Given the results displayed in figures 12.3 and 12.4 it could be qualifications that explain the apparent association between volunteering and social trust. In other words, people who have high qualifications tend to be members of voluntary organizations and to report high levels of trust in other people and this may be behind the association we found in figure 12.1.

To control for a variable in contingency tables we look within its categories. For example, to control for qualifications when assessing the effect of volunteering on social trust, we look separately at those with different levels of qualifications. Complex tables can get quite hard to read and interpret systematically, and one way to help think through the different possible causal influences is to draw a more complex causal path model.

12.3 Causal path models for three variables

The set of paths of causal influence, both direct and indirect, that we want to begin to consider are represented in figure 12.5. In this causal model we are trying to explain social trust, the base is therefore the belief that 'You can't be too careful'. The base categories selected for the explanatory variables are having lower levels of qualifications and not being a member of a voluntary organization, to try and avoid negative paths. Each arrow linking two variables in a causal path diagram represents the direct effect of one variable upon the other, controlling all other relevant variables. The rule for identifying the relevant variables was given in chapter 11: when we are assessing the direct effect of one variable upon another, any third variable which is likely to be causally connected to both variables and prior to one of them should be controlled. Coefficient b in figure 12.5 shows the direct effect of being in a voluntary association on the belief that most people can be trusted. To find its value, we focus attention on the proportion who say that most people can be trusted, controlling for level of qualifications. In order to understand how to do this it is easiest to refer to actual figures rather than discussing the principles in the abstract. We therefore first need to use SPSS to help us create a three-way contingency table that takes account of all three variables we are interested in.

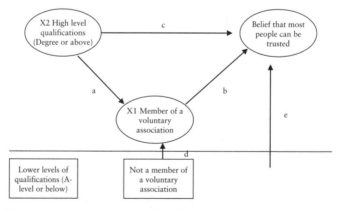

Figure 12.5 Social trust by membership of voluntary association and level of qualifications: causal path diagram.

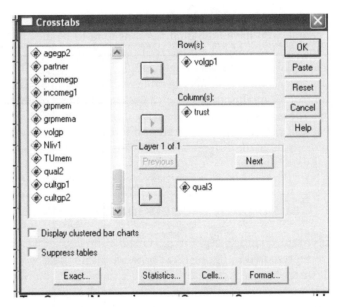

Figure 12.6   Screenshot of the Crosstabs dialogue box – creating a three-way contingency table.

Within SPSS the Crosstabs procedure can be used to provide a three-way table. As shown in figure 12.6, the control variable is entered into the 'Layer' section of the dialogue box.

This produces figure 12.7, which is in effect two separate tables, the first showing the association between volunteering and social trust for those with a degree or higher and beneath it a table showing the association between volunteering and social trust for those with A-level qualifications or lower.

We can capture the relationships that are demonstrated in this table more simply if we just focus on the proportion of individuals who say that 'Most people can be trusted' in each of four groups – high qualified volunteers, high qualified non-volunteers, low qualified volunteers and low qualified non-volunteers. These proportions are displayed in figure 12.8 together with the associated *d* statistics. The effect of being a volunteer is obtained by subtracting the proportion of those who are not members of a voluntary association from the proportion of people who are currently a member of a voluntary association. But qualifications must be controlled because it is connected to both volunteering and social trust and prior to both of them. So two different calculations are made, the effect of volunteering among the highly qualified is 0.593 – 0.566, or + 0.027, and that among the less well qualified is 0.544 − 0.411 or + 0.133. We have therefore obtained two *d*s – one for the highly qualified and one for the less well qualified.

How is a single number summary of the *d*s to be found? For the purposes of this chapter, we will simply take the arithmetic mean; the *d* among the well qualified is +0.027, among those with A-levels or lower qualifications is +0.133, so the average effect (coefficient *b*) is +0.08. Like all summaries, this average *d* only

Figure 12.7   Extract from SPSS output showing a three-way contingency table.

Currently a member of a voluntary group? * Attitudes towards trusting people * qual3 Crosstabulation

qual3					Attitudes towards trusting people		Total
					Can't be too careful	People can be trusted	
Degree or higher	Currently a member of a voluntary group?	No	Count		76	99	175
			% within Currently a member of a voluntary group?		43.4%	56.6%	100.0%
		Yes	Count		22	32	54
			% within Currently a member of a voluntary group?		40.7%	59.3%	100.0%
	Total		Count		98	131	229
			% within Currently a member of a voluntary group?		42.8%	57.2%	100.0%
Alevel eqiv or lower	Currently a member of a voluntary group?	No	Count		303	211	514
			% within Currently a member of a voluntary group?		58.9%	41.1%	100.0%
		Yes	Count		36	43	79
			% within Currently a member of a voluntary group?		45.6%	54.4%	100.0%
	Total		Count		339	254	593
			% within Currently a member of a voluntary group?		57.2%	42.8%	100.0%

makes sense if the coefficients being averaged are broadly similar. We will discuss what to do if they are not in section 12.6. There are, of course, more sophisticated and sensitive ways of combining the two ds. One fairly obvious procedure would be to weight each d by the number of cases it was based on. But for now we will keep the process as simple as possible.

The effect of being a volunteer ($+0.08$) on social trust is seen to be pretty small. Indeed by controlling for level of qualifications we have reduced the size of d from 0.114 to 0.08. The original effect of being a volunteer in figure 12.2 ($+0.114$) was spuriously high. It was a product of the fact that the well qualified are more likely to be members of organizations and the well qualified are also more likely to express high levels of social trust. The operation of these two education effects is not, however, strong enough to actually reverse the sign of the relationship between volunteering and social trust. The general conclusion still holds: those who are currently members of voluntary associations have somewhat higher levels of social trust than those who do not participate in their community in this way.

We can assess the direct effect of qualifications on social trust controlling for volunteering in the same way. Among those who are members of voluntary organizations, 0.593 of those with high level qualifications and 0.544 of those with lower level qualifications state that most people can be trusted – a difference of $+0.049$ (see figure 12.8). Among those who are not members of a voluntary association, the difference is $+0.155$. The average (coefficient c) is therefore $+0.102$.

Figure 12.8 Social trust by highest level of qualifications and membership of a voluntary association.

	Degree or above	N	A-level or below	N
Not a member of a voluntary group	0.566	175	0.411	514
Currently a member of a voluntary group	0.593	54	0.544	79
d	0.027		0.133	
Average value of d = 0.08				

So the direct effect of high level qualifications (+0.102) is seen to be somewhat stronger than the direct effect of being a volunteer (+0.08).

Being highly qualified also has an indirect effect upon levels of social trust because those with high levels of qualifications are more likely to be members of voluntary groups, and, as we have seen, those who are currently members of a voluntary association are somewhat more likely to express trust in other people. It is not necessary to control for anything, since in this particular model there are no other variables connected to both qualifications and volunteering and prior to one of them (if the logic of this escapes you then re-read chapter 11; these are complex ideas that repay repetition). We therefore consider the effect of qualifications on volunteering as shown in the original bivariate table in figure 12.3. While 0.226 of the well qualified respondents were volunteers, only 0.137 of the less well qualified respondents were, a difference of +0.089. So coefficient *a* is +0.089. Causal path models are excellent devices for forcing the data analyst to look at the appropriate marginal relationships in tables.

There are also two paths, *d* and *e*, in figure 12.5 which represent the other unspecified causes; all variables in a model which have causal paths leading to them must also have arrows reminding us of the proportion unpredicted by the model. The values are obtained from the proportion of the base groups who are in the non-base categories of the response variables. Path *d* is given by the proportion of the less well qualified who are volunteers (0.137 to be precise, from figure 12.3). And path *e* reminds us that some less well qualified respondents who were not members of a voluntary association said that most people could be trusted; the value of coefficient *e* is therefore 0.411 (figure 12.9). These paths are the final coefficients to be entered on the quantified model (figure 12.9).

We can be sure that the model in figure 12.9 is better than that derived from figure 12.2. However, we cannot even be sure that it has got the causal effects absolutely right. Their accuracy still depends upon the correctness of our assumptions about causal order and the operation of other variables. If we had either specified the causal order incorrectly, or failed to control for other important variables, the coefficients would be meaningless. Worse, nothing in the data themselves would alert us to this fact. Science is a collective enterprise; over time, researchers build up a body of wisdom which tells them which are the important variables to include when modelling a particular process, and which must be controlled.

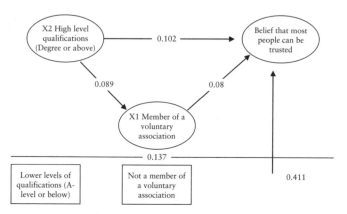

Figure 12.9 Assigning coefficients to figure 12.5.

12.4 More complex models: going beyond three variables

Clearly there are likely to be many other factors or 'variables' that will have an influence, both on volunteering behaviour and on social trust. For example, in the model discussed above we have not considered gender or age, and both of these may have an impact on all of the variables in our model. As can be seen from the discussion above, it becomes quite complicated even to calculate the direct and indirect causal paths when we have a simple model with three variables. We therefore need to go beyond these paper and pencil techniques if we are going to build more complex models that aim to compare the impact of a number of different explanatory variables on an outcome variable such as social trust. The following section describes the conceptual foundations that underlie models to examine the factors influencing a simple dichotomous (two-category) variable.

12.5 Logistic regression models

In chapter 9, regression analysis was introduced as a method for predicting the values of a continuously distributed dependent variable from an independent, or explanatory, variable. The principles behind logistic regression are very similar and the approach to building models and interpreting the models is virtually identical. However, whereas regression (more properly termed Ordinary Least Squares regression, or OLS regression) is used when the dependent variable is continuous, a binary logistic regression model is used when the dependent variable can only take two values. In many examples this dependent variable indicates whether an event occurs or not and logistic regression is used to model the **probability** that the event occurs. In the example we have been discussing above, therefore, logistic regression would be used to model the probability that an individual believes that most people can be trusted. When we are just using a single explanatory variable, such as volunteering, the logistic regression can be written as

$$\text{Prob(event)} = \frac{1}{1 + e^{-\beta X}}$$

or more specifically

$$\text{Prob(trust)} = \frac{1}{1 + e^{-\beta \textit{volunteering}}}$$

In order to estimate this model using SPSS select 'Regression' and then 'Binary Logistic' from the 'Analyze' menu (see figure 12.10).

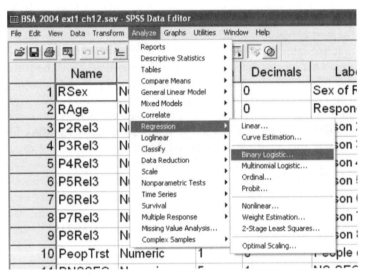

Figure 12.10   Screenshot of SPSS demonstrating Binary Logistic regression command.

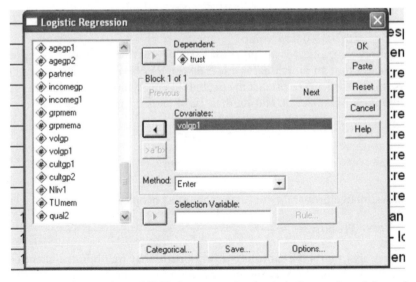

Figure 12.11   Screenshot of SPSS demonstrating Logistic Regression dialogue box.

Next specify the dependent variable as 'trust' (this is what we are aiming to predict), and then select 'volgp1' from the list of variables and place it in the Covariates box (see figure 12.11). This is where we list all the independent or 'explanatory' variables. In this first example we will just focus on one explanatory variable but a whole list of explanatory variables could be added here.

Logistic regression models can include both categorical and continuous explanatory variables or 'covariates', so the next stage is to specify which explanatory variables in the model are categorical, and which category is to be treated as the base or reference category. To do this, click on the 'Categorical' button and then transfer the variable 'volgp1' into the list of categorical covariates. In this example the first category should be used as the reference category as this is the category that indicates that an individual is **not** currently a member of a voluntary organization. This means that in the model the coefficient will be for those who are members of a voluntary association. Make sure the 'First' reference category is checked and then click on the 'Change' button (see figure 12.12). Next click on the 'Continue' button. By clicking on 'Paste' the following syntax will then be pasted into a syntax window and you can highlight this and run the commands in order to estimate this most basic model with just one explanatory variable.

```
LOGISTIC REGRESSION trust
/METHOD = ENTER volgp1
/CONTRAST (volgp1)=Indicator(1)
/CRITERIA = PIN(.05) POUT(.10) ITERATE(20) CUT(.5) .
```

The parameter estimates for this very simple model are shown in figure 12.13.

The logistic regression equation for predicting the probability of an individual saying that people can be trusted is therefore

$$\text{Prob(trust)} = \frac{1}{1 + e^{-z}}$$

Where $Z = -0.201 + 0.458(\text{volgp1})$.

Remember that volgp1 is an indicator variable and that a value of 1 on this variable indicates that an individual is a member of a voluntary group. We can therefore use the coefficients to predict the probability of an individual who is a member of a voluntary organization stating that 'most people can be trusted'.

$$Z = 0.257$$

$$1 + e^{-z} = 1.773$$

And the estimated probability of saying that most people can be trusted is therefore

$$\text{Prob(trust)} = \frac{1}{1 + e^{-z}} = \frac{1}{1 + e^{-0.257}} = \frac{1}{1.773} = 0.564$$

We can see that this is the same as the proportion that we obtained in the contingency table in figure 12.1 examining the association between volunteering and social trust. This may seem like a very convoluted method to obtain a simple

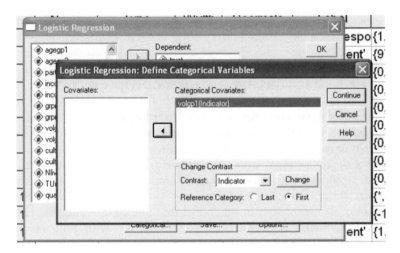

Figure 12.12 SPSS screenshot demonstrating the specification of categorical covariates in the model.

Figure 12.13 Parameter estimates.

Variables in the Equation

		B	S.E.	Wald	df	Sig.	Exp(B)
Step 1ᵃ	volgp1(1)	.458	.191	5.757	1	.016	1.581
	Constant	-.201	.077	6.887	1	.009	.818

a. Variable(s) entered on step 1: volgp1.

proportion, and indeed for a model with just one explanatory variable the more straightforward route is to create a contingency table. However, the purpose here is to demonstrate the links between logistic regression and contingency tables so that we can move on to estimate more complex models.

Using the same model, **for an individual who is not a member of a voluntary association**, the variable volgp1 takes the value 0 and so Z is equivalent to the constant term -0.201. In this case

$$1 + e^{-z} \text{ is } 2.223$$

$$\frac{1}{2.223} = 0.450$$

And the probability of saying most people can be trusted for someone who is not a member of a voluntary group is therefore 0.450.

Looking back at figure 12.13, we can also see that there is a significance value associated with the coefficient. This is in the column labelled 'Sig.'. We first introduced significance values (or p values) in chapter 7 as a way of judging whether a result found in the sample was likely to be 'significant', i.e. whether it is also likely to be found in the population represented by a specific sample. In the context of logistic regression the P value in the column labelled Sig. provides an indication of whether the coefficient is significantly different from 0. For large sample sizes, such as in this example, the test that a specific coefficient is 0 can be based on the Wald statistic, which has a chi-squared distribution when it is squared.

12.6 Estimating a more complex model

The advantage of the binary logistic regression method over the construction of a simple contingency table is the ability to estimate a more complex model with several different explanatory variables. Let's start by following the logic discussed above and estimate a model with two explanatory variables, namely 1) being a member of a voluntary association and 2) level of qualifications. In this more complex model the syntax is as follows:

```
LOGISTIC REGRESSION trust
  /METHOD = ENTER volgp1 degree
  /CONTRAST (volgp1)=Indicator(1) /CONTRAST (degree)=Indicator(1)
  /CRITERIA = PIN(.05) POUT(.10) ITERATE(20) CUT(.5) .
```

This model can also be run from the menus in the same way that was shown in figures 12.10 to 12.12. Note that trust is still the dependent variable but this time there are two 'Contrast' subcommands, one for each explanatory variable. The parameter estimates for this model with two explanatory variables are shown in figure 12.14.

Figure 12.14 Variables in the Equation

		B	S.E.	Wald	df	Sig.	Exp(B)
Step 1[a]	volgp1(1)	.382	.194	3.899	1	.048	1.466
	degree(1)	.543	.159	11.719	1	.001	1.721
	Constant	-.340	.087	15.218	1	.000	.711

[a] Variable(s) entered on step 1: volgp1, degree.

We can see that both variables in the model are significant because the p values in the 'Sig.' column are less than .05. However, the coefficient for the volunteering variable is only just less than 0.05 at 0.048 and this coefficient has been reduced from .458 to .382 by the inclusion of qualifications in the model. This confirms what we found when constructing a three-way contingency table above, namely that being a member of a voluntary association has less of an impact on social trust once the prior variable 'qualifications' has been controlled.

Next, let's estimate an even more complex model that also includes income, sex and age. In this example, to keep everything as simple as possible, each of these variables is entered as dichotomous explanatory variables. The income variable indicates whether household income is greater or less than £20,000 per annum, and the age variable indicates whether individuals are 45 and under (young) or 46 and over (old), while the sex variable is coded 1 for men and 2 for women. The syntax for this slightly more complex model is given below (once again this could also be run using the menus as described above).

LOGISTIC REGRESSION trust
/METHOD = ENTER volgp1 degree RSex incomegp agegp1
/CONTRAST (volgp1)=Indicator(1) /CONTRAST (degree)=Indicator(1)
/CONTRAST (RSex)=Indicator(1) /CONTRAST
(incomegp)=Indicator(1) /CONTRAST (agegp1)=Indicator(1)
/CRITERIA = PIN(.05) POUT(.10) ITERATE(20) CUT(.5).

Examining the coefficients and their associated significance in figure 12.15, we can see that qualifications and income are highly significant, age is not too far from being significant (p = 0.09), but sex and being a member of a voluntary organization are not significant. In other words, although in our very first model we found that being a member of a voluntary group did appear to have a significant impact on social trust, making individuals more trusting, once we have controlled for variables such as qualifications and income, being a member of a voluntary group is no longer significant. Rather, it is those with high level qualifications (degree and above) and those who have a relatively high household income (£20,000 per year or more) who are most likely to say that most people can be trusted. The evidence from this model, based on analysis of the Social Attitudes Survey 2004, would therefore suggest that there is perhaps less of a link between engagement in community life and trust than Putnam has supposed.

Figure 12.15 Parameter estimates for the model with five explanatory variables predicting 'trust'.

Variables in the Equation

		B	S.E.	Wald	df	Sig.	Exp(B)
Step 1[a]	volgp1(1)	.221	.212	1.085	1	.298	1.247
	degree(1)	.479	.176	7.398	1	.007	1.615
	RSex(1)	.184	.157	1.364	1	.243	1.201
	incomegp(1)	.672	.167	16.168	1	.000	1.959
	agegp1(1)	.274	.162	2.877	1	.090	1.315
	Constant	-.867	.199	19.060	1	.000	.420

a. Variable(s) entered on step 1: volgp1, degree, RSex, incomegp, agegp1.

In the model above, age was included as a categorical dichotomous explanatory variable in order to keep the model as simple as possible. We can see that the coefficient for age is reasonably large and positive (0.274) suggesting that those in the older age group are more trusting than those in the younger age group. However, this did not reach significance as the associated p value is only 0.09. One problem with the interpretation here is that by collapsing age into a dichotomous variable we have lost a lot of information. When individuals answered questions in the 2004 British Social Attitudes Survey, their age last birthday was recorded, but in the model above we have placed those who are 20 in the same category as those who are 40 (by classifying them all as 'young') and those who are 46 in the same category as those who are 70 (by classifying them as 'old'). As was noted above, one of the advantages of the logistic regression model is that it is possible to include both categorical and continuous explanatory variables in the model. Let us therefore now re-estimate exactly the same model, but include the original age variable rather than a dichotomous summary of age. The syntax is now as shown below, the variable agegp1 has been replaced by RAge and because this is a continuous variable there is no associated 'CONTRAST' subcommand.

```
LOGISTIC REGRESSION trust
    /METHOD = ENTER volgp1 degree RSex incomegp RAge
    /CONTRAST (volgp1)=Indicator(1) /CONTRAST (degree)=Indicator(1)
    /CONTRAST (RSex)=Indicator(1) /CONTRAST
    (incomegp)=Indicator(1)
    /CRITERIA = PIN(.05) POUT(.10) ITERATE(20) CUT(.5).
```

The model coefficients are displayed in figure 12.16.

Figure 12.16 Model coefficients to predict 'trust' using the original age variable.

Variables in the Equation

		B	S.E.	Wald	df	Sig.	Exp(B)
Step 1[a]	volgp1(1)	.222	.211	1.110	1	.292	1.249
	degree(1)	.510	.178	8.211	1	.004	1.666
	RSex(1)	.181	.157	1.323	1	.250	1.198
	incomegp(1)	.714	.172	17.181	1	.000	2.042
	RAge	.010	.005	3.867	1	.049	1.010
	Constant	-1.238	.333	13.846	1	.000	.290

a. Variable(s) entered on step 1: volgp1, degree, RSex, incomegp, RAge.

We can see that in the new model the continuous age variable is just significant (p = .049), but the coefficient associated with age appears very low at just 0.010. The reason for this is that age is now measured in years so for every additional year of age the probability of stating that most people can be trusted increases by a very small marginal amount. However, the coefficient for an individual who is 60 years old will still be 0.4 greater than the coefficient for an individual aged 20 and so age can be seen to have a substantial effect.

One problem with entering a continuous variable such as age into the model in this way is that it assumes that there is a linear association between age and trust (this is discussed more fully in chapter 10). One simple way to investigate this is to create a variable for age with several different categories and inspect the coefficients to check whether the relationship is reasonably linear. Alternatively, age can be transformed into age squared (i.e. a quadratic) as described in chapter 10, and included in the model.

12.7 Interpreting the coefficients in a logistic regression model

Although it is possible to use the method above to calculate the individual probabilities for the different groups represented in the model, it is useful to have a more intuitive method for interpreting the coefficients. In linear regression (introduced in chapter 9) the interpretation of the regression coefficient is relatively straightforward. Thinking graphically, it is the slope of the regression line through the points on the scatterplot. When there is more than one explanatory variable in the model it can be interpreted as the estimated change in the dependent variable for a one unit change in the explanatory variable, assuming that the values of all the other variables in the model are held constant. This also means that the value of a coefficient will depend on the other explanatory variables that the researcher has decided to include in the model. It is also true that in a logistic regression model the value of a coefficient will depend on the other variables in the model. However, unfortunately the interpretation of that coefficient is not as intuitive as the slope of a line. The value of a coefficient for Variable A 'VARA' in a logistic regression indicates the increase in the log odds of the dependent variable if VARA increases by one unit. For example in figure 12.16, the coefficient of 0.51 associated with the variable 'degree' could be interpreted that having a degree increases an individual's *log* odds of 'trusting' people by 0.51 because log odds are difficult to interpret. SPSS also provides the values for Exp(B) (i.e. e^B) so that it can be seen that having a degree increases an individual's odds of trusting people by a factor of approximately 1.67 compared with an individual who does not have a degree. Further information about interpreting logistic regression models can be found in Norusis (2005).

12.8 Estimating a more complex model – interactions

Although the models in figures 12.15 and 12.16 are considerably more complex than the model with just one or two explanatory variables they are still relatively straightforward in that all the explanatory variables are considered separately. In this section we move on to consider more complex models which include 'interaction terms'.

Generalizations are at the heart of social scientific activity. We aim to discover causal processes which could potentially affect everyone in society. When we find that having high levels of qualifications makes people more likely to trust others, we assume that the reasons for this are general. We suppose that the increased likelihood would operate for anyone who had high levels of qualifications – whatever their age or gender.

When no generalization can be made about the causal process at work, we say that there is an **interaction** in the relationships. An interaction can be formally defined as a situation in which the effect of one variable upon another depends upon the value of a third variable; when asked how much effect X has on Y, we are forced to answer: 'it depends'. Interactions are sometimes also called 'conditional relationships'. In other words, the relationship varies under different conditions.

To illustrate this point, let us examine a further set of findings from the 2004 Social Attitudes Survey. In addition to asking respondents about membership of organizations, social participation and social trust, the Social Attitudes Survey also includes questions about party identification and views on whether it is appropriate for government to play a central role in redistributing wealth and providing welfare payments for the least well-off in society. It is therefore possible to

Figure 12.17   Bivariate relationship between party identification and views on welfare.

Government should spend more on welfare benefits for the poor		
	Disagree	Agree	N
Conservative	0.747	0.253	676
Labour	0.515	0.485	804
Liberal Democrat	0.535	0.465	325
Total	0.605	0.395	1805

Source: Analysis of British Social Attitudes Survey 2004.

examine the link between political leanings and attitudes, for different groups within society. For example, figure 12.17 shows the bivariate relationship between party identification (simplified to Conservative, Labour or Liberal Democrat) and agreement with the statement: '*The government should spend more money on welfare benefits for the poor, even if it leads to higher taxes.*'

We can see that, as we might well predict, in comparison with the Conservatives, both Labour and Liberal Democrat supporters are more likely to agree with the statement that Government should spend more on welfare benefits for the poor. However, we might expect the relationship between attitudes and party identification to differ among people of different generations. In particular, over the past decade, the political parties could be argued to have realigned themselves somewhat so that the Liberal Democrats have campaigned explicitly for social justice and stated that it would not rule out higher taxes in order to have more money for public spending. It therefore makes good sense for us to control for age when looking at the relationship between party identification and attitudes on welfare spending. The cross-tabulation is shown in figure 12.18.

Once age is controlled, the association between party identification and views on welfare spending changes somewhat. Among those aged 46 or more, the relationship is as it seemed from the bivariate table: those who support the Labour Party are more likely than the Conservatives or the Liberal Democrats to agree with higher spending on welfare for the poor, even at the risk of higher taxes. But among the more recent generations aged 45 or under, the relationship is slightly different in that it is those who identify with the Liberal Democrats who are *most*

Figure 12.18   Proportion agreeing with higher spending on welfare by party identification by age.

Government should spend more on welfare benefits for the poor		
	45 and under	46 plus	N
Conservative	0.116	0.33	676
Labour	0.377	0.57	804
Liberal Democrat	0.381	0.53	325
Total	0.292	0.466	1805
Labour d	0.261	0.24	
Lib Dem d	0.265	0.2	

Source: Analysis of British Social Attitudes Survey 2004.

Figure 12.19 The impact of party identification and age on attitudes to welfare spending [Model 1].

Variables in the Equation

		B	S.E.	Wald	df	Sig.	Exp(B)
Step 1[a]	agegp1(1)	.879	.106	68.865	1	.000	2.408
	conlablib			101.958	2	.000	
	conlablib(1)	1.134	.117	94.508	1	.000	3.109
	conlablib(2)	1.043	.146	51.064	1	.000	2.838
	Constant	-1.689	.119	200.169	1	.000	.185

a. Variable(s) entered on step 1: agegp1, conlablib.

Note that conlablib(1) = Labour supporters and conlablib(2) = Liberal supporters

likely to support higher welfare spending. The patterns of attitudes are not that different for the two age groups, but the result is sufficiently different for us to feel uncomfortable about averaging the two effects. There is, in short, some evidence of an interaction present. The association between party identification and attitudes to welfare spending depends upon one's age.

Once some evidence of an interaction has been found in simple exploratory analysis it is worth building this interaction effect into a logistic regression model to be able to test formally whether the patterns of results for the two age groups are sufficiently different to be statistically significant. If you have mastered estimating and interpreting a simple logistic regression model, using a package such as SPSS, it is relatively straightforward to include an interaction term. Let us now therefore estimate and inspect two models. The first includes just the 'main effects' or explanatory variables age and party identification, with attitudes to welfare spending as the dependent variable. The second includes both the main effects and the interaction term. In both models the first category of each variable is set as the base or reference category (as discussed above). In other words the coefficients in the model will be for the older age group and for those supporting the Labour Party and the Liberal Democrat Party.

We can see that both age group and party identification are significantly associated with attitudes to welfare spending. The first positive coefficient in column B indicates that older people are more in favour of spending more on welfare than younger people (because the younger age group was used as the reference category). The positive coefficient for conlablib(1) 1.134 indicates that those who support the Labour Party are more likely to agree with higher welfare spending than the Conservatives (the reference category). The positive coefficient for conlablib(2) 1.043 indicates that those who support the Liberal Democrats are more likely to agree with higher welfare spending than the Conservatives. In addition, the fact that the coefficient for Labour supporters is slightly higher than the coefficient for Liberal Democrat supporters echoes the bivariate relationship that we observed in figure 12.18, namely that Labour supporters are slightly more in favour of higher welfare spending than are Liberal Democrat supporters.

In order to estimate a model including the interaction term between party identification and age group, we follow the same procedure described above for estimating a logistic regression model with main effects. In addition we highlight the two variables that form the interaction term (by highlighting one variable and then pressing the Control key while highlighting the second variable) and include this interaction in the list of covariates by clicking on the button marked '>a*b>' as shown in figure 12.20.

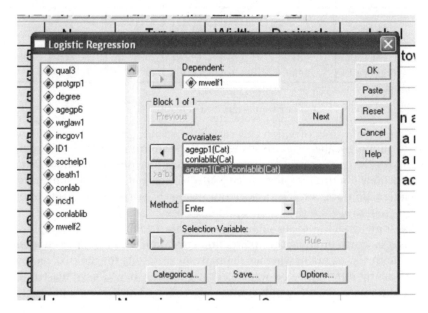

Figure 12.20 Screenshot demonstrating a logistic regression including an interaction term.

The model including interaction effects is displayed in figure 12.21. We can see that there are now two additional coefficients in the model, one for the interaction between age and identification with the Labour Party (agegp1(1) by conlablib(1)) and one for the interaction between age and identification with the Liberal Democrat Party(agegp1(1) by conlablib(2)). The fact that these both have associated p values in the Significance column of the table that are less than 0.05 shows that there is a 'significant' interaction. The coefficients attached to the interactions are also both negative whereas the coefficients associated with the main effects of age group and political party supported are both positive. This can be interpreted to mean that those who are in the older age group and are supporters of the Liberal Democrat or Labour parties are not as likely to agree with higher spending on welfare as would be expected from the model with just the main effects. Another way of understanding this is to say that the association between an individual's party allegiance and his or her views on welfare spending are dependent on age group. This is the key to what we mean by an interaction; the association between two variables is dependent on the value or status of a third variable. In this example, and looking back at figure 12.18, we can see that the interaction is not very strong. Indeed, it is theoretically possible for the relationship between two variables to completely reverse from being a positive association to being a negative association, dependent on the level of a third variable.

However, in the social sciences this is extremely rare as you will discover for your-self in Exercise 12.4 which gives you the opportunity to explore some of the data from the British Social Attitudes Survey.

12.9　Age and cohort effects

Age is always an ambiguous variable in survey research. Unless one has data from repeated surveys across time, there is no way of telling whether one is dealing with pure age effects, pure period effects or an interaction between the two, termed generation or cohort effects. If we had several surveys at our disposal, and those aged 45 or less were always more in favour of higher spending on welfare, regardless of when the survey was undertaken, this would be an example of a pure age effect. If we found that responses in later surveys were more favourable towards welfare spending among respondents of all ages, this would be interpreted as a pure period effect. When age and period interact, we may assume we are dealing with the unique experiences of a generation growing up under particular conditions.

Because there are interactions by age in figure 12.21, it is likely that we are dealing with a generation effect. However, because the data come from a survey conducted at one point in time, we cannot tell if the relationship is conditional upon age or period. If, for example, we were to find the same results in the Social Attitudes Survey in the year 2020, we could assume that these results are conditional upon age. The increase in the availability of longitudinal data, discussed in the next chapter, has made it more possible to start disentangling age effects and period effects.

Figure 12.21　The impact of party identification and age on attitudes to welfare spending [Model 2 including interaction terms].

Variables in the Equation

		B	S.E.	Wald	df	Sig.	Exp(B)
Step 1[a]	agegp1(1)	1.327	.225	34.631	1	.000	3.769
	conlablib			48.291	2	.000	
	conlablib(1)	1.533	.229	44.897	1	.000	4.634
	conlablib(2)	1.550	.266	33.881	1	.000	4.710
	agegp1 * conlablib			5.829	2	.054	
	agegp1(1) by conlablib(1)	-.544	.268	4.115	1	.043	.580
	agegp1(1) by conlablib(2)	-.724	.321	5.083	1	.024	.485
	Constant	-2.034	.201	102.414	1	.000	.131

a. Variable(s) entered on step 1: agegp1, conlablib, agegp1 * conlablib.

12.10　Conclusion

In this chapter, techniques for building up systems of the joint influence of vari-ables have been outlined, firstly using differences in proportions as the measure of strength of effect, and then moving on to look at the coefficients in logistic regression models as a measure of association. Causal path diagrams have been extended to three variables to show how the factors are hypothesized to interrelate. These diagrams are useful because they force explicit decisions to be made about the causal order of the variables, and lessen the risk that the analyst will control for the wrong variables. They force consideration of the marginal relationship between the variables where this might be important. The techniques of control used in contingency tables involved literally holding a variable constant by considering its categories one at a time. This process takes place automatically when a logistic regression model is estimated. This means that the results displayed in a logistic regression model indicate the impact of each explanatory variable on the dependent variable, once all the other variables in the model are controlled for.

The techniques themselves are identical whether the variable being controlled is a prior or an intervening variable in the relationship being investigated. The interpretation of the result is, however, very dependent on which is the test variable. If the relationship between two variables disappears when a prior variable is controlled, the original effect has been explained away. If it disappears when an intervening variable is controlled, the mechanism linking the two variables has been interpreted.

Learning exactly which proportions to calculate in a contingency table, which variables to control for by looking within their categories, and which to ignore by collapsing over their categories, takes some practice. There is no quick substitute.

Exercises

12.1 Data from the 1984 Social Attitudes Survey, reported in the original edition of this book, showed that those with high household incomes are more inclined to say that they would break an unjust law than the poor. Draw up a causal path diagram depicting the relationships you would expect to hold if party support were introduced as a test factor. Then inspect the table in figure 12.22.

Figure 12.22 People's inclination to break the law by household income.

	Conservative		Not Conservative	
	Poor	Rich	Poor	Rich
Might break law	25	105	89	157
Would not break law	149	219	236	205

Source: Data from the 1984 Social Attitudes Survey.

Are the relationships as you predicted?

12.2 Figure 12.23 shows where a sample of school-leavers who had either been on a government Youth Opportunities Scheme (YOPS) or been unemployed for six weeks by the beginning of October 1978 had ended up by April 1979. The sample was obtained by selecting one in five of the 42 per

cent of people who left school in Scotland in 1977–8 with few or no qual-
ifications (i.e. without at least a grade O in the Scottish Certificate of
Education). The table shows whether the respondent had tried to obtain an
O grade pass or not.

Figure 12.23 Destination of school-leavers April 1979.

	October	April 1979			
	1978	Job	Unemp.	YOPS	Other
Sat O grade but failed	YOPS	89	35	56	2
	Unemployed	71	41	48	2
Did not sit O grade	YOPS	159	92	93	4
	Unemployed	145	235	129	7

Source: Raffe (1981: 483).

The purpose of the Youth Opportunities Scheme was to prepare the less
qualified for employment. On this evidence, did it succeed? In order to
answer the question, dichotomize the response variable and present the
table in proportional terms. Is it possible to summarize the relationships
you find in a linear causal model?

12.3   The table in figure 12.24 summarizes the results of a simple logistic regression model, with no interaction terms, where the dependent variable is
agreement or disagreement with the statement 'Income differences in
Great Britain are too large'. The model is effectively predicting the probability that an individual will *agree* with the statement that income differences are too large. By inspecting the coefficients in the column labelled
'B' and the associated significance values, what can you say about the
impact that age, qualifications and household income have on these attitudes about inequality?

Figure 12.24 Logistic regression model SPSS output (dependent variable is
agreement or disagreement with the statement 'Income differences
in Great Britain are too large').

Variables in the Equation		B	S.E.	Wald	df	Sig.	Exp(B)
Step 1(a)	Age 46+	0.22	0.11	3.74	1	0.053	1.25
	Degree	−0.42	0.12	11.31	1	0.001	0.66
	Household annual income £20K+	−0.57	0.12	22.66	1	0.000	0.56
	Constant	1.00	0.12	72.39	1	0.000	2.71

Source: Analysis of British Social Attitudes Survey 2004.

12.4   What can you discover from the dataset BSA2004_Teach.sav about the factors which have an impact on people's responses to the question 'Can you trust people in government to do what is right?' Pay particular attention to whether there are any possible interactions between variables that you think might be worth exploring and whether they are significant.

13

Longitudinal Data

13.1 Introduction

For the most part this book has been concerned with cross-sectional data and the techniques for exploring cross-sectional datasets. In this final chapter we turn our attention to longitudinal data and provide an introduction to some of the key features of longitudinal research and analysis. We have already encountered some examples of longitudinal data in previous chapters. For example, chapter 3 introduced the National Child Development Study which collected data on over 17,000 babies born in one week of 1958 and has continued to track these individuals throughout their lives. In chapter 6 we used another longitudinal dataset, the eleventh cohort of the Youth Cohort Study, to examine the association between parental occupation and an individual's main activity at age 19. Longitudinal social research offers unique insights into process, change and continuity over time in phenomena ranging from individuals, families and institutions to whole societies. The majority of longitudinal data take human subjects as the unit of analysis, and therefore longitudinal data commonly record change at an individual or 'micro' level (Ruspini, 2002). They can be contrasted with cross-sectional data that record the circumstances of individuals (or other research units) at just one particular point in time.

It is important to distinguish longitudinal data from the time series data presented in chapter 5. As we will see later in this chapter, although time series data can provide us with a picture of aggregate change, it is only longitudinal data that can provide evidence of change at the level of the individual. Time series data could perhaps be understood as a series of snapshots of society, whereas longitudinal research entails following the same group of individuals over time and linking information about those individuals from one time point to another. For example, in a study such as the British Household Panel Survey (see the appendix to this chapter on the accompanying website) individuals are interviewed each year about a range of topics including income, political preferences and voting. This makes it possible to link data about individuals over time and examine, for example, how an individual's income may rise (or fall) year on year and how their political preferences may change.

The first part of this chapter provides a brief introduction to longitudinal research design and focuses on some of the issues in collecting longitudinal data and problems of attrition. The second part of the chapter then provides a brief conceptual introduction to the analysis of longitudinal data. It is beyond the scope of this book to provide a detailed discussion of specialist statistical techniques for dealing with longitudinal data, such as event history analysis, and the final section therefore gives a summary of some books and resources that can be used to look at this topic in more depth.

13.2 Collecting longitudinal data

Prospective and retrospective research designs

Longitudinal data are frequently collected using a **prospective** longitudinal research design, i.e. the participants in a research study are contacted by researchers and asked to provide information about themselves and their circumstances on a number of different occasions. This is often referred to as a *panel study*. However, it is not necessary to use a longitudinal research design in order to collect longitudinal data and there is therefore a conceptual distinction between longitudinal data and longitudinal research (Featherman, 1980; Scott and Alwin, 1998; Taris, 2000). Indeed, the **retrospective** collection of longitudinal data is very common. In particular, it has become an established method for obtaining basic information about the dates of key life events such as marriages, separations and divorces and the birth of any children (i.e. event history data). This is clearly an efficient way of collecting longitudinal data and obviates the need to re-contact the same group of individuals over a period of time.

A potential problem is that people may not remember the past accurately enough to provide good quality data. While some authors have argued that recall is not a major problem for collecting information about dates of significant life events, other research suggests that individuals may have difficulty remembering dates accurately, or may prefer not to remember unfavourable episodes or events in their lives (Mott, 2002; Dex, 1995; Dex and McCulloch, 1998; Jacobs, 2002).

Large-scale quantitative surveys often combine a number of different data collection strategies so they do not always fit neatly into the classification of prospective or retrospective designs. In particular, longitudinal event history data are frequently collected retrospectively as part of an ongoing prospective longitudinal study. For example, the British Household Panel Survey is a prospective panel study. However, in addition to the detailed questions asked every year about current living conditions, attitudes and beliefs, in the 1992 and 1993 waves of the BHPS, respondents were asked to provide information about their past employment experiences and their relationship histories.

A further type of prospective panel study is a linked panel, which uses census data or administrative data (such as information about hospital treatment or benefits records). This is the least intrusive type of quantitative longitudinal research study as individuals may well not be aware that they are members of the panel. Unique personal identifiers are used to link together data that were not initially collected as part of a longitudinal research study. For example, a 1 per cent sub-sample of records from the 1971 British Census has been linked to records for the same sample of individuals in 1981, 1991 and 2001. This is known as the Longitudinal Study of the British Census. A similar study linking the 1991 and 2001 Census records for 5 per cent of the population of Scotland was officially launched in March 2007.

Cohort studies

A cohort has been defined as an 'aggregate of individuals who experienced the same event within the same time interval' (Ryder, 1965, p. 845). The most obvious type of cohort used in longitudinal quantitative research is the birth cohort i.e. a sample of individuals born within a relatively short time period. We might also choose to study samples of a cohort of people who got married, who were released from prison, or who started at university in a particular month or year.

Cohort studies allow an explicit focus on the social and cultural context that frames the experiences, behaviour and decisions of individuals. For example, in the case of the 1958 British Birth Cohort study (known as the National Child Development Study), it is important to understand the cohort's educational experiences in the context of profound changes in the organization of secondary education during the 1960s and 1970s, and the rapid expansion of higher education, which was well underway by the time cohort members left school in the mid 1970s (Bynner and Fogelman, 1993).

Comparisons between cohorts can also help to clarify how individuals of different ages may respond differently to particular sets of historical circumstances. This emphasis on the importance of understanding individuals' lives and experiences as arising out of the intersection of individual agency and historical and cultural context has become articulated as the life course paradigm. The term 'life course' 'refers to a sequence of socially defined events and roles that the individual enacts over time' (Giele and Elder, 1998, p. 22). Research adopting the life course paradigm tends to use both qualitative and quantitative data (Elder, 1974; Laub and Sampson, 1998; Giele, 1998).

Figure 13.1 provides a brief summary of a small selection of quantitative studies that have used different longitudinal panel designs, focusing on those that are commonly used in Britain, North America and Europe.

Problems of attrition

A major methodological issue for longitudinal studies in comparison with cross-sectional studies is the problem of attrition, i.e. the drop out of participants through successive waves of a prospective study. Each time individuals in a sample are re-contacted there is the risk that some will refuse to remain in the study, some will be untraceable, and some may have emigrated or died. In the United States, the National Longitudinal Study of Youth (1979) is regarded as the gold standard for sample retention against which other surveys are evaluated (Olsen, 2005).

Figure 13.1 Examples of longitudinal studies.

Study	Type	Country	Date started	Frequency of data collection	Main focus	Key reference or website
Panel Study of Income Dynamics	Household	USA	1968	Annual	Income	http://psidonline.isr.umich.edu/ McGonalgle and Schoeni (2006)
National Longitudinal surveys	Cohort	USA	1966, 1971 etc.	Annual	A series of cohort studies started at different times and with cohorts of different ages, with a primary focus on employment	www.bls.gov/nls/ NLS Handbook 2005 www.bls.gov/nls/handbook/ nlshndbk.htm
Survey of Income and Program participation	Household	USA	1984	Every 4 months	Income support	www.bls.census.gov/sipp/ SIPP users Guide 2001 available in PDF at http://www.bls.census. gov/sipp/pubs.html
National Longitudinal Study of Children and Youth	Cohort of children aged 0–11	Canada	1994	Every 2 years	Well-being and development of children into early adult life	www.statcan.ca/english/sdds/

Study	Type	Country	Year(s)	Frequency	Focus	Source
British Birth Cohort Studies: National Survey of Health and Development; National Child Development Study; British Cohort Study 1970; Millennium Cohort Study	Cohort	Great Britain	1946, 1958, 1970 and 2000	Varies, but generally every 2 to 3 years at early stages of children's development And every 4 years in adult life	Health and child development with a broader focus in adult life (the 1946 cohort study is more specifically focused on health)	www.cls.ioe.ac.uk/ www.nshd.mrc.ac.uk/ Ferri, Bynner and Wadsworth (2003); Dex and Joshi (2005)
Longitudinal Study of the Census in England and Wales	Linked panel using Census data	England and Wales	1971	Links decennial census data	Demographic and employment topics included in the census	www.celsius.lshtm.ac.uk/ Blackwell et al (2005)
German Socio-economic Panel	Household study	West Germany and now includes the former GDR	1984	Annual	Broad focus on living conditions, social change, education and employment	www.diw.de/english/sop/
European Community Household Panel	Household study	European Community	1994	Annual	Living conditions, employment, income, health and housing	www.iser.essex.ac.uk/epag/dataset.php Berthoud and Iacovou (2002)

Olsen reports that in 2002, 23 years after the first data collection, there were 9,964 respondents eligible for interview and of these 7,724 (77.5 per cent) were successfully interviewed.

The prospective nature of the majority of longitudinal studies means that information will have been collected in earlier sweeps about members of the sample who are not contacted, or refuse participation, in later sweeps. This makes it possible to correct for possible distortion in results due to missing cases. In quantitative research, weights may be applied or models may be constructed explicitly to adjust for missing data. In both qualitative and quantitative studies new members of the panel may be brought in, and/or studies may over-sample particular groups from the outset in anticipation of uneven attrition.

There are a number of ways in which sample retention can be maximized in longitudinal studies. These include: using targeted incentive payments; allowing respondents to choose the mode in which they are interviewed, i.e. by telephone or in a face-to-face interview (Olsen, 2005); collecting 'stable addresses' such as the address of parents or other relatives who are less likely to move than the respondent themselves and can subsequently be used to trace the respondent; making regular contact with respondents and asking them to confirm their current address and notify the research group of changes of address.

13.3 Examining change over time

One way of looking at change over time is to conduct two surveys asking the same questions at different points in historical time. This is known as a repeated cross-sectional survey. The British Social Attitudes Survey, discussed in more detail in chapter 12, is an example of a repeated cross-sectional survey. Each year a similar core set of questions about values and attitudes are asked of a new cross-sectional sample of individuals. This makes it possible to look at aggregate change over time. For example, using the British Social Attitudes Survey we know that in 1984, 75 per cent of adults over 18 stated that the gap between the richest and poorest in Britain was 'too large'. This increased to a high of 87 per cent in 1995 and subsequently declined slightly to 78 per cent in 2003 (Summerfield and Gill, 2005). Opinion polls, discussed in chapter 5, are another example of a repeated cross-sectional design. These focus on the specific issue of which political party respondents support.

Figure 13.2 shows the actual British General Election results for the whole of the United Kingdom for 1992 and 1997. These elections have been chosen for analysis because they involve a huge swing from Conservative to Labour so that the Conservative majority of 22 seats in the 1992 election was transformed into a Labour majority of 178 seats just five years later. This type of repeated cross-sectional information gives an indication of aggregate change over time. For example, we can see that between 1992 and 1997, Labour's share of the vote increased substantially (from 34.4 per cent to 43.2 per cent) while the Conservatives' vote collapsed from 41.9 per cent to 30.7 per cent. In addition we can see that the turnout decreased from 77.7 per cent to 71.3 per cent. However, what is not clear from figure 13.2 is whether the people who voted Labour in 1992 also all voted Labour

Figure 13.2 British General Election results 1992 and 1997.

	1992 British General Election % vote	1997 British General Election % vote
Labour	34.4	43.2
Conservative	41.9	30.7
Liberal Democrat	17.8	16.8
Others	5.8	9.3
Total turnout	**77.7**	**71.3**

Source: UK Election Statistics 1945–2003 (House of Commons Library Research paper 03/59).

Figure 13.3 British Household Panel Study self-reported voting 1992 and 1997 (Great Britain only).

BHPS self-reported retrospective voting 1992 and 1997		
	1992 British General Election % vote	1997 British General Election % vote
Labour	37.8	51.6
Conservative	44.2	30.2
Liberal Democrat	15.7	14.7
Others	2.3	3.6
% claiming to have voted	84.7	82.3

Source: Analysis of data from the British Household Panel Study 1992 and 1997.

in 1997. It is also uncertain whether the 71.3 per cent of people who turned out to vote in 1997 also voted in 1992, or whether a different section of the population voted in the two elections. This cannot be deduced from the actual election results and this type of information is not available from repeated cross-sectional studies. This is because from the election results, and in repeated cross-sectional surveys, there is no way of linking information about an individual's behaviour (i.e. voting) in 1992 and their behaviour in 1997.

However, by using evidence from longitudinal studies such as the British Household Panel Survey or the British Birth Cohort studies it is possible to track how individual behaviour changes over time. As a starting point, for initial comparison, data from a longitudinal survey such as the British Household Panel Study may be presented in a similar way to the General Election results. Figure 13.3 shows the percentage of respondents from the BHPS reporting that they had voted for each party in 1992 (wave 2) and 1997 (wave 7). Note that these data have been weighted using the cross-sectional respondent weights provided in the BHPS dataset to make the data as close as possible to the British population. However there are still likely to be differences between the figures here and those for the 1992 and 1997 General Elections because the BHPS does not include individuals from Northern Ireland or from north of the Caledonian Canal in Scotland. The data were collected in the autumn of 1992 and 1997 respectively and therefore respondents are being asked to remember how they voted just a few months prior to the survey. The numbers in figure 13.3 tell a very similar story to those in figure 13.2 with Labour's share of the vote increasing and the Tories' share of the vote decreasing dramatically. However, we can see that the percentage of respondents claiming to have voted in the 1992 and 1997 elections is considerably higher than the actual turnout. This is a common problem in social surveys because respondents are inclined to give a socially desirable response to interviewers when asked whether they voted in the last election.

However, this type of presentation of information from the BHPS, as if it is a series of cross-sectional surveys, does not fully exploit the longitudinal nature of the data. In the BHPS, each individual has a unique identification number which makes it possible to link their responses in one survey to their responses in a survey in a different year. This means, for example, that it is possible to examine how individuals' voting behaviour in 1992 relates to their voting behaviour in 1997.

13.4 Transition tables

Transition tables are not dissimilar to the contingency tables that were introduced in chapters 6 and 7. However, they have a longitudinal dimension in that the two variables that are being cross-tabulated can be understood as a single categorical variable that has been measured at two time points. For example, the transition table shown in figure 13.4 uses data from the BHPS to examine how voting behaviour of individuals changed between 1992 and 1997. In this table the rows describe voting behaviour in 1992 and the columns describe voting behaviour in 1997. In this table longitudinal respondent weights for wave 7 (i.e. 1997) have been applied. Row percentages have been calculated so that it is possible to see, for example, how the voting behaviour of those voting Conservative in 1992 changed by 1997. We can see that whereas 86.5 per cent of Labour voters in the 1992 election stayed loyal to the party and voted Labour again in 1997, only 62.6 per cent of Conservative voters stayed loyal and just under a half (48.6 per cent) of Liberal Democrats voted for the party in both 1992 and 1997. It is also interesting to note that of those who reported that they didn't vote in 1992, approximately a half (51.8 per cent) also reported not voting in 1997. However, approximately three out of ten (29.6 per cent) of those who report that they didn't vote in 1992 report voting Labour in 1997. A similar pattern of results is presented by Kellner (1997). He uses data from an NOP poll of 17,073 voters who were surveyed as they left polling stations on election day in 1997. This asked individuals both about how they had just voted and about how they remembered voting in 1992. Kellner's analysis suggests that nearly three in ten (29 per cent) of those who recalled voting Conservative in 1992 switched parties in the 1997 election compared with just 10 per cent of those who recalled voting Labour. However, one of the disadvantages of the methodology used in this NOP poll is that it only collects data from those who voted in 1997 (i.e. those surveyed as they left the polling stations) whereas analysis of data from the BHPS provides information on the whole sample whether or not they voted in the 1992 or 1997 elections.

Figure 13.4 Transition table cross-tabulating individuals' votes in 1992 by individuals' votes in 1997 (row percentages).

Vote in 1992		Didn't vote	Conservative	Labour	Libdem	Other	Total
							Vote in 1997
Didn't vote	Count	424	61	242	62	29	818
	% within 1992 vote	51.8	7.5	29.6	7.6	3.5	100
Conservative	Count	255	1,362	318	188	54	2,177
	% within 1992 vote	11.7	62.6	14.6	8.6	2.5	100
Labour	Count	168	20	1,648	49	20	1,905
	% within 1992 vote	8.8	1.0	86.5	2.6	1.0	100
Libdem	Count	82	49	276	404	21	832
	% within 1992 vote	9.9	5.9	33.2	48.6	2.5	100
Other	Count	16	3	34	8	43	104
	% within 1992 vote	15.4	2.9	32.7	7.7	41.3	100
Total	**Count**	945	1,495	2,518	711	167	5,836
	% within 1992 vote	16.2	25.6	43.1	12.2	2.9	100

Source: Analysis of data from the British Household Panel Study 1992 and 1997.

Figure 13.5 Transition table cross-tabulating individuals' votes in 1992 by individuals' votes in 1997 (column percentages).

Vote in 1992		Didn't vote	Conservative	Labour	Libdem	Other	Total
							Vote in 1997
Didn't vote	Count	424	61	242	62	29	818
	% within 1997 vote	44.9	4.1	9.6	8.7	17.4	14.0
Conservative	Count	255	1362	318	188	54	2177
	% within 1997 vote	27.0	91.1	12.6	26.4	32.3	37.3
Labour	Count	168	20	1648	49	20	1905
	% within 1997 vote	17.8	1.3	65.4	6.9	12.0	32.6
Libdem	Count	82	49	276	404	21	832
	% within 1997 vote	8.7	3.3	11.0	56.8	12.6	14.3
Other	Count	16	3	34	8	43	104
	% within 1997 vote	1.7	0.2	1.4	1.1	25.7	1.8
Total	**Count**	945	1495	2518	711	167	5836
	% within 1997 vote	100	100	100	100	100	100

Source: Analysis of data from the British Household Panel Study 1992 and 1997.

The same data from the BHPS can be analysed slightly differently if we calculate the column percentages in the transition table (see figure 13.5). This suggests for example that in the 1997 election the Labour Party gained slightly more votes from people who reported that they had voted Tory in 1992 (12.6 per cent) than people who reported that they had voted Liberal Democrat in 1992 (11.0 per cent). We can also see that nearly 10 per cent of the Labour vote in 1997 came from people who reported that they didn't vote in the 1992 election.

This type of analysis can be refined by further disaggregating the sample by age. For example, the transition tables in figures 13.4 and 13.5 can be constructed separately for different age groups in order to understand more about patterns of individual voting over time for different sections of the population. Exercise 13.1 asks you to interpret separate transition tables for those aged under 40 in 1992 and those aged 40 or over.

13.5 Poverty dynamics

In chapter 4 we focused on ways of measuring income inequalities and figure 4.5 in that chapter provided a picture of how income inequality has changed over time in Britain. Once again this approach can only provide a picture of aggregate change over time. Large-scale government surveys, such as the Family Resources Survey, used to inform publications such as Households Below Average Income (HBAI), are repeated cross-sectional studies. These sources cannot provide information about how an individual's income, or how household income, changes from one year to the next. The annual HBAI publication therefore also draws on the BHPS in order to provide additional information about the persistence of poverty over time. The extent to which individuals living in households with low incomes are simply experiencing temporary fluctuations in income, or are persistently experiencing low income, is clearly an important issue. The persistence of poverty over time for individuals or households can only be addressed by using longitudinal data.

The 2005/6 edition of the HBAI reported that there had been a reduction in persistent low income for children over the period from 1991–4 to 2001–4. Persistent low income is defined as living in a household with below 60 per cent of median income for at least three out of four consecutive years. Whereas 20 per cent of children were found to have lived in a household with persistent low income in the years 1991–4, this had reduced to 13 per cent in the period 2001 to 2004. These figures relate to income before housing costs (see the first panel of table 7.1 of HBAI 2005–2006). Persistent low income had not however dropped as substantially for other groups (such as working-age adults or pensioners). Overall, considering all individuals, the percentage experiencing persistent low income fell from 12 per cent in 1991–4 to ten per cent in 2001 to 2004. A more detailed discussion of income mobility and poverty dynamics using data from the first two waves of the BHPS is provided by Jarvis and Jenkins (1995).

In their 1995 paper, Jarvis and Jenkins analyse poverty dynamics by classifying people into one of four groups according to whether their incomes are above or below a wave 1 low-income threshold and a wave 2 low-income threshold. Jarvis and Jenkins use two different ways of defining low income (a) the poorest deciles i.e. those in the bottom ten per cent of the income distribution and (b) those earning less than half of the 1991 average income (i.e. £109 per week). To simplify matters we will just focus here on reproducing the results using half of the 1991 average income as the cut off. Jarvis and Jenkins examined the proportion of the sample that was in one of four groups defined by their income in 1991 and 1992. Group A had less than half 1991 mean income in both 1991 and 1992 (i.e. they are low

Figure 13.6 Low income dynamics 1991 and 1992, data from the BHPS.

Low income dynamics a summary

Group	Income relative to low income cut-off (Half 1991 mean income)		Percentage in group
	1991	1992	
A	Below	Below	10.1
B	Below	Above	7.1
C	Above	Below	6.4
D	Above	Above	76.4

Source: Adapted from the summary table on page ii of Jarvis and Jenkins (1995).

income stayers). Group B is defined as having less than half 1991 average income in 1991, but incomes above this cut off in 1992 (i.e. low income escapers). Group C is defined as having incomes above the cut off in 1991 but then having incomes below the cut off in 1992 (low income entrants); and group D is defined as having incomes above the cut off in both 1991 and 1992 (high income stayers). The distribution of individuals in each of these groups is shown in figure 13.6.

We can see that there was a significant degree of low income turnover in Britain in the early 1990s. Approximately a quarter of the sample were found to have incomes below the cut off of half 1991 mean income at either one or both of the times they were interviewed in 1991 and 1992. This type of simple longitudinal analysis revealed that the number of people experiencing low income at least once during the two years is substantially greater than the proportion with low income indicated by a cross-sectional snapshot of either the 1991 income distribution or the 1992 income distribution. Further analysis revealed that the types of people who were most likely to be in group A 'low income stayers' were those who were in lone parent families in 1991, those in families where no one was in work and the elderly.

There is a strong argument for targeting anti-poverty policies at those who experience persistent income poverty. However, it is problematic to put this into practice until we have a clearer understanding of the processes involved in movements into and out of low income. Further research is therefore needed into poverty dynamics and this requires the careful analysis of longitudinal data (Smith and Middleton, 2007).

13.6 Approaches to the analysis of longitudinal data

The examples of analysing longitudinal data in this chapter have focused on the use of longitudinal data to provide very simple descriptive summaries of change over time. This type of analysis does not require any specialized statistical tools or complex models. Rather the fact that information has been recorded for the same individuals over a number of years is exploited to provide a better profile of individual behaviour and circumstances over time than would be possible with cross-sectional data. However, it would be wrong to imply that this is all there is to longitudinal analysis. Indeed there is now an extensive literature on the statistical analysis of longitudinal data with good introductions for social scientists provided by Allison (1984); Yamaguchi (1991); Ruspini (2002); Dale and Davies (1994). It is beyond the scope of this chapter (and this book) to provide more than a very brief summary of the main approaches to longitudinal analysis. This final section therefore aims to provide a brief accessible introduction to longitudinal analysis that will hopefully inspire some readers to pursue the topic further.

There are perhaps two main approaches to the analysis of longitudinal data. The first is an extension of the simple analyses shown above and can be conceptualized as 'Repeated measures analysis'. This type of analysis takes as its focus the changes in an individual attribute over time. For example weight, performance score, attitude, voting behaviour, reaction time, depression, etc. In particular, psychologists often use repeated measures of traits, dispositions or psychological well-being to examine which factors may promote change or stability for individuals. This approach can also be used to investigate what type of effect a particular life event may have on individual functioning. For example, several studies examining the potential consequences of parental divorce for children have compared behavioural measures and measures of performance in maths and reading in addition to other outcomes, before and after a parental divorce (Cherlin et al., 1991; Elliott and Richards, 1991; Ni Bhrolchain et al., 1995). The second main type of longitudinal analysis is commonly known as Event history analysis or Event history modelling. Here the focus is on the timing of events or the duration until a particular event occurs, rather than changes in attributes over time.

13.7   Event history modelling

In many respects event history modelling resembles more widely understood regression techniques, such as ordinary least squares regression and logistic regression (where the dependent variable is dichotomous) introduced in chapter 9 and chapter 12. The emphasis is on determining the relative importance of a number of independent variables or 'covariates' for 'predicting' the outcome of a dependent variable. However, event history modelling differs from standard multiple regression in that the dependent variable is not a measurement of an individual attribute (such as income or qualifications), rather it is derived from the occurrence or non-occurrence of an event, which is *temporally* marked; for example, age at first partnership or length of unemployment. Standard regression techniques are not appropriate in the case of event history data, which focus on the timing of events, for two reasons. First is the problem of what duration value to assign to individuals or cases that have not experienced the event of interest by the time the data are collected – these cases are termed 'censored cases'. A second problem, once a sample is observed longitudinally, is the potential for the values of some of the independent covariates to change. The issue then arises as to how to incorporate these 'time-varying' covariates into the analysis.

These two problems have led to the development of modelling techniques specifically intended for the analysis of event history data. In essence, these techniques allow us to evaluate the relative importance of a number of different variables, or 'covariates' for predicting the chance, or *hazard*, of an event occurring. The hazard is a key concept in event history analysis, and is sometimes also referred to as the hazard rate or hazard function. It can be interpreted as the probability that an event will occur at a particular point in time, given that the individual is at risk at that time. The group of individuals who are at risk of the event occurring are therefore usually referred to as the *risk set*.

Approaches to event history modelling

One of the most common approaches within the social sciences is to use Cox's proportional hazard models or 'Cox Regression' (Cox, 1972). This provides a method for modelling time-to-event data and allows the inclusion of predictor variables (covariates). For example, a model could be estimated for duration of marriage based on religion, age at marriage or level of education. Cox regression will handle the censored cases correctly, and it will provide estimated coefficients for each of the covariates, allowing an assessment of the relative importance of multiple covariates and of any interactions between them. Cox regression is known as a continuous time approach because it is assumed that the time that an event occurs is measured accurately.

Although the Cox model is one of the most popular and widely applied approaches it has two main disadvantages. First, it is relatively inflexible in terms of modelling duration dependence i.e. for specifying exactly how the hazard may change over time, and second, it makes it difficult to incorporate time varying covariates. For this reason, many researchers, with an explicit interest in how the probability of an event occurring changes over time, prefer to use a 'discrete-time' approach. This requires that the data have a specific format. A separate unit of analysis is created for each discrete time interval. Each record therefore corresponds to a person/month or person/year (depending on the accuracy with which events have been recorded). Once the data have been reconfigured in this way, the unit of analysis is transferred from being the individual case to being a person/year and logistic regression models can be estimated for the dichotomous dependent variable (whether the event occurred or not) using maximum likelihood methods (Allison, 1984). This approach facilitates inclusion of explanatory variables that vary over time because each year, or month, that an individual is at risk is treated as a separate observation. It is also easy to include more than one measure of duration. Discrete time methods are therefore thought to offer a preferable approach when the researcher wants to include several time-varying covariates. A good example is provided by Heaton and Call's research on the timing of divorce (Heaton and Call, 1995). This analytic approach is also used by those looking at recidivism and wanting to understand the timing and correlates of repeat offending (Baumer, 1997; Gainey et al., 2000; Benda, 2003).

13.8 Causality in cross-sectional and longitudinal research

Information about the temporal ordering of events is generally regarded as essential if we are to make any claims about a causal relationship between those events. Given the importance of establishing the chronology of events in order to be confident about causality we can see that longitudinal data are frequently to be preferred over cross-sectional data. In some substantive examples even when data are collected in a cross-sectional survey, it is clear that one event or variable precedes another. For example, in an analysis that focuses on the impact of school-leaving age on occupational attainment there is unlikely to be confusion about the temporal ordering of the variables. However, there are a number of examples where the use of cross-sectional survey data prevents researchers from determining the causal ordering of variables.

For example, there is a considerable body of research that has shown a strong association between unemployment and ill health. This can either be interpreted to imply that unemployment causes poor health or that those who are in poor health are more likely to become unemployed and subsequently find it more difficult to find another job, i.e. there is a selection effect such that ill-health might be described as causing unemployment (Bartley, 1991; Blane et al., 1993). In this case, longitudinal data would be needed to follow a sample of employed individuals and determine whether their health deteriorated if they became unemployed, or conversely whether a decline in health led to an increased probability of becoming unemployed.

In quantitative studies, longitudinal data are also valuable for overcoming the problems of disentangling maturational effects and generational effects. As Dale and Davies (1994) explain, cross-sectional data that examine the link between age and any dependent variable confound cohort and life-course effects. For example, if analysis of a cross-sectional survey demonstrates a link between age and preference for a particular political party, it is possible that it is the life experiences of different cohorts, who have grown up in rather different historical contexts, that leads individuals of different generations to form distinct and enduring party loyalties. However, an alternative explanation of the observed association would be that individuals change their political allegiances as they grow older.

13.9 Conclusion

This chapter has aimed to give a brief introduction to the collection and analysis of longitudinal data. It has demonstrated that even without using sophisticated statistical techniques longitudinal data can be tabulated using transition tables to give a simple picture of changes in individual behaviour or circumstances over time. New variables can then be created based on individual trajectories and these can then be used as dependent variables in subsequent analyses.

Although longitudinal data are expensive to collect, the first part of the chapter has highlighted the fact that there are a great many sources of longitudinal data available for secondary analysis. In particular, Britain has a long heritage of collecting longitudinal data on cohorts of individuals born in 1946, 1958, 1970 and more recently around the time of the Millennium. This means that there are now excellent sources of data that provide information about individuals' lives from birth and well into adult life.

Exercises

13.1 The tables in figure 13.7 show reported voting behaviour in 1992 and 1997 separately for those aged under 40 and those aged 40 and over in 1997.

(a) Are those in the older or younger age group most likely to stay loyal to the Conservative Party in the 1992 and 1997 elections?

(b) What are the main differences in the reported voting patterns of the older and younger groups in these two elections?

(c) Calculate what percentage of the older and younger groups report voting for the same party (or consistently not voting) in the 1992 and 1997 elections. Is this what you would expect?

Figure 13.7 Transition table cross-tabulating individuals' votes in 1992 by individuals' votes in 1997 (row percentages) disaggregated by age group.

Aged under 40 years			Vote in 1997					
			Didn't vote	Conservative	Labour	Libdem	Other	Total
Vote in 1992	Didn't vote	Count	270	40	170	32	20	532
		% within 1992 vote	50.8	7.5	32.0	6.0	3.8	100
	Conservative	Count	142	395	140	76	17	770
		% within 1992 vote	18.4	51.3	18.2	9.9	2.2	100
	Labour	Count	107	11	653	23	13	807
		% within 1992 vote	13.3	1.4	80.9	2.9	1.6	100
	Libdem	Count	51	18	105	153	9	336
		% within 1992 vote	15.2	5.4	31.3	45.5	2.7	100
	Other	Count	12	0	20	4	24	60
		% within 1992 vote	20	0	33.3	6.7	40	100
Total		Count	582	464	1088	288	83	2505
		%	23.2	18.5	43.4	11.5	3.3	100

Figure 13.7 (continued)

Aged 40 plus			Vote in 1997					
			Didn't vote	Conservative	Labour	Libdem	Other	Total
Vote in 1997	Didn't vote	Count	155	21	72	30	9	287
		% within 1992 vote	54.0	7.3	25.1	10.5	3.1	100
	Conservative	Count	113	967	178	112	38	1408
		% within 1992 vote	8.0	68.7	12.6	8.0	2.7	100
	Labour	Count	61	9	995	26	7	1098
		% within 1992 vote	5.6	0.8	90.6	2.4	0.6	100
	Libdem	Count	32	32	171	251	12	498
		% within 1992 vote	6.4	6.4	34.3	50.4	2.4	100
	Other	Count	4	3	14	4	20	45
		% within 1992 vote	8.9	6.7	31.1	8.9	44.4	100
Total		**Count**	365	1032	1430	423	86	3336
		%	10.9	30.9	42.9	12.7	2.6	100

Source: Analysis of data from the British Household Panel Study 1992 and 1997.

13.2 Using the teaching dataset based on the National Child Development Study (NCDS_ExpData_teach.sav) use the Crosstabs command in SPSS to create a transition table to examine individuals' movements between social classes measured at age 42 and age 46 (SC42 and SC46).

(a) What percentage of individuals are in the same social class at age 42 and age 46?

(b) What percentage of those who were professionals at age 42 are still professionals at age 46?

(c) Focusing on those who were professionals at age 42, which social class are they most likely to move into if they do not stay in the professional social class?

References

Abbott, A. (1992), 'What do cases do?' in C. Ragin and H. S. Becker (eds), *What is a Case?* Cambridge: Cambridge University Press, pp. 53–82.

Allen, J. (2006), *Worry about Crime in England and Wales: Findings from the 2003/4 and 2004/5 British Crime Survey.* Home Office Online report 15/06.

Allison, P. D. (1984), *Event History Analysis: Regression for Longitudinal Event Data.* Beverley Hills: Sage.

Atkinson, A. B. (1983), *The Economics of Inequality* (2nd edn). Oxford: Clarendon Press.

Balnaves, M. and Caputi, P. (2001), *Introduction to Quantitative Research Methods: An Investigative Approach.* London: Sage.

Banks, J. and Johnson, P. (1993), *Children and Household Living Standards* (IFS Reports, R42 978-1-873357-21-7). London: The Institute for Fiscal Studies.

Bartley, M. (1991), 'Health and labour force participation: stress, selection and the reproduction costs of labour power'. *Journal of Social Policy, 20,* 327–64.

Bateson, N. (1984), *Data Construction in Social Surveys.* London: Allen and Unwin.

Baumer, E. (1997), 'Levels and predictors of recidivism: the Malta experience'. *Criminology, 35,* 601–28.

Benda, B. B. (2003), 'Survival analysis of criminal recidivism of boot camp graduates using elements from general and developmental explanatory models'. *International Journal of Offender Therapy and Comparative Criminology, 47,* 89–110.

Berthoud, R. and Iacovou, M. (2002), *Diverse Europe: Mapping Patterns of Social Change Across the EU.* Economic and Social Research Council. www.iser.essex.ac.uk/epag/pubs/reports/pdf/diverse_europe_full.pdf

Beveridge, W. H. (1909), *Unemployment: A Problem of Industry.* London: Longmans, Green and Co.

Bickel, P. J., Hammel, E. A. and O'Connell, J. W. (1975), 'Sex bias in graduate admissions: data from Berkeley'. *Science,* **187**: 398–404.

Bird, D. (2004), 'Technical report – methodology for the 2004 annual survey of hours and earnings'. *Labour Market Trends, 112,* 417–64.

Blackwell, L., Akinwale, B., Antonatos, A. and Haskey, J. (2005), 'Opportunities for new research using the post-2001 ONS longitudinal study'. *Population Trends, 121,* 8–16.

Blane, D., Smith, G. and Bartley, M. (1993), 'Social selection: what does it contribute to social class differences in health?'. *Sociology of Health and Illness, 15,* 1–15.

Booth, C. (1892), *The Life and Labour of the People of London.* An online archive of Booth's investigations is available at: http://booth.lse.ac.uk/static/b/index.html

Brant, J. D. and Chalk, S. M. (1985), 'The use of automatic editing in the 1981 Census'. *Statistical News, 68,* 13–15.

Butler, N. R. and Bonham, D. G. (1963), *Perinatal Mortality*. London: E. and S. Livingstone.

Bynner, J. and Fogelman, K. (1993), 'Making the grade: education and training experiences', in E. Ferri (ed.), *Life at 33: The Fifth Follow-up of the National Child Development Study*, pp. 36–59. London: National Children's Bureau.

Bynner, J. and Parsons, S. (2003), 'Social participation, values and crime', in E. Ferri, B. J and M. Wadsworth (eds), *Changing Britain, Changing Lives: Three Generations at the Turn of the Century*. London: Institute of Education, University of London.

Byrne, D. (2002), *Interpreting Quantitative Data*. London: Sage.

Campbell, D. T. (1951), 'On the possibility of experimenting with the "bandwagon effect"'. *International Journal of Opinion and Attitude Research*, 5, 251–60.

Carmines, E. G. and Zeller, R. A. (1979), *Reliability and Validity Assessment*. Thousand Oaks, California: Sage.

Cartwright, N. (2004), 'From causation to explanation and back', in B. Leiter (ed.), *The Future for Philosophy*. Oxford University Press (pp. 230–45).

Chadwick-Jones, J. K., Nicholson, N. and Brown, C. (1982), *Social Psychology of Absenteeism*. New York: Praeger.

Chamberlain, R., Chamberlain, G., Howlett, B. and Claireaux, A. (1975), *British Births 1970*. London: Heinemann Educational.

Cherlin, A. J., Furstenberg, F., Chase-Lansdale, P. L., Kiernan, K., Robins, P. K., Morrison, D. R. and Teitler, J. O. (1991), 'Longitudinal studies of effects of divorce on children in Great Britain and the United States'. *Science Technology & Human Values*, 252.

Courtenay, G. (1996), *Youth Cohort Study of England and Wales, 1991–1993; Cohort Five, Sweep One to Three [computer file]*. Colchester, Essex: UK Data Archive [distributor].

Cowell, F. A. (1977), *Measuring Inequality*. London: Philip Allan.

Cox, D. R. (1972), 'Regression models and life tables'. *Journal of the Royal Statistical Society, B, 34*, 187–202.

Curtice, J. (1997), 'So how well did they do? The polls in the 1997 election'. *Journal of the Market Research Society, 39*, 449–61.

Dale, A. and Davies, R. (1994), *Analyzing Social and Political Change: A Casebook of Methods*. London: Sage.

Davie, R., Butler, N. and Goldstein, H. (1972), *From Birth to Seven: The Second Report of the National Child Development Study*. London: Longman.

Davis, J. A. (1976), 'Analyzing contingency tables with linear flow graphs: d systems', in D. Heise (ed.), *Sociological Methodology*. San Francisco: Jossey Bass.

—— (1985), *The Logic of Causal Order*. Beverly Hills, California: Sage.

Dex, S. and Joshi, H. (2005), *Children of the 21st Century: From Birth to Nine Months*. Bristol: The Policy Press.

Dex, S. (1995), 'The reliability of recall data: a literature review'. *Bulletin de methodologie sociologique, 49*, 58–80.

Dex, S. and McCulloch, A. (1998), 'The reliability of retrospective unemployment history data'. *Work Employment and Society, 12*, 497–509.

DfES (2003), *The Future of Higher Education: Foreword*. London: Department for Education and Skills.

—— (2003), *Widening Participation in Higher Education*. London: Department for Education and Skills.

Dixon, M. and Paxton, W. (2005), 'The state of the nation: an audit of social injustice in the UK', in N. Pearce and W. Paxton (eds), *Social Justice: Building a Fairer Britain*. London: Politico's Publishing Ltd.

Douglas, J. W. B. (1964), *The Home and the School: A Study of Ability and Attainment in the Primary School*. London: Macgibbon and Kee.

Department for Work and Pensions (DWP) (2005), *Households Below Average Income: An Analysis of the Income Distribution 1994/5–2003/04*. London: Department for Work and Pensions.

Eales, M. J. (1988), 'Depression and anxiety in unemployed men'. *Psychological Medicine,* *18*, 935–45.

Easterlin, R. (1974), 'Does economic growth improve the human lot? Some empirical evidence', in P. A. David and M. W. Reder (eds), *Nations and Households in Economic Growth*, pp. 89–126. New York: Academic Press.

Elder, G. H. (1974), *Children of the Great Depression: Social Change in Life Experience.* Chicago: University of Chicago Press.

Elliott, B. J. and Richards, M. P. M. (1991), 'Children and divorce: educational performance and behaviour before and after parental separation'. *International Journal of Law and the Family*, *5*, 258–76.

Elliott, J. (2005), *Using Narrative in Social Research: Qualitative and Quantitative Approaches.* London: Sage.

Erikson, R. and Goldthorpe, J. H. (1992), *The Constant Flux: Study of Class Mobility in Industrial Societies.* Oxford: Clarendon Press.

Featherman, D. L. (1980), 'Retrospective longitudinal research: methodological considerations'. *Journal of Economics and Business*, *32*, 152–69.

Ferri, E., Bynner, J. and Wadsworth, M. E. J. (2003), *Changing Britain, Changing Lives: Three Generations at the Turn of the Century.* London: Institute of Education.

Fiegehan, G. C., Lansley, P. S. and Smith, A. D. (1977), *Poverty and Progress in Britain 1953–73.* Cambridge: Cambridge University Press.

Floud, R. and Wachter, K. W. (1982), 'Poverty and physical stature: evidence on the standard of living of London boys 1770–1870'. *Social Science History*, *6*, 422–52.

Fogelman, K. (ed.) (1983), *Growing Up in Great Britain*. London: Macmillan.

Förster, M. and d'Ercole, M. M. (2005), *Income Distribution and Poverty in OECD Countries in the Second Half of the 1990s.* OECD Directorate for Employment, Labour and Social Affairs. http://ideas.repec.org/p/oec/elsaab/22-en.html

Gainey, R. R., Payne, B. K. and O'Toole, M. (2000), 'The relationship between time in jail, time on electronic monitoring, and recidivism: an event history analysis of a jail-based program'. *Justice Quarterly*, *17*, 733–52.

Galton, F. (1907), 'One vote one value', *Nature* (Letter to the Editor).

Giele, J. Z. (1998), 'Innovation in the typical life course', in J. Z. Giele and G. H. Elder (eds), *Methods of Life Course Research: Qualitative and Quantitative Approaches*, pp. 231–63. London: Sage.

Giele, J. Z. and Elder, G. H. (1998), *Methods of Life Course Research: Qualitative and Quantitative Approaches.* Thousand Oaks, California: Sage.

Gillies, D. (2005) 'An action-related theory of causality', *British Journal of the Philosophy of Science*, *56*, 823–42.

Goldthorpe, J. H. (1980), *Social Mobility and Class Structure in Modern Britain*. Oxford: Oxford University Press.

Goldthorpe, J. H. (1997), 'The "Goldthorpe" class schema: some observations on conceptual and operational issues in relation to the ESRC review of government social classifications', in D. Rose and K. O'Reilly (eds), *Constructing Classes: Towards a New Social Classification for the UK*. Swindon: ESRC/ONS.

Goldthorpe, J. H., Llewellyn, C. and Payne, C. (1987), *Social Mobility and Class Structure in Modern Britain*. (2nd edn). Oxford: Clarendon Press.

Goodenough, F. (1926), *Measurement of Intelligence by Drawings*. New York: World Book Company.

Goodman, A. and Oldfield, Z. (2004), *Permanent Differences? Income and Expenditure Inequality in the 1990s and 2000s* (IFS Reports, R66). London: The Institute for Fiscal Studies.

Goyder, J. (1987), *The Silent Minority: Non-Respondents to Survey Interviews.* Cambridge: Polity Press.

Hakim, C. (1979), 'Census confidentiality in Britain', in M. Bulmer (ed.), *Censuses, Surveys and Privacy*. London: Macmillan.

Hakim, C (1982), *Secondary Analysis in Social Research: A Guide to Data Sources and Methods with Examples*. London: Allen and Unwin.

Halpern, D. (2005), *Social Capital*. Cambridge: Polity.

Halsey, A. H., Heath, A. and Ridge, J. (1980), *Origins and Destinations: Family, Class and Education in Modern Britain*. Oxford: Clarendon.

Heaton, T. B. and Call, V. R. A. (1995), 'Modeling family dynamics with event history techniques'. *Journal of Marriage and the Family, 57*, 1078–90.

Hoaglin, D. C., Mosteller, F. and Tukey, J. W. (2006), *Exploring Data Tables, Trends, and Shapes* (4th edn). Chichester: John Wiley and Sons.

Hollway, W. and Jefferson, T. (2000), *Doing Qualitative Research Differently: Free Association, Narrative and the Interview Method*. London: Sage.

Hough, M. and Mayhew, P. (1983), *The British Crime Survey: First Report*. London: HMSO.

Hume, D. (1748), An Enquiry Concerning Human Understanding. Reprinted (e.g.) in Hume, An Enquiry concerning Human Understanding ed. E. Steinberg. Indianapolis: Hackett, 1977.

Hunter, A. A. (1973), 'On the validity of measures of association: the nominal-nominal, two by two case'. *American Journal of Sociology, 79*, 99–109.

Huxley, A. (1958), *Brave New World Revisited*. New York: Harper and Row.

Jacobs, S. C. (2002), 'Reliability and recall of unemployment events using retrospective data'. *Work, Employment and Society, 16*, 537–48.

Jarvis, S. and Jenkins, S. P. (1995), 'Do the poor stay poor? New evidence about income dynamics from the British Household Panel Survey' (Occasional Paper 95-7). Colchester: ESRC Research Centre on Micro-Social Change, University of Essex. www.irc.essex.ac.uk/pubs/occpaps/pdf/op95-2_text.pdf

Jenkins, S. P. and Micklewright, J. (2007), 'New directions in the analysis of inequality and poverty' (ISER Working Paper 2007–11). Colchester: University of Essex. www.iser. essex.ac.uk/pubs/workpaps

Jones, F. (2007), 'The effect of taxes and benefits on household income 2005–06'. London: Office for National Statistics. www.statistics.gov.uk/cci/article.asp?ID=1804

Jowell, R. and Airey, C. (eds) (1984), *British Social Attitudes: The 1984 Report*. Aldershot: Gower and Social and Community Planning Research.

Jowell, R. and Witherspoon, S. (eds) (1985), *British Social Attitudes: The 1985 Report*. Aldershot: Gower and Social and Community Planning Research.

Jowell, R., Witherspoon, S. and Brook, L. (eds) (1986), *British Social Attitudes: The 1986 Report*. Aldershot: Gower and Social and Community Planning Research.

Kellner, P. (1997), 'Why the Tories were trounced', in P. Norris and N. T. Gavin (eds), *Britain Votes 1997* (pp. 108–23). Oxford: Oxford University Press.

Kruskal, J. B. (1978), 'Transformations of statistical data', in W. H. Kruskal and J. M. Tanur (eds), *The International Encyclopaedia of Statistics* (vol. 2, pp. 1044–56). New York: Free Press, Macmillan.

Laub, J. H. and Sampson, R. J. (1998), 'Integrating quantitative and qualitative data', in J. Z. Giele and G. H. Elder (eds), *Methods of Life Course Research: Qualitative and Quantitative Approaches* (pp. 213–30). Thousand Oaks, CA: Sage.

Layard, R. (2005), *Happiness: Lessons from a New Science*. London: Penguin Books Ltd.

Le Grand, J. (1985), *Inequalities in Health: The Human Capital Approach*. London: London School of Economics, Suntory Toyota Centre Welfare State Programme, no. 1.

Mackie, J. L. (1974), *The Cement of the Universe: A Study of Causation*. Oxford: Clarendon.

Marsh, C. (1985), 'Do polls affect what people think?', in C. Turner and E. Martin (eds), *Surveys of Subjective Phenomena* (vol. 2, pp. 565–91). New York: Russell Sage Foundation.

—— (1988), *Exploring Data: An Introduction to Data Analysis for Social Scientists* (1st edn). Cambridge: Polity Press.

Mirlees-Black, C., Mayhew, P. and Percy, A. (1996), The 1996 British Crime Survey: England and Wales Home Office Statistical Bulletin, Issue 19/96. Research and Statistics Directorate. London: Home Office.

Mosteller, F. and Tukey, J. W. (1977), *Data Analysis and Regression: A Second Course in Statistics*. Reading, Mass.: Addison-Wesley.

Mott, F. (2002), 'Looking backward: post hoc reflections on longitudinal surveys', in E. Phelps, F. Furstenberg and A. Colby (eds), *Looking at Lives : American Longitudinal Studies of the Twentieth Century*. New York: Russell Sage.

Ní Bhrolcháin, M. (2001), '"Divorce effects" and causality in the social sciences'. *European Sociological Review, 17*, 33–57.

Ní Bhrolcháin, M., Chappell, R. and Diamond, I. (1995), *How do children of disrupted families fare in young adulthood?* (Working paper 95–8): University of Southampton.

Norusis, M.J. (2007), *SPSS 15.0 Guide to Data Analysis*. London: Prentice-Hall.

—— (2005), *SPSS 13.0 Statistical Procedures Companion*. New Jersey, USA: Prentice-Hall.

Olsen, R. J. (2005), 'The problem of respondent attrition: survey methodology is key'. *Monthly Labor Review, 128*, 63–70.

Park, A., Curtice, J., Thomson, K., Bromley, C. and Phillips, M. (eds) (2004), *British Social Attitudes: The 21st Report*. London: Sage Publications.

Park, A., Curtice, J., Thomson, K., Bromley, C., Phillips, M. and Johnson, M. (eds) (2005), *British Social Attitudes: The 22nd Report. Two Terms of New Labour: The Public's Reaction*. London: Sage Publications.

Park, A., Curtice, J., Thomson, K., Jarvis, L. and Bromley, C. (eds) (2003), *British Social Attitudes: The 20th Report. Continuity and Change Over Two Decades*. London: Sage Publications.

Piketty, T. and Saez, E. (2003), 'Income inequality in the United States 1913–1998'. *Quarterly Journal of Economics, 118*, 1–39.

Plewis, I., Calderwood, L., Hawkes, D. and Nathan, G. (2004), *National Child Development Study and 1970 British Cohort Study Technical Report: Changes in the NCDS and BCS70 Populations and Samples over Time*. London: Centre for Longitudinal Studies, Institute of Education, University of London.

Povey, D. and Prime, J. (1999), *Recorded Crime Statistics: England and Wales, April 1998 to March 1999. Home Office Statistical Bulletin 18/99*. London: Home Office.

Pringle, M., Butler, N. and Davie, R. (1966), *11,000 Seven Year Olds*. London: Longman.

Putnam, R. (2000), *Bowling Alone: The Collapse and Revival of American Community*. London: Simon and Schuster.

Raffe, D. (1981), 'Special programmes in Scotland: the first year of YOP'. *Policy and Politics, 9*, 471–87.

Reese, R. A. (2005), 'Boxplots'. *Significance, 2*, 134–5.

Rickards, L., Fox, K., Roberts, C., Fletcher, L. and Goddard, E. (2004), *Living in Britain, No. 31, Results from the 2002 General Household Survey*. London: Her Majesty's Stationery Office (HMSO).

Robinson, R., O'Sullivan, T. and Le Grand, J. (1985), 'Inequality and housing'. *Urban Studies, 22*, 249–56.

Ruspini, E. (2002), *Introduction to Longitudinal Research*. London: Routledge.

Russell, B. (1913), 'On the notion of cause'. *Proceedings of the Aristotelian Society, 13*, 1–26.

Ryder, N. B. (1965), 'The cohort as a concept in the study of social change'. *American Sociological Review, 30*, 843–61.

Saez, E. and Veall, M. R. (2003), 'The evolution of high incomes in Canada, 1920–2000'. *National Bureau of Economic Research Working Paper Series, No. 9607*.

Samuelson, P. A. and Nordhaus, W. D. (1985), *Economics*. (12th edn). New York: McGraw-Hill.

Scott, J. and Alwin, D. (1998), 'Retrospective versus prospective measurement of life histories in longitudinal research', in J. Z. Giele and G. H. Elder (eds), *Methods of Life*

Course Research: Qualitative and Quantitative Approaches (pp. 98–127). Thousand Oaks, CA: Sage.

Seers, D. (1979), 'The meaning of development', in D. Lehmann (ed.), *Development Theory: Four Critical Studies*. London: Frank Cass.

Siltanen, J., Jarman, J. and Blackburn, R. M. (1995), *Gender Inequality in the Labour Market: Occupational Concentration and Segregation*. Geneva: International Labour Office.

Smith, A. (2006), *Crime Statistics: An Independent Review* (carried out for the Secretary of State for the Home Department) http://www.homeoffice.gov.uk/rds/pdfs06/crime-statistics-independent-review-06.pdf

Smith, N. and Middleton, S. (2007), *A Review of Poverty Dynamics Research in the UK*, Joseph Rowntree Foundation. http://www.jrf.org.uk/bookshop/eBooks/2040-poverty-dynamics-review.pdf

Summerfield, C. and Gill, B. (2005), *Social Trends No. 35*. (35th edn). (vol. 35). Basingstoke, Hampshire: Palgrave Macmillan.

Taris, T. W. (2000), *A Primer in Longitudinal Data Analysis*. London: Sage.

Tawney, R. H. (1964), *Equality* (1931), with an introduction by Richard M. Titmuss. London: Unwin.

Thomas, R. (1999), 'The politics and reform of unemployment and employment statistics', in D. Dorling and S. Simpson (eds), *Statistics in Society: The Arithmetic of Politics* (pp. 324–34). London: Arnold.

—— (2005), 'Is the ILO definition of unemployment a capitalist conspiracy?' *Radical Statistics*, 4–22.

Todd, J. and Butcher, B. (1982), *Electoral Registration in 1981*. London: HMSO.

Tukey, J. W. (1977), *Exploratory Data Analysis*. Reading, Mass.: Addison-Wesley.

Velleman, P. F. and Hoaglin, D. C. (1981), *Applications, Basics and Computing of Exploratory Data Analysis*. Boston: Duxbury.

Wachter, K. W. (1981), 'Graphical estimation of military heights'. *Historical Methods, 14*.

Wadsworth, M. E. J., Montgomery, S. M. and Bartley, M. J. (1999), 'The persisting effect of unemployment on health and social well-being in men early in working life'. *Social Science and Medicine, 48*, 1491–9.

Walker, A., Kershaw, C. and Nicholas, S. (2006), *Crime in England and Wales 2005/2006*. London: Home Office. www.homeoffice.gov.uk/rds/crimeew0506.html

Wilson, P. R. and Elliot, D. J. (1987), 'An evaluation of the postcode address file as a sampling frame and its use within OPCS'. *Journal of the Royal Statistical Society (A), 150*, 230–40.

World Bank (2000), *World Bank, World Development Indicators (WDI)*. Manchester: University of Manchester, ESDS International (MIMAS).

Yamaguchi, K. (1991), *Event History Analysis*. Newbury Park, California: Sage.

Index

Abbott, Andrew 237
absenteeism 238–9, 245–7, 248–50
absolute value 39
accuracy *see* rounding
adjacent value **167**
age 15
  and cohort effects 273
  and social trust 267–8
  see also fear of crime
aggregate change over time 282
aggregate level data 52
alcohol
  consumption 10, 11, 16, 17, 18, 58,
  59
  units 10
analysis of variance 161, 183–8
anatomy of a straight line 194
Annual Survey of Hours and Earnings
  52, 53
arithmetic mean *see* mean
asymmetric measure of association
  147
Atkinson, A.B. 88, 89
attrition 279–82
average 37–40
  see also, mean, median
axis 192
  see also X-axis and Y-axis

bar chart **13–14**, 18, 19, 21, 32
  in SPSS 30, 31
  three-dimensional 122
  see also clustered bar chart
base category 143
base for comparison 143
basic needs 224
Beveridge, William 161
BHPS *see* British Household Panel Survey

bimodal distribution 15, 37
birth cohort **62**
bivariate relationships *see also* causal
  explanations **113–15**, 192
Blair, Tony 96, 97, 107
Booth, Charles 8
bounded number **119**
boxplot 161, **167**, 175, 215–16
boxplots, multiple 171, 181–2
breaking the smooth 110
British Crime Survey 99, 142
British Household Panel Survey 80, 277
British Social Attitudes Survey 76, 254–5,
  282
Byrne, David 238

Campbell, D. T. 242
capital gains 77–8
car ownership 22
  see also households with no car or
  van
case 7, 8, 25
categorical variable 12
causal
  explanations 233–51
  laws 235
  models 62
causal path model 113–15, 143–4, 238–9,
  245–6, 258
causality 113–15, 141, 235–53
  and correlation 236–7
  and longitudinal research 290
  see also complex causality, multiple
  causality and reciprocating systems
cause of diseases 235–6
cell frequency **123**, 128
censored cases 288, 289
Census of Population 8

censuses 214
British, content 80–1
British, 2001 191
United States 80
central tendency *see also* mean, median 48
chi-square 148–57, 256, 257
in SPSS 156–7
distribution 151
and sample size 155
class 11, 113–14, 119–26, 292
background 121–6, 292
NS-SEC 11, 117, 119, 120
Registrar General's 11
socio-economic group 11
clustered bar chart 54, 55
see also bar chart
coefficients of a straight line, derivation
198
cohabitation 23, 24
cohort 118
comparisons 279
effects 273, 290
studies 279
column percentages 124–6, 128, 129, 284
columns 122
complex causality 238
Compute command (SPSS) 60
conditional fit **172**
Conservative party 106–7
and inequality 87
support for 282–6
constant **195**
adding or subtracting 58, 59, 60
multiplying or dividing by 58
see also intercept
contingency table 121–4
interpretation 155–6
in SPSS 129–30
continuous variable 12
control 240–1, 257–8
controlling
for intervening variables 248–50
for prior variables 244–7, 255–8
correlation **193**
counterfactual dependence 235
covariates 264
Cox Proportional hazard models 289
crime
rates 94, 96–8
trends over time 93–9, 110–11
recorded 98
see also fear of crime
Crosstabs command (SPSS) 129, 136,
259
cubing *see* transformation
cumulative distribution 83

cumulative income shares 83, 84
curvy lines 225–7

d (measure of effect size) 144–7, 256, 257,
259–260
data 9, 19, 57
collection 9
matrix 9,11
data=fit+residual 38
decile 43
ratio 86
decimal places 45
decomposition 86
degrees of freedom 154–5, **184**
for T-test 180
dependent variable 186, 202, 262, 264
deprivation 191
see also households with no car or van
and income
depth (of quartiles) 41
Descriptive statistics (SPSS) 47, 48
Descriptives command (SPSS) 64, 65
direct effects *see* effect
discrete time event history analysis 289
distorter variable 251
distribution 13, 21, 22, 215
see also bimodal, uniform and unimodal
distribution
divorce 289
dQ (midspread) 43, 44
dummy variable 143

earned income 78
earnings
inequality 73
by gender *see also* Equal Pay Act 71–3
East Midlands, unemployment rates 166
economic activity 162
economically inactive **162**
education 117–18
educational variables 225
effect 113–15, **173**
direct and indirect 238–9
in contingency tables 143–144
elaboration 242, 250
Elder, Glen 279
elderly 287
elections
General, Britain 1992 100
General Election results (Britain) 282–3
endpoint smoothing 109–10
enhancer variables 251
Equal Pay Act 72–3
equation for a straight line 194
equivalence scale 79
ethnicity 152–3

European Community Household Panel 281
European working hours 54, 55
European Working Time Directive 54, 55
event history
    analysis 288–9
    data 278
    modelling 288–9
expected frequencies 150–1
Expenditure and Food Survey 80
experiments 240–4
explanations 235, **236, 247**
explanatory variable 113–15, 141–2, 173, 192, 256, 266–7
Exploratory Data Analysis (EDA) 2
extreme values (extremes) 40, 43, 165, 169

F statistic 184
Family Resources Survey 9, 80, 81
far outlier **171**
fear of crime 141–6
    and ethnicity 152–3
    and gender 148
    measurement 146
final goods 213
fit 38
    see also data=fit+residual
fitting a resistant line 196–9
    in SPSS 199–204
floor effect 16, 215
flow 77
frequencies table (SPSS) 47, 48, 49

Galton, Sir Francis 39
Gaussian distribution 66–71, 147, 222
    pattern in residuals 107
    see also normal distribution
GDP *see* Gross Domestic Product
gender
    and absenteeism 245–7
    and alcohol consumption 159
    and graduate admissions 248
    see also earnings, fear of crime, working hours
gender differences, mathematics 175–180
General Elections, see *elections*
General Household Survey 9
German Socio-Economic Panel 281
Gini coefficient 86, 87, 88, 90, 224
GNI *see* Gross National Income
Goldthorpe, John 117, 120
Gross Domestic Product **214**
Gross National Income 213
    alternative measures of welfare 224–5
    per capita 215–17, 223
    per capita and life expectancy 225

half-slope **198**
hanning 105–8
    skip mean 105
happiness 77, 210, 224
hazard 289
    see also Cox Proportional hazard models
height 69, 111–12
higher education 117–18
histogram 13, 15, 16, 17, 32, 108, 165, 166, 174, 205–6
    compared with boxplot 167
household 19
    disposable income (historical changes) 76
    expenditure 61
    size 23, 24,
    size and poverty 140
    survey 8
Households Below Average Income 80, 286
households with no car or van 193–4
Hume, David 235, 236

income 21, 77
    disposable 82
    distribution 83
    earned 78
    equivalized 79
    measurement 79
    original 78, 82, 87
    persistent low 286–7
    post-tax 82, 87
    pre-tax 83
    transfer 78
    unearned 78
    see also Households Below Average Income and Survey of Personal Incomes
independent variable *see also* explanatory variable 202
indirect effects *see* effect
individual agency 237
individual level data 52
inequality 76, 86, 224, 275
    measurement 77
    trends in 88, 89
inferential statistics 155–6, 158, **183**
inflow table 124–6
inner fence **167**
intentionality 237
interactions 269–73
intercept **195, 198**
interlocked quotas 100
interquartile range 41, 171

interval
  level variable 175
  scale 12, 175, 186
intervening variables 243–4
IQ (intelligence) tests 66
Iraq war (2003) 107
item non-response 127
iteration 105

Jarvis, S 286
Jenkins, S. P. 286

Kellner, Peter 284

labelling data 126
labour force **162**
Labour Force Survey 162
Labour party
  and crime 96, 97
  and inequality 87–8
  and opinion polls 101, 104, 106–7
  support for 282–3
labour-contract 120
ladder of powers **219–21**, 227
Layard, Richard 77
level 15, 35, 37, 39, 171
  measures of 35, 37
levels of measurement 12
Levene's test for equality of variances 180
Liberal Democrat party 107
  and opinion polls 104, 106–7
  support for 283–6
life course 279
life expectancy 224–6
linear regression **196**
linear relationships 193, 194–9
linked panel study 278
locational summaries 44
log transformation 217–19, 227
logarithm **217–19**
  in excel 217
logistic regression
  in SPSS 263–9
  interpreting coefficients 268–9
  regression models 262–73
lone parents 191–5, 287
longitudinal data 277–92
Longitudinal Study of the British Census 279
Lorenz curves 83, 84, 85, 86, 90

main effects 271
marginal distribution 123
marginal relationships 261
marginals **123**
Marine Society **112**

mathematics tests 62, 63, 175, 206
mean (arithmetic mean) 35, **40**, 42, 45,46, 53, 54, 55
  in SPSS 47
measures of deprivation 191
median 35, 38, 41, 45, 53, 54, 55, 71–2, 165, 218
  grand 173
  in SPSS 47
micro-level data 52
midspread 41, 44, 46
  in SPSS 47
Mill, John Stewart 117
Millennium Cohort Study 280
Millennium Development Goals 212–13
missing data 11, 127
missing values 11
  in SPSS 29
monotonic relationship 193, **194**
MORI 100–1
multiple boxplots *see* boxplots, multiple
multiple causality **238**
multiplication by a constant 58, 59, 60
Murray, Charles 191

National Accounts 81
National Child Development Study 62–70, 140,175–77, 206–9, 277
National Crime Recording Standard 99
national income 212
  see also Gross National Income
National Longitudinal Study of Youth 279, 280
NCDS *see* National Child Development Study
negative numbers, logs of 222
negative relationship 193, 206, 250
New Deal for Lone Parents 191
New Earnings Survey 71–2
nominal scale 12, 20
nominal variable 129, 186
non-linear relationships 225–6
normal distribution 66–7, 147, 151
  see also Gaussian distribution
notifiable offences 98
NS-SEC *see* class
null hypothesis **152**, 177, 179, 183, 185

observed frequencies 150–1
occupation 7, 119
  see also class
odds 120
oneway analysis of variance 183–8
  in SPSS 186–8
  multiple comparisons 185
opinion data 128

opinion polls 99, 241–2, 282, 284
  see also MORI
ordinal scale 12
ordinal variable 129, 132
original income *see* income
outer fences **167**
outflow table 124–6
outliers 15, 22, 167, **168–9**, 172, 201
  see also far outlier

p values 151, 265
Panel Study of Income Dynamics 280
parents
  interest in education 181–6
  occupation 119–26
party identification and welfare views
  269–73
Pearson, Karl **156–7**, 247
percentage 61, **119**, 124–6
  see also column, row and total
    percentages
percentage tables 124–6
percentiles 43
pie chart 13, 14, 21, 32
  in SPSS 27, 28, 29
population 8
positive relationship 193, 194, 207, 224,
  250
Post Hoc tests (SPSS) 187
poverty dynamics 286–7
  see also income
power transformations 219–22
prior variable 242–3
probability 119–120, 151, 153
proportion 119, 142–7
prospective longitudinal design 278
prosperity 76
Putnam, Robert 254

qualifications and social trust 257–8
quantile groups 81
quantile shares 81
quantiles 43, 81
quartiles 41, 73, 165, 218
Quetelet, Adolphe 67
quota sample *see* sample

R square 202, 206
random sample *see* sample
range 40, 44, 46
  in SPSS 48
reading comprehension test 62, 63
recidivism 289
reciprocating systems (of causality) 243
Recode command (SPSS) 132–4
recoding 18, 19, 130, 135

redistribution 85
reference category 271
region 20, 21
  official (Government Office) 164
Registrar General's Social Class *see* class
regression coefficient 203, 208
regression
  inspection of residuals 204–6, 208–9
  predicated values 203–5
relatives 61
repeated cross-sectional design 282
repeated measures analysis 288
residual 37, 38, 172–4, 204
  and resistant lines 197–9
  in multiple batches **172–4**
  see also data=fit+residual
residuals and regression, inspection using
  SPSS 204–6
resistant measures 46, 53
response variable 113–15, 141–2, 173,
  192
retrospective collection of data 278
risk set **289**
rounding 13
row percentages 124–6, 128, 129, 284
rows 122
Russell, Bertrand 235

sample 8, **9**
  calculation of standard deviation 42
  clustered 19
  quota 100
  random **8**, 100
  retention in longitudinal studies 282
scale independence 85, 88
scaling 58, 59, 60
scatterplot **192–3**
  in SPSS 199
Scottish Longitudinal Study 279
Select cases command (SPSS) 50, 51
service relationship 120
shape 15, 37, 172
sigma (the sum of) 40
significance tests 117, 147–53
significant difference 179
Simpson's paradox 247–8
skewed distribution 16, 21, 22, 169
slope **195**, **198**
smoothing 94, 101, 102
  end values 103, 109, 110
  iterations 105
  mean 104
  median 103, 104, 105, 106
  residuals 103, 104, 107, 108
social capital 255–6
social change 22, 23

social conditions 2
social desirable response 284
social participation 255–6
socio-economic groups *see* class
sources 127
spread 15, 171, 222–3
SPSS *see* Statistical Package for the Social
    Sciences
spurious component 247
spurious relationship 247, 256
stable addresses 282
standard deviation 42, 43, 45, 68
    in SPSS 47
standardized distribution 68
standardized variables 61–6
    in SPSS 64–5
Statistical Package for the Social Sciences
    3, 24
    commands 26
    Data Editor 25
    menus 25, 26
    Output 25, 26
    Syntax 25, 26, 48
    tutorials 26
statistical significance 151
statistics, general 2
STDEV (Excel) 43
step 167
stock 77
straggle 16, 215, 221
summaries of three 102
summary measure 63
Summary statistics (SPSS) 49
suppressor variables 251
Survey of Personal Incomes 81
symmetric measure of association 146–7

T-statistic 176
    See also T-test
tables 117–38, 141–58, 254–74
    see also contingency table, percentage
    table
Tebbit, Norman 163
Temporary command (SPSS) 50
test factors 244, 249
three-variable contingency table 136–8
    in SPSS 259
time series 93, 277
time varying covariates 288–9
total percentages 124–6
transfer income 78
transformation 169, 217–24
transition tables 285–6
truncating 13

trust 254–62
    thick and thin 254
T-test 175–81
    equal variances 180
    formula 176
    in SPSS 177–80
Tukey 2, 46, 94, 185, 228
Twyman's law 46
type 1 error 153–4
type 2 error 153–4
typical 37

unbending lines 225–6
unearned income *see* income
unemployed, long term 191–2
unemployment 93, 161–7, 206–7, 290
    and health 290
    rate and owner occupied housing 206–7
    rates 96
    rates, across Europe 162–163
    rates, by local area 164
    rates, by region 163, 170–1
    rates, East Midlands 166
    statistics 162
    time trends 93
uniform distribution 66
unimodal distribution 15, 37
unit of analysis 7, 9, 79, 174, 191, 206,
    289
United Nations 212
unusual value *see* outlier

value labels (SPSS) 134–5
variable 7, 8, 25
variable labels (SPSS) 134–5
variance 42
varying digits 12,13
voluntary group membership 255–8
voting behaviour 282–6

Wald statistic 266
wealth 77
working hours 35, 36, 38, 39, 44, 49, 52,
    53
    by gender 36, 54, 55
World Bank 213, 214

X-axis 192

Y-axis 192
Youth Cohort Study 118–26, 277
Youth Opportunities Scheme 274–5

Z scores 64